THE KEY

STUDENT STUDY GUIDE

nce 10 Academic
2D)

THE KEY student study guide is designed to help students achieve success in school. The content in each study guide is 100% curriculum aligned and serves as an excellent source of material for review and practice. To create this book, teachers, curriculum specialists, and assessment experts have worked closely to develop the instructional pieces that explain each of the key concepts for the course. The practice questions and sample tests have detailed solutions that show problem-solving methods, highlight concepts that are likely to be tested, and point out potential sources of errors. ***THE KEY*** is a complete guide to be used by students throughout the school year for reviewing and understanding course content, and to prepare for assessments.

Rao,Gautam,1961 –
THE KEY – Science 10 Academic Ontario

1. Science – Juvenile Literature. I. Title

Castle Rock Research Corporation
2340 Manulife Place
10180 – 101 Street
Edmonton, AB T5J 3S4

4 5 6 FP 13 12 11

Publisher
Gautam Rao

Contributors
Darrol Colgur
Crystal Talbot
Melissa Tesche

CASTLE ROCK
RESEARCH CORP

Dedicated to the memory of Dr. V. S. Rao

THE KEY—Science 10

THE KEY consists of the following sections:

KEY Tips for Being Successful at School gives examples of study and review strategies. It includes information about learning styles, study schedules, and note taking for test preparation.

Class Focus includes a unit on each area of the curriculum. Units are divided into sections, each focusing on one of the specific expectations, or main ideas, that students must learn about in that unit. Examples, definitions, and visuals help to explain each main idea. Practice questions on the main ideas are also included. At the end of each unit is a test on the important ideas covered. The practice questions and unit tests help students identify areas they know and those they need to study more. They can also be used as preparation for tests and quizzes. Most questions are of average difficulty, though some are easy and some are hard—the harder questions are called *Challenger Questions*. Each unit is prefaced by a ***Table of Correlations***, which correlates questions in the unit (and in the practice tests at the end of the book) to the specific curriculum expectations. Answers and solutions are found at the end of each unit.

KEY Strategies for Success on Tests helps students get ready for tests. It shows students different types of questions they might see, word clues to look for when reading them, and hints for answering them.

Practice Tests includes one to three tests based on the entire course. They are very similar to the format and level of difficulty that students may encounter on final tests. In some regions, these tests may be reprinted versions of official tests, or reflect the same difficulty levels and formats as official versions. This gives students the chance to practice using real-world examples. Answers and complete solutions are provided at the end of the section.

For the complete curriculum document (including specific expectations along with examples and sample problems), visit www.edu.gov.on.ca/eng/curriculum/secondary.

THE KEY *Study Guides* are available for many courses. Check www.castlerockresearch.com for a complete listing of books available for your area.

For information about any of our resources or services, please call Castle Rock Research at 905.625.3332 or visit our website at http://www.castlerockresearch.com.

At Castle Rock Research, we strive to produce an error-free resource. If you should find an error, please contact us so that future editions can be corrected.

CONTENTS

KEY Tips for Being Successful at School

KEY TIPS FOR BEING SUCCESSFUL AT SCHOOL

KEY FACTORS CONTRIBUTING TO SCHOOL SUCCESS

In addition to learning the content of your courses, there are some other things that you can do to help you do your best at school. Some of these strategies are listed below.

- **KEEP A POSITIVE ATTITUDE**—always reflect on what you can already do and what you already know.
- **BE PREPARED TO LEARN**—have ready the necessary pencils, pens, notebooks, and other required materials for participating in class.
- **COMPLETE ALL OF YOUR ASSIGNMENTS**—do your best to finish all of your assignments. Even if you know the material well, practice will reinforce your knowledge. If an assignment or question is difficult for you, work through it as far as you can so that your teacher can see exactly where you are having difficulty.
- **SET SMALL GOALS FOR YOURSELF WHEN YOU ARE LEARNING NEW MATERIAL**—for example, when learning the parts of speech, do not try to learn everything in one night. Work on only one part or section each study session. When you have memorized one particular part of speech and understand it, then move on to another one, continue this process until you have memorized and learned all the parts of speech.
- **REVIEW YOUR CLASSROOM WORK REGULARLY AT HOME**—Review to be sure that you understand the material that you learned in class.
- **ASK YOUR TEACHER FOR HELP**—your teacher will help you if you do not understand something or if you are having a difficult time completing your assignments.
- **GET PLENTY OF REST AND EXERCISE**—concentrating in class is hard work. It is important to be well-rested and have time to relax and socialize with your friends. This helps you to keep your positive attitude about your school work.
- **EAT HEALTHY MEALS**—a balanced diet keeps you healthy and gives you the energy that you need for studying at school and at home.

How to Find Your Learning Style

Every student learns differently. The manner in which you learn best is called your learning style. By knowing your learning style, you can increase your success at school. Most students use a combination of learning styles. Do you know what type of learner you are? Read the following descriptions. Which of these common learning styles do you use most often?

- **Linguistic Learner**: You may learn best by saying, hearing, and seeing words. You are probably really good at memorizing things such as dates, places, names, and facts. You may need to **write and then say out loud** the steps in a process, a formula, or the actions that lead up to a significant event.

- **Spatial Learner**: You may learn best by looking at and working with pictures. You are probably really good at puzzles, imagining things, and reading maps and charts. You may need to use strategies like **mind mapping and webbing** to organize your information and study notes.

- **Kinaesthetic Learner**: You may learn best by touching, moving, and figuring things out using manipulative. You are probably really good at physical activities and learning through movement. You may need to **draw your finger over a diagram** to remember it, **"tap out" the steps** needed to solve a problem, or **"feel" yourself writing** or typing a formula.

SCHEDULING STUDY TIME

You should review your class notes regularly to ensure that you have a clear understanding of all the new material you learned. Reviewing your lessons on a regular basis helps you to learn and remember ideas and concepts. It also reduces the quantity of material that you need to study prior to a test. Establishing a study schedule will help you to make the best use of your time.

Regardless of the type of study schedule you use, you may want to consider the following suggestions to maximize your study time and effort:

- Organize your work so that you begin with the most challenging material first.
- Divide the subject's content into small, manageable chunks.
- Alternate regularly between your different subjects and types of study activities in order to maintain your interest and motivation.
- Make a daily list with headings like "Must Do," "Should Do," and "Could Do."
- Begin each study session by quickly reviewing what you studied the day before.
- Maintain your usual routine of eating, sleeping, and exercising to help you concentrate better for extended periods of time.

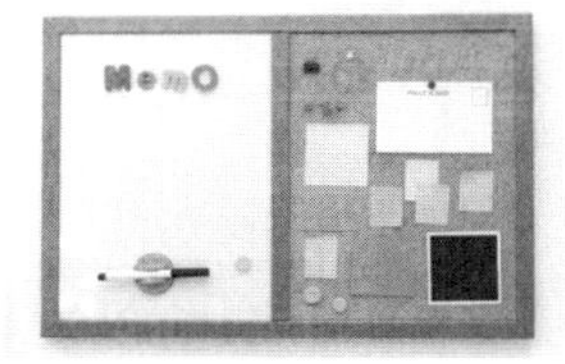

Creating Study Notes

Mind-Mapping or Webbing

- Use the key words, ideas, or concepts from your reading or class notes to create a mind map or web (a diagram or visual representation of the given information). A mind map or web is sometimes referred to as a knowledge map.

- Write the key word, concept, theory, or formula in the centre of your page.

- Write down related facts, ideas, events, and information and then link them to the central concept with lines.

- Use coloured markers, underlining, or other symbols to emphasize things such as relationships, time lines, and important information.

- The following examples of a Frayer Model illustrate how this technique can be used to study scientific vocabulary.

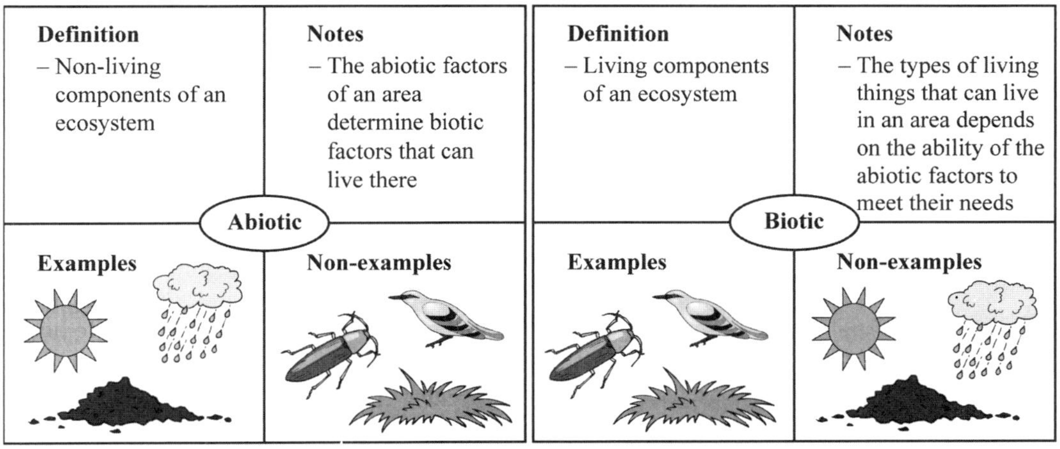

INDEX CARDS

To use index cards while studying, follow these steps:

- Write a key word or question on one side of an index card.
- On the reverse side, write the definition of the word, answer to the question, or any other important information that you want to remember.

What is the difference between heat and thermal energy?

What is the difference between heat and thermal energy?

Thermal energy is the total energy of the particles in a solid, liquid, or gas. Heat is the amount of thermal energy transferred between objects.

SYMBOLS AND STICKY NOTES—IDENTIFYING IMPORTANT INFORMATION

- Use symbols to mark your class notes. For example, an exclamation mark (!) might be used to point out something that must be learned well because it is a very important idea. A question mark (?) may highlight something that you are not certain about, and a diamond (◊) or asterisk (*) could highlight interesting information that you want to remember.
- Use sticky notes when you are not allowed to put marks in books.
- Use sticky notes to mark a page in a book that contains an important diagram, formula, explanation, etc.
- Use sticky notes to mark important facts in research books.

KEY STRATEGIES FOR REVIEWING

Reviewing textbook material, class notes, and handouts should be an ongoing activity. Spending time reviewing becomes more critical when you are preparing for tests. You may find some of the following review strategies useful when studying during your scheduled study time.

- Before reading a selection, preview it by noting the headings, charts, graphs, and chapter questions.
- Before reviewing a unit, note the headings, charts, graphs, and chapter questions.
- Highlight key concepts, vocabulary, definitions, and formulas.
- Carefully read over each step in a procedure.
- Draw a picture or diagram to help make the concept clearer.

KEY STRATEGIES FOR SUCCESS: A CHECKLIST

Review, review, review: review is a huge part of doing well at school and preparing for tests. Here is a checklist for you to keep track of how many suggested strategies for success you are using. Read each question and then put a check mark (✓) in the correct column. Look at the questions where you have checked the "No" column. Think about how you might try using some of these strategies to help you do your best at school.

***KEY* Strategies for Success**	**Yes**	**No**
Do you attend school regularly?		
Do you know your personal learning style—how you learn best?		
Do you spend 15 to 30 minutes a day reviewing your notes?		
Do you study in a quiet place at home?		
Do you clearly mark the most important ideas in your study notes?		
Do you use sticky notes to mark texts and research books?		
Do you practise answering multiple-choice and written-response questions?		
Do you ask your teacher for help when you need it?		
Are you maintaining a healthy diet and sleep routine?		
Are you participating in regular physical activity?		

Biology

BIOLOGY: TISSUES, ORGANS, AND SYSTEMS OF LIVING THINGS

Table of Correlations

	Specific Expectation	Practice Questions	Unit Test Questions	Practice Test 1	Practice Test 2
10.2.B1	evaluate the importance of medical and other technological developments related to systems biology, and analyse their societal and ethical implications				
10.2.B1.1	*analyse, on the basis of research, ethical issues related to a technological development in the field of systems biology (e.g., cloning, stemcell research, live organ transplants, transgenic transplants), and communicate their findings*	1, 2	1, 2		1
10.2.B1.2	*assess the importance to human health and/or society of medical imaging technologies (e.g., ultrasound, X-rays, computerized axial tomography [CT or CAT] scan, magnetic resonance imaging [MRI], microscopy, biophotonics) used in Canada in diagnosing or treating abnormalities in tissues, organs, and/or systems*	3, 4	3, 4	1	
10.2.B1.3	*describe public health strategies related to systems biology (e.g., cancer screening and prevention programs; vaccines against the human papillomavirus [HPV] and measles, mumps, and rubella [MMR]; AIDS education), and assess their impact on society*	5, 6	5, 6	2	
10.2.B2	investigate cell division, cell specialization, organs, and systems in animals and plants, using research and inquiry skills, including various laboratory techniques				
10.2.B2.1	*use appropriate terminology related to cells, tissues, organs, and systems of living things, including, but not limited to: absorption, anaphase, capillaries, concentration, differentiation, diffusion, meristematic, mesophyll, phloem, prophase, red blood cells, regeneration, stomate, and xylem*	12	7		2
10.2.B2.2	*examine cells under a microscope or similar instrument to identify the various stages of mitosis in plants and animals*	7, 8, 9	8, 9	3	3
10.2.B2.3	*examine different plant and animal cells (e.g., cheek cells, onion cells) under a microscope or similar instrument, and draw labelled biological diagrams to show how the cells' organelles differ*	13, 14, 15	10, 11	4	4
10.2.B2.4	*investigate, using a microscope or similar instrument, specialized cells in the human body or in plants, focusing on different types of cells (e.g., bone, muscle, leaf, root cells), and draw labelled biological diagrams to show the cells' structural differences*	22, 23	12		5
10.2.B2.5	*investigate the rate of cell division in cancerous and non-cancerous cells, using pictures, videos, or images, and predict the impact of this rate of cell division on an organism*	19	13	5	
10.2.B2.6	*investigate, through a laboratory or computer simulated dissection of a plant, worm, fish, or frog, the interrelationships between organ systems of a plant or an animal (e.g., between the root system and leaf system in a plant; between the digestive system and circulatory system in an animal)*	26, 27, 28	14		6
10.2.B2.7	*use a research process to investigate a disease or abnormality related to tissues, organs, or systems of humans or plants (e.g., heart disease, tobacco mosaic virus, wheat rust)*	16	15	6	

Table of Correlations

Specific Expectation		Practice Questions	Unit Test Questions	Practice Test 1	Practice Test 2
10.2.B3	demonstrate an understanding of the hierarchical organization of cells, from tissues, to organs, to systems in animals and plants				
10.2.B3.1	*describe the cell cycle in plants and animals, and explain the importance of mitosis for the growth of cells and repair of tissues*	10, 11	16, 17	7	7
10.2.B3.2	*explain the importance of cell division and cell specialization in generating new tissues and organs (e.g., the division of stem cells into specialized cells such as muscle cells or nerve cells in humans; the division of meristematic cells to expand and differentiate plant tissue)*	17, 18	18, 19	8	8
10.2.B3.3	*explain the links between specialized cells, tissues, organs, and systems in plants and animals (e.g., muscle cells and nerve cells form the tissue found in the heart, which is a component of the circulatory system; granum and thylakoid structures act as solar collectors in the chloroplast to produce carbohydrates for plant growth)*	20, 21	20, 21	9	
10.2.B3.4	*explain the primary functions of a variety of systems in animals (e.g., the circulatory system transports materials through the organism; the respiratory system supplies oxygen to and removes carbon dioxide from the body)*	24, 25	22, 23		9
10.2.B3.5	*explain the interaction of different systems within an organism (e.g., the respiratory system brings oxygen into the body, and the circulatory system transports the oxygen to cells) and why such interactions are necessary for the organism's survival*	29, 30	24, 25	10	10

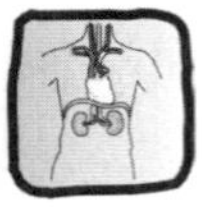

10.2.B1.1 *analyse, on the basis of research, ethical issues related to a technological development in the field of systems biology (e.g., cloning, stemcell research, live organ transplants, transgenic transplants), and communicate their findings*

Ethics in Biology

Researchers, doctors, and the public are often asked to consider issues in bioethics. Ethics deal with whether an action is right or wrong, and bioethics are actions specific to medicine and biology.
The number of bioethical issues seems to grow as technology advances, and now includes topics such as cloning, stem cell research, live organ transplants, and transgenic transplants.

Cloning

Cloning refers to the process of creating a biological unit (parts of DNA, a cell, or an entire organism) that is genetically identical to the parent.
Cloning can occur naturally, and many plants, bacteria, and insects use cloning as a method of reproduction—this is often referred to as asexual reproduction. While scientists have been able to make copies of DNA fragments and whole cells for many years, they were only able to successfully clone the first large animal just over a decade ago. The sheep, named Dolly, was created from a single adult cell. This breakthrough brought with it many questions about the ethics of cloning, such as the following:

- Is cloning whole organisms ethical?
- Who should be able to use this technology?
- Should scientists be allowed to clone every organism, including humans?

Use the following information to answer the next question.

Nudibranchs, more commonly known as sea slugs, possess unique toxins that make them unpalatable to predators.
These toxins have brought nudibranchs to the attention of pharmaceutical companies because of the potential for their toxins to be used in drugs and anti-cancer treatments.

1. The **main** ethical concern for a pharmaceutical company developing new drugs from natural sources such as nudibranch toxins is
   A. the right to patent the new drug
   B. privacy of patients in the drug trials
   C. potential impacts on nudibranch populations
   D. proper training for doctors on the use of the new drug

Use the following information to answer the next question.

DNA screening is a valuable tool for determining whether or not a person is genetically predisposed to certain diseases.

Open Response

2. Outline three **major** ethical issues related to the use of DNA screening.

10.2.B1.2 *assess the importance to human health and/or society of medical imaging technologies (e.g., ultrasound, X-rays, computerized axial tomography [CT or CAT] scan, magnetic resonance imaging [MRI], microscopy, biophotonics) used in Canada in diagnosing or treating abnormalities in tissues, organs, and/or systems*

Medical Imaging Technologies

Medical imaging technologies are used by doctors and researchers to create pictures of the human body. Technologies such as ultrasound, X-rays, CT scans, MRIs, and microscopes allow medical professionals to more accurately diagnose and treat health problems.

X-Rays

The first X-ray taken in 1895 was one of the earliest forms of medical imaging. An X-ray machine is like a big camera that uses X-rays instead of visible light to produce the image on the film. X-rays are shot through the body. Bone, muscles, and other soft tissues all absorb X-rays differently, so when the X-rays pass through the body, the image that results on the film shows the different tissue layers as different shades of grey.

Ultrasound

Ultrasound is sound waves that have a frequency higher than humans are able to hear. It is commonly used as a medical imaging technology. Ultrasound waves are projected into the tissues. The waves are reflected back toward the sensor. Different layers of soft tissue reflect the waves to different degrees, creating a real-time image of the tissue. Ultrasound technology is thought to have few health risks, and it is often used during pregnancy to check the progress and health of a developing fetus.
Unlike MRI and CT machines, ultrasound machines are relatively inexpensive and portable, making them more easily accessible to the public.

Magnetic Resonance Imaging

A magnetic resonance imaging (MRI) machine uses a powerful magnetic field to create an image of the internal structures in the body. The human body is composed mainly of water molecules which interact with the magnetic field to form the image the doctor sees on the screen. An MRI gives good contrast between different layers of soft tissues such as organs, muscle, and the brain. Doctors often use MRIs to diagnose tumors, brain injuries, and ligament or muscle damage.

3. Which type of radiation is used to assess tissue injuries?

A. X-ray **B.** Infrared

C. Ultraviolet **D.** Gamma ray

Open Response

4. Explain what biophotonics are and some possible applications.

10.2.B1.3 *describe public health strategies related to systems biology (e.g., cancer screening and prevention programs; vaccines against the human papillomavirus [HPV] and measles, mumps, and rubella [MMR]; AIDS education), and assess their impact on society*

Canadian Public Health Strategies

Many countries, including Canada, have some form of government-provided health care that is funded by the public's tax dollars. Public health strategies are ways of protecting and informing the public so the need for health care is reduced.

Public Health Agency of Canada

The Canadian Government's health-care agency is the Public Health Agency of Canada (PHAC). The primary goal of the PHAC is to limit the pressure on the Canadian health-care system by providing Canadians with the knowledge and tools necessary to understand and manage their health-care issues accordingly. The PHAC works to prevent and control chronic and infectious diseases, and it is responsible for responding to public health emergencies.

Immunization and vaccine programs are one way the PHAC prevents diseases. Measles used to be a very common and potentially serious childhood disease that affected a high proportion of the nation's children. When a vaccination program was introduced, the incidence of the rate of infection fell to less than 1% of the rate without the vaccination.

Some diseases, such as AIDS, do not have vaccines or cures. Education programs are aimed at awareness and preventing the spread of disease. By raising the awareness of the disease's symptoms and mode of transmission, public health agencies hope that the public will make informed decisions that reduce their likelihood of contracting the disease.

There is no vaccine against cancer, and while some forms are preventable, many are not. The earlier cancer is found, the more likely it is to be treatable. The PHAC has cancer-screening programs aimed at early detection of the disease. In 1993, the PHAC launched the Canadian Breast Cancer Initiative, aimed at reducing the number of women who die from breast cancer. Along with education and awareness, the PHAC began encouraging women over 30 and those considered at higher risk of breast cancer to get screened each year. The pink ribbon has become a recognizable symbol of the fight against breast cancer.

CHALLENGER QUESTION

5. Which of the following scenarios would **not** be the responsibility of the Public Health Agency of Canada?

- **A.** A Canadian spinach farm sells produce that might be contaminated with *E. coli* bacteria.
- **B.** The number of parents choosing to vaccinate their children is dropping.
- **C.** An effective new technique is developed to screen for colon cancer.
- **D.** A new strain of flu emerges, and cases are occurring in Canada.

Use the following information to answer the next question.

> Recent shifts in the genetics of some influenza viruses have led to the emergence of new more pathogenic strains of the flu. In an attempt to limit the spread of these new strains, the public health coordinator for the Public Health Agency of Canada will need to develop ways to raise public awareness about this issue.

Open Response

6. Briefly outline three ways that a public health coordinator could raise public awareness about the emergence of new strains of the flu.

____
____
____
____
____

10.2.B2.2 *examine cells under a microscope or similar instrument to identify the various stages of mitosis in plants and animals*

10.2.B3.1 *describe the cell cycle in plants and animals, and explain the importance of mitosis for the growth of cells and repair of tissues*

10.2.B2.1 *use appropriate terminology related to cells, tissues, organs, and systems of living things, including, but not limited to: absorption, anaphase, capillaries, concentration, differentiation, diffusion, meristematic, mesophyll, phloem, prophase, red blood cells, regeneration, stomate, and xylem*

THE CELL CYCLE AND MITOSIS

Cells multiply through a process called mitosis, where a cell divides into two identical copies of itself. The different stages of mitosis can be examined using a microscope. Before a cell can undergo mitosis, however, it must prepare itself in a stage called interphase. This sequence of events, as cells prepare themselves to divide and then do so during mitosis, is called the cell cycle.

THE CELL CYCLE

The cell cycle consists of two phases: interphase and mitosis. Only 10% of the cell cycle is spent dividing and undergoing mitosis. Ninety percent of the time, during **interphase**, a cell is growing, metabolizing nutrients to produce energy, replicating DNA, and performing various other cellular functions. This diagram depicts a cell cycle.

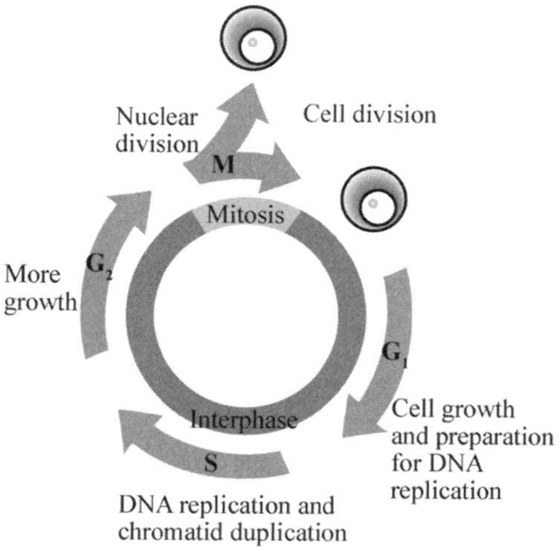

Interphase is divided into three distinct phases. The cell enters the first stage of interphase, known as the **Gap 1** (G_1) phase, once the cell has completed mitosis. The cell begins to grow and prepare itself for DNA replication. The cell produces proteins and enzymes that are necessary to replicate DNA.

The next phase is the **synthesis** (S) phase of interphase. Proteins and enzymes replicate DNA found in one chromatid to produce a duplicate chromatid. This ensures that mitosis begins with paired chromosomes, each consisting of two identical chromatids (called **sister chromatids**) attached together at the centromere. The cell continues growing throughout this phase.

During **Gap 2** (G_2), the cell begins its preparations for mitosis. Chemical switches determine if the DNA has been properly replicated and if the cell is ready to divide. Depending upon the condition checks performed by these chemical switches, the cell either enters the M (mitosis) stage or enters a cell death stage called **apoptosis**.

If DNA has been properly replicated, mitosis (M) occurs.

Mitosis

Mitosis is the mechanism that allows the nuclei of cells to split and provide each daughter cell with a complete set of chromosomes during cellular division.

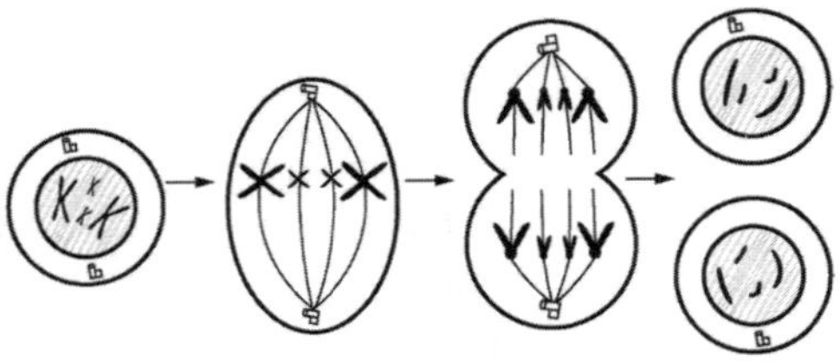

Prophase Metaphase Anaphase Telophase

The first phase of mitosis is known as **prophase**. During prophase, chromosomes thicken and condense, the nuclear membrane disappears, and spindle fibers begin to radiate from centrioles. One centriole begins moving toward one pole of the cell, and the other centriole moves to the opposite pole.

The next phase is called **metaphase**. Paired chromosomes line up at the equatorial plate (centre of the cell), and spindle fibers radiating from the centrioles attach to the centromere of each paired chromosome.

During **anaphase**, spindle fibers shorten, and the paired chromosomes separate to become individual chromosomes. Each paired chromosome is made up of two identical sister chromatids. When the chromatids split from each other, they become *individual* chromosomes. Each individual chromosome contains the same genetic information as the sister it split from.

During the last phase of mitosis, called **telophase**, an important event called **cytokinesis** occurs. The cytoplasm divides, and two daughter cells are produced. The nuclear membrane reforms, and the chromosomes decondense. After telophase is completed, the cell cycle continues, and each daughter cell is ready to enter the G_1 phase of interphase.

The Importance of Mitosis

Mitosis allows a single mother cell to split into two identical daughter cells. The genetic information in the new daughter cells will be exactly the same as the genetic information in the mother cell.
Plants and animals are able to grow because of mitosis.

Tissues expand as cells reproduce through mitosis. This process also allows for the repair of some types of damaged tissues, when dead or dying cells are replaced by new daughter cells. Skin cells, for example, are replaced constantly as they are sloughed off. Mitotic division occurs at a rate fast enough to replace the dead skin cells.

7. Which of the following diagrams depicts metaphase?

A.

B.

C.

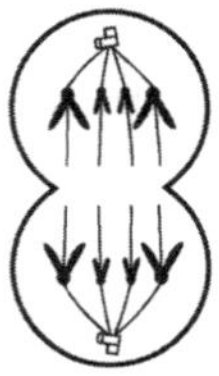

D.

8. Which of the following events takes place during prophase?

A. The cell divides.

B. The nucleus shrinks in size.

C. The cell membrane disappears.

D. The nuclear membrane disappears.

Use the following information to answer the next question.

Down syndrome is a genetic disorder caused by an extra copy of the 21st chromosome. Babies born with Down syndrome have three copies of chromosome 21 and can have a range of developmental, cognitive, and physical impairments. Down syndrome can be diagnosed during an amniocentesis or at birth by examining the chromosomes of a cell.

Open Response

9. Identify the stage of mitosis that is **best** for examining the number of chromosomes, and explain why.

____

____

10. After mitotic cell division, the number of chromosomes in the daughter cells is

A. twice the parent cell

B. equal to the parent cell

C. one-half of the parent cell

D. one-fourth of the parent cell

11. Which of the following biological outcomes is **not** a result of mitosis?

A. Maintenance of genetic composition

B. Introduction of genetic variation

C. Repair of skin wounds

D. Growth of organs

12. The process of somatic body cells dividing to create more body cells is called

A. fusion **B.** mating

C. mitosis **D.** meiosis

10.2.B2.3 *examine different plant and animal cells (e.g., cheek cells, onion cells) under a microscope or similar instrument, and draw labelled biological diagrams to show how the cells' organelles differ*

Animal and Plant Cells

Plant cells are similar to animal cells in that they have many of the same organelles. However, unlike animal cells, plant cells have cell walls and chloroplasts.

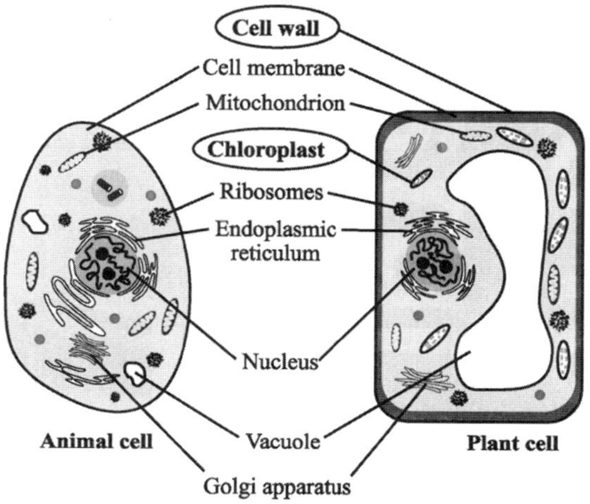

Cell wall– The cell wall provides structural support for the cell. It helps the cell stand up against gravity and to resist turgor pressure, allowing the plant to grow tall and the plant cells to expand as they fill with water.

Chloroplasts– Chloroplasts contain the green pigment known as chlorophyll, which uses energy from the sun in photosynthesis.

13. Which of the following statements comparing cheek cells and onion cells is **true**?

A. Neither cheek cells nor onion cells have a cell wall.

B. Cheek cells have a cell wall, onion cells do not.

C. Onion cells have a cell wall, cheek cells do not.

D. Both cheek cells and onion cells have a cell wall.

CHALLENGER QUESTION

Use the following information to answer the next question.

Cell Types

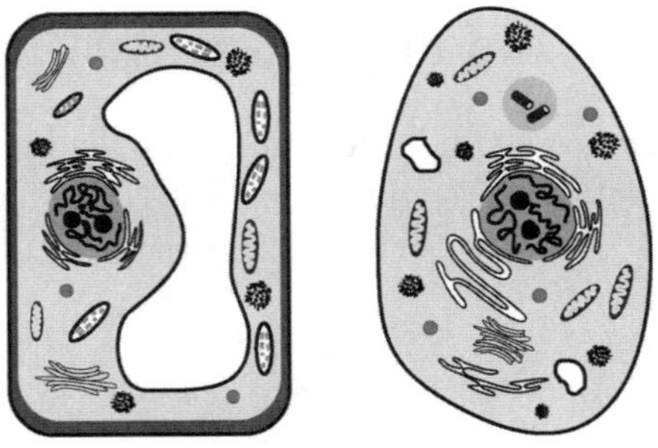

14. Which statement correctly describes the features of Cell 1 and Cell 2?

A. Only Cell 1 has a nucleus.

B. Only Cell 2 has cytoplasm.

C. Only Cell 1 is capable of photosynthesis.

D. Only Cell 2 is capable of cellular respiration.

CHALLENGER QUESTION

Use the following information to answer the next question.

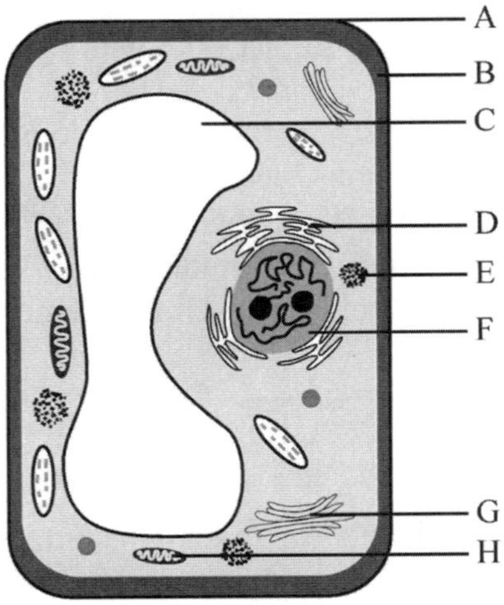

The structure of a eukaryotic cell

Open Response

15. Match each labeled organelle in the diagram with its name.

Organelle Name	Letter
Vacuole	______
Cell membrane	______
Nucleus	______
Mitochondria	______
Cell wall	______
Endoplasmic reticulum	______
Golgi apparatus	______
Ribosome	______

10.2.B2.7 *use a research process to investigate a disease or abnormality related to tissues, organs, or systems of humans or plants (e.g., heart disease, tobacco mosaic virus, wheat rust)*

Diseases in Living Systems

A disease is an abnormal state of a tissue, organ, or organ system that has negative effects on the organism's function. There are thousands of different diseases that affect plants and animals. Each disease is usually accompanied by specific symptoms that indicate something is wrong in the organism. It is on the basis of these symptoms that the disease can be identified and treated.

Causes of Disease

Diseases have many causes: genetic mutations, pathogens, viruses, and even poor lifestyle choices. Heart disease is one of the leading causes of death in North America. Heart disease is a general term that covers many conditions affecting the function of the heart. A poor diet can lead to the buildup of plaque in the arteries and walls of the heart, which will restrict the flow of blood. Genetic problems can occur with the sinoatrial node (natural pacemaker) in the heart, causing an irregular heartbeat. Valvular diseases affect the heart's ability to completely fill with blood and the ability to pump blood to the extremities of the body. Heart disease, like most human disease, has a number of foundations dedicated to the study and cure of the disease. Most foundations also aim to increase public awareness of the condition and have factual information available in their pamphlets and websites. These foundations are excellent places to start researching a disease.

Plants are also susceptible to disease. In fact, the first virus was discovered in a plant. Discolored and mottled leaves led scientists to discover the tobacco mosaic virus, which affects plants in the tobacco family. Wheat rust, which is caused by a fungus, is another disease that affects plants. Spores of the fungus land on the leaves of a plant and find a stoma (the opening for gas exchange on the leaf).
The fungus then grows into the plant, stealing its nutrients and causing sickness in the plant. Although most plant diseases are not transferable to humans, much research goes into them because of the economic damage they cause, especially to cash crops like tobacco, wheat, or bananas.

Use the following information to answer the next question.

A healthy lifestyle can help prevent diseases such as cirrhosis of the liver. The liver removes bacteria and toxins from the blood, makes proteins needed for blood clotting, and produces bile that aids in the absorption of fats. Cirrhosis of the liver impairs these and other important functions of the liver. Cirrhosis of the liver can be caused by heavy alcohol consumption and obesity.

16. Cirrhosis is a liver disease characterized by

A. scarring of the liver tissue

B. shrinking of the liver tissue

C. the decay of the liver tissue

D. the deposit of waste in the liver tissue

10.2.B3.2 *explain the importance of cell division and cell specialization in generating new tissues and organs (e.g., the division of stem cells into specialized cells such as muscle cells or nerve cells in humans; the division of meristematic cells to expand and differentiate plant tissue)*

10.2.B2.5 *investigate the rate of cell division in cancerous and non-cancerous cells, using pictures, videos, or images, and predict the impact of this rate of cell division on an organism*

Cell Division and Specialization

Plants and animals are complex organisms with levels of cellular organization that require specialized cells. In both animal and plant embryos, the first cells are undifferentiated, meaning they are still general cells and are able to become a wide variety of specialized cell types. Once a cell is specialized, it cannot produce cells of a different type. As the plant or animal develops, most cells specialize to become tissues and organs. Some cells remain undifferentiated—this includes stem cells in animals and meristem cells in plants.

Stem Cells

Stem cells are undifferentiated animal cells. Embryos begin as stem cells, then differentiate into specialized cells, such as blood cells, bone cells, muscles cells, and neurons. These specialized cells form the tissues and organs that make up the adult organism. Adults have a limited number of stem cells that are able to repair and regenerate damaged tissues. Adult stem cells are important in maintaining the normal replacement of tissues including skin, blood, and intestinal linings.

Meristem Cells

Meristem is plant tissue that is made up of undifferentiated cells. Meristematic tissue is responsible for plant growth, and it is a region of rapid cell division. Cells from the meristem can differentiate and specialize. There are many areas of meristematic tissue on plants, including the tips of roots, the apex of new growth, within the cambium, and at floral sites.

Cell Division in Cancerous Cells

Cancer refers to a group of diseases in which cells do not divide at normal rates. Cancerous cells divide at much higher rates than healthy cells. The newly divided cells are clustered together, creating a lump called a tumor. Three characteristics are typically used to distinguish a harmful (malignant) tumor from a non-harmful (benign) tumor:

1. Cells in malignant tumors experience **uncontrolled growth**, meaning they do not self-regulate or stop dividing on their own.
2. Malignant tumors begin to **invade** and intrude on neighboring tissues. This can create blockages or interfere with the function of tissues and organs.
3. **Metastasis** is the ability of a tumor to break into smaller pieces and spread to other areas of the body through the bloodstream and the lymphatic system. The cells that spread are still dividing uncontrollably, and they form new tumors in other areas of the body.

17. Which of the following disadvantages of multicellularity occurs because cells are specialized in a division of labour?

A. The power of regeneration is lost in some cells.

B. Old, injured cells that die cannot be replaced by new cells.

C. The outer cells must form a protective layering to protect the internal cells.

D. The complexity of the organism increases, and some cells become obsolete.

Use the following information to answer the next question.

Plant tissues consist of two basic types: meristematic tissue and permanent tissue. Meristematic tissues are composed of actively dividing cells.

18. Which of the following plant parts will contain the **greatest** percentage of meristematic tissue cells?

A. Ripe fruits **B.** Shoot tips

C. Xylem vessels **D.** Matured leaves

Use the following information to answer the next question.

A scientist conducted a research project comparing the growth of non-cancerous cells (colony A) to cancerous cells (colony B) by culturing each type in separate petri dishes. The results of the study were collected and plotted on a graph.

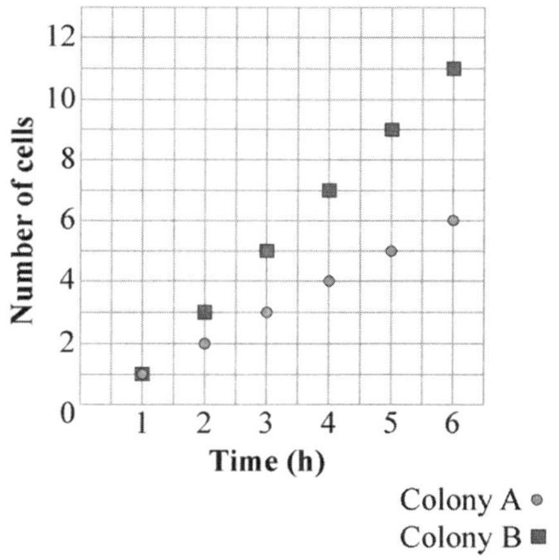

19. Which of the following conclusions can be drawn from the graph?

A. The rate of cell division is higher in cancerous cells than in regular cells.

B. Cell division in cancerous cells causes tumours.

C. Cancerous cells are larger than regular cells.

D. Cancerous cells are transmitted by contact.

10.2.B3.3 *explain the links between specialized cells, tissues, organs, and systems in plants and animals (e.g., muscle cells and nerve cells form the tissue found in the heart, which is a component of the circulatory system; granum and thylakoid structures act as solar collectors in the chloroplast to produce carbohydrates for plant growth)*

10.2.B2.4 *investigate, using a microscope or similar instrument, specialized cells in the human body or in plants, focusing on different types of cells (e.g., bone, muscle, leaf, root cells), and draw labelled biological diagrams to show the cells' structural differences*

Cellular Specialization, Tissues, Organs, and Organ Systems

In multicellular organisms, cells are specialized to perform certain functions, so they can have very different cell structures. Groups of similarly specialized cells form tissues, and these tissues function together to form an organ. Many organs make up an organ system. Muscle, bone, nerve, blood, guard, tracheids, and vessel element cells are examples of specialized cells in plants and animals.

Specialized Cell Types

The shape and size of a cell is influenced by the function it performs. For example, blood cells are small, concave, disc-shaped, and do not have a nucleus. This permits the red blood cells to flow easily through the blood vessels as they transport oxygen and carbon dioxide gases between the lungs and body tissues.

Red blood cell

In comparison, nerve cells are usually long, thin, and branched. This permits nerve cells to connect with each other and other types of cells, thereby allowing for the communication of information in the form of electrical impulses between different parts of the body.

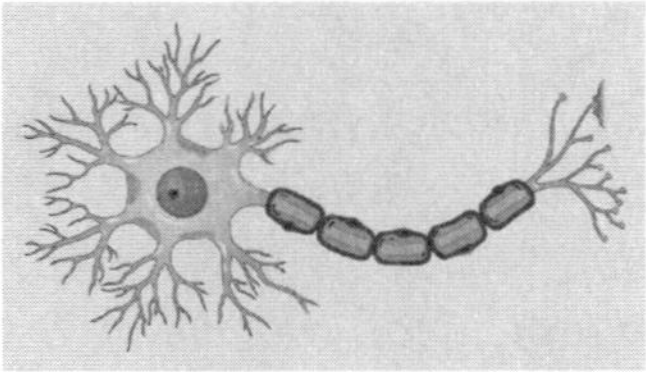

Nerve cell (neuron)

In plants, the bean-shaped guard cells in leaves expand and contract, regulating the stomata opening during gas exchange.

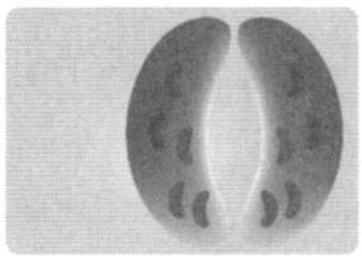

Guard cells of stomata

Structural Organization of Multicellular Organisms

The structure of every multicellular organism is organized according to the functions it carries out:

1. Cells – the basic structural unit of all living organisms.
2. Tissues – cells that perform similar functions form a tissue.
3. Organs – tissues that perform similar functions form an organ.
4. Organ systems – a group of organs that work together to perform a function forms an organ system.
5. Organism – formed by the combination of its organ systems.

The following chart shows the organization of cells, tissues, organs, and organ systems for a plant.

Cells	Tissues	Organs	Related Organs	Organ Systems
Protective epithelial cells	Dermal tissue	Epidermis	Leaf, stem, root	Shoot system and root system
Transport cells	Vascular tissue	Xylem	Leaf, stem, root	Shoot system and root system
		Phloem		
Photosyn-thetic and storage cells	Ground tissue	Cortex in roots or shoots (food storage) Mesophyll in leaves (photosynthe-sis)	Leaf, stems, roots, bark	Shoot system and root system

The following diagram shows the different levels of the structures of the shoot system in a plant.

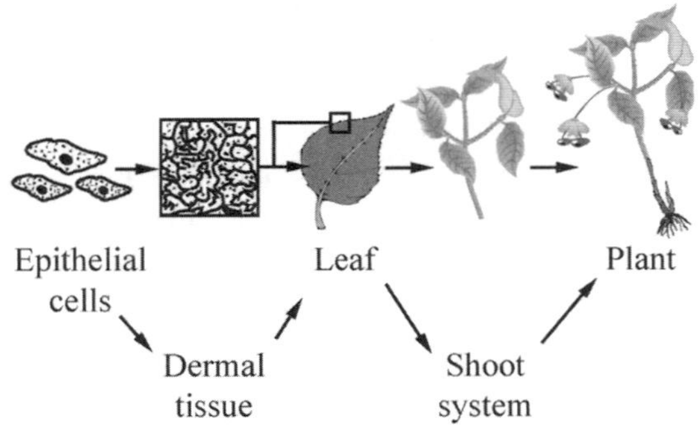

The following chart shows the organization of cells, tissues, organs, and organ systems for an animal.

Cells	Tissues	Related Organs	Organ Systems	Functions
Bone	Connec-tive tissue	Bones	Skeletal system	Supportive structures
Blood		Heart, blood vessels	Cardiovas-cular system	Transport functions
Muscle cells	Smooth muscle tissue	Stomach, blood vessels	Digestive and Cardio-vascular systems	Digestion and transport functions
	Skeletal muscle tissue	Limbs	Muscular system	Movement and support
	Cardiac muscle tissue	Heart	Cardiovas-cular system	Transport functions (gener-ates blood flow)
Nerve cells	Nervous tissue	Brain, spinal chord	Nervous system	Coordination and transportation of stimuli

Cells	Tissues	Related Organs	Organ Systems	Functions
Squamous		Skin, linings of digestive and respiratory tracts		
Cuboidal	Epithelial tissue	Linings of digestive and respiratory tracts	Skin, digestive system, respiratory system	Protection, digestion, respiration;. ciliated cells help in the movement of particles along the tract
Ciliated columnar		Lining of respiratory tract		
Stratified squamous		Skin		

The following diagram shows the different levels of the structures of the cardiovascular in a human.

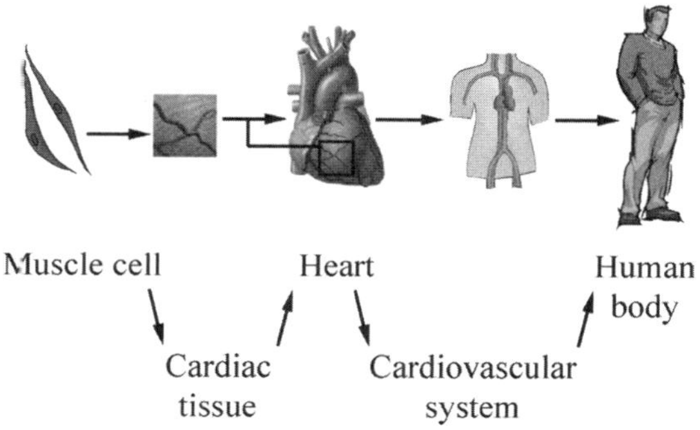

Unlike the somatic cells, the reproductive cells in multicellular organisms do not form tissues, organs, or systems. In other words, they do not form the organs they are found in. Instead, they are found separately within the reproductive organs.
For example, the sperm of a male organism is found within the testes, while the egg of a female organism are found within the ovaries.

20. From the simplest to the most complex, what are the levels of structural organization in living things?

A. Cells, organs, tissues, organ systems, and organisms

B. Organs, organ systems, cells, tissues, and organisms

C. Organ systems, organs, cells, tissues, and organisms

D. Cells, tissues, organs, organ systems, and organisms

CHALLENGER QUESTION

Use the following information to answer the next question.

Chloroplasts are involved in trapping solar energy and converting it into chemical energy through the production of glucose.

21. The region of the chloroplast in which the collection of solar energy for the production of glucose occurs is the

A. outer membrane **B.** inner membrane

C. thylakoid **D.** stroma

Use the following information to answer the next question.

In a technique called fluorescent labelling, a fluorescent molecule is attached to a certain structure within a cell. The cell is then illuminated with a laser that causes the fluorescent molecule to glow brightly. The structure within the cell to which the fluorescent molecule is attached can be observed under a fluorescent microscope. Biologists at the University of Toronto use this technique to study cell activity.

22. Fluorescent molecules are attached to the mitochondria in several different cell types. When viewed under a fluorescent microscope, which of the following cell types would glow **most** brightly?

A. Fat cells **B.** Skin cells

C. Blood cells **D.** Muscle cells

Use the following information to answer the next question.

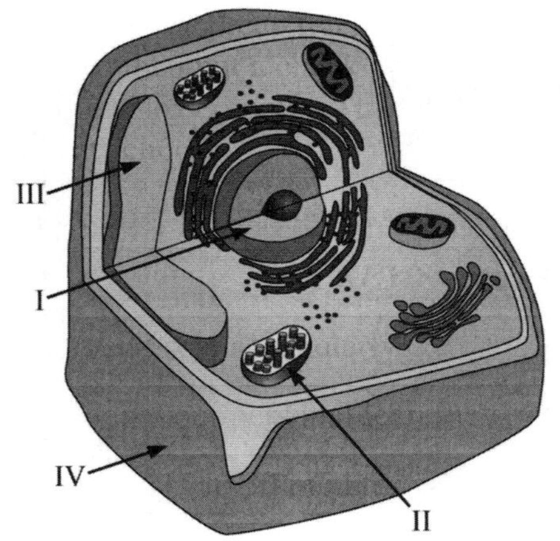

Diagram of a plant cell with four labelled organelles

23. The organelle of a plant cell that is responsible for photosynthesis is labelled

A. I **B.** II

C. III **D.** IV

10.2.B3.4 *explain the primary functions of a variety of systems in animals (e.g., the circulatory system transports materials through the organism; the respiratory system supplies oxygen to and removes carbon dioxide from the body)*

Organ Systems

An organ system is a group of organs and tissues working together for similar purpose. Animals have many organ systems that help them to live and perform daily functions.

Functions of Organ Systems in Animals

The **digestive system** takes food and breaks it down by enzymatic, chemical, and mechanical means into a form that can be absorbed by the intestines and delivered to the cells. The processes carried out in the digestive tract are as follows: ingestion (eating), digestion (breaking down nutrients by chemical and mechanical means), absorption of nutrients (bringing digested nutrients through the intestinal wall into the bloodstream), and egestion (elimination of waste by defecation). The system consists of the mouth, esophagus, stomach, small and large intestines, liver, pancreas, and various other glands.

The **circulatory system** transports and distributes materials from one part of the body to another (e.g., oxygen, carbon dioxide, metabolic wastes, blood cells, hormones, enzymes, antibodies, nutrients, heat, etc.). The circulatory system consists of the heart, arteries, capillaries, veins, and blood.

The **respiratory system** accomplishes gas exchange—it brings oxygen into the body and expels carbon dioxide, water vapour, and heat. This system consists of the lungs and conducting passageways. More specifically it includes the nose, pharynx, larynx, trachea, bronchi, bronchioles, and alveoli.

The **immune system** defends against micro-organisms and cancer cells. This system consists of lymph tissue (thymus, tonsils, lymph nodes), antibodies, and several types of white blood cells.

The **excretory system** accomplishes filtration of blood as well as the removal of excess substances, water, and toxic waste (urea). The excretory system consists of the kidneys, ureters, bladder, and urethra.

The **endocrine system** makes and controls the release of hormones (chemical messengers) that travel from one part of the body to the other through the bloodstream. Hormones control growth, development, and reproduction. Many organs and glands comprise this system including the hypothalamus, pituitary, thyroid, pancreas, parathyroid, liver, kidneys, ovaries, and testes.

The **reproductive system** creates gametes (sperm and eggs), and accomplishes reproduction and development. Female reproductive organs and structures include the uterus, ovaries, fallopian tubes and vagina. Male reproductive organs and structures include the testes, vas deferens, seminal vesicles, prostate gland, Cowper's gland, penis, and urethra.

The **nervous system** provides voluntary and involuntary control of the body's activities and responds to environmental stimuli. The organs and structures involved are the brain, spinal cord, nerves, and sensory receptors.

The **skeletal system** provides structural support. Structures in the skeletal system that support, move, and protect the body are bones, ligaments, tendons, and cartilage.

The **muscular system** controls locomotion, movement, and creation of pressure. Smooth or circular muscle pushes food, blood, or gametes through tubes; cardiac muscle creates force to push blood through blood vessels; and skeletal muscles shorten to change the position of bones, allowing locomotion.

The **integumentary system** protects against the external environment and invasion by micro-organisms. This system consists of skin, hair, and nails.

24. The body system that releases hormones that control specific functions within the body is called the

A. integumentary system

B. circulatory system

C. endocrine system

D. nervous system

Use the following information to answer the next question.

The ____*i*____ system and ____*ii*____ in the human body act together, to coordinate and maintain all the body's homeostatic functions.

25. This statement is **best** completed by the information in which of the following rows?

A.

i	*ii*
respiratory	lungs

B.

i	*ii*
digestive	stomach

C.

i	*ii*
circulatory	heart

D.

i	*ii*
nervous	brain

10.2.B3.5 *explain the interaction of different systems within an organism (e.g., the respiratory system brings oxygen into the body, and the circulatory system transports the oxygen to cells) and why such interactions are necessary for the organism's survival*

10.2.B2.6 *investigate, through a laboratory or computer simulated dissection of a plant, worm, fish, or frog, the interrelationships between organ systems of a plant or an animal (e.g., between the root system and leaf system in a plant; between the digestive system and circulatory system in an animal)*

Interdependence of Organ Systems

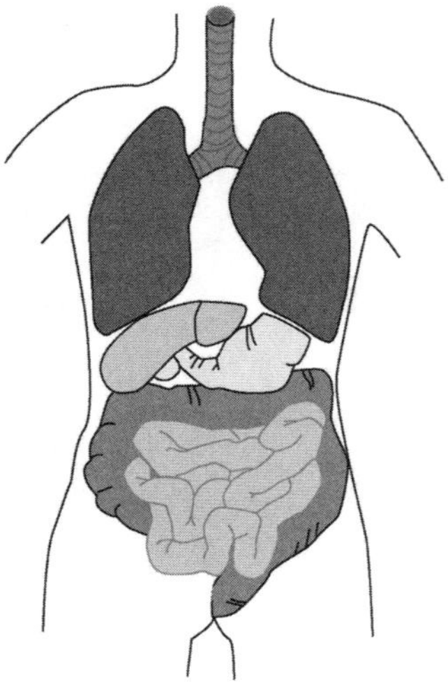

Cellular and organ specialization has led to division of labour within multicellular organisms, but this does not mean that one system can function independently of the others. All body systems are linked. One life function may require the involvement of several organ systems.
The following list includes examples of interdependencies in the structure and function of organ systems:

- The respiratory system brings oxygen into the body, and the circulatory system carries oxygen from the lungs to the cells. The same is true for the delivery of carbon dioxide from the tissues back to the lungs.
- The digestive system is responsible for breaking down food to a size that can be absorbed into cells, and the circulatory system must deliver those nutrients from the gut to each cell.
- The endocrine glands produce hormones, and the circulatory system delivers the hormones from the site where they are produced to the site where they will act.
- The skeletal system is important for support of the body, but the body cannot move without the attachment of the muscles of the muscular system to the bones. Similarly, the muscular system is quite useless without commands from the nervous system (brain, spinal cord, nerves).
- The kidneys of the excretory system remove urea and other wastes from the blood, and the circulatory system supplies the kidneys with blood that needs to be cleaned and returns the clean blood back to the body.

Example

The following example examines the interactions of several organ systems that occur in the process of urea elimination following consumption of a high protein meal:

1. The digestive system breaks down protein into amino acids, deaminating (removing NH_2 groups) extra amino acids to make urea.
2. Urea is carried by the circulatory system to the kidneys of the excretory system.
3. The kidneys filter the urea from the blood and send the urea through the ureters to the bladder.
4. When the bladder is full, a signal is sent to the nervous system, and the nervous system responds with the urge to urinate.
5. The muscular system contracts tissues surrounding the bladder, creating pressure that moves urine through the urethra to be expelled from the body.

CHALLENGER QUESTION

Use the following information to answer the next question.

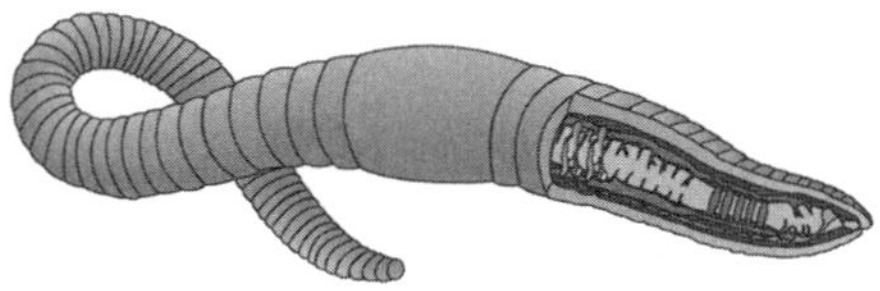

Latashia dissected an earthworm along the sagittal plane, exposing its dorsal and ventral blood vessels.

Open Response

26. Name and briefly describe the body system to which these vessels belong and how that system interacts with the integumentary system.

____

____

____

____

____

Use the following information to answer the next question.

Diagram of Vertebrate Hearts

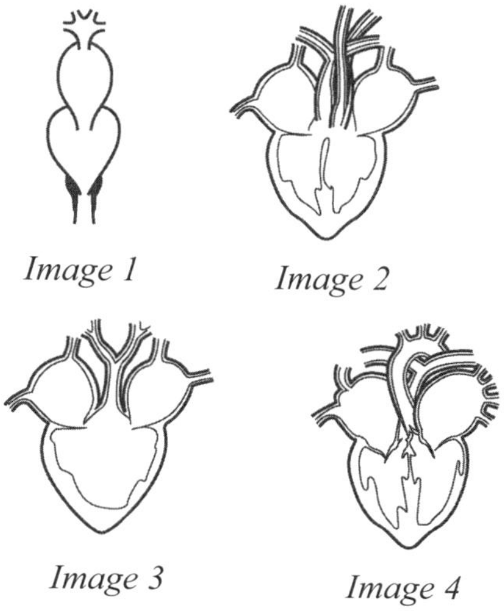

Numerical Response

27. Match each heart to its respective vertebrate group. (Record your answer as a four-digit number.)

Vertebrate	Heart Number
Amphibian	________
Mammal	________
Reptile	________
Fish	________

CHALLENGER QUESTION

Use the following information to answer the next question.

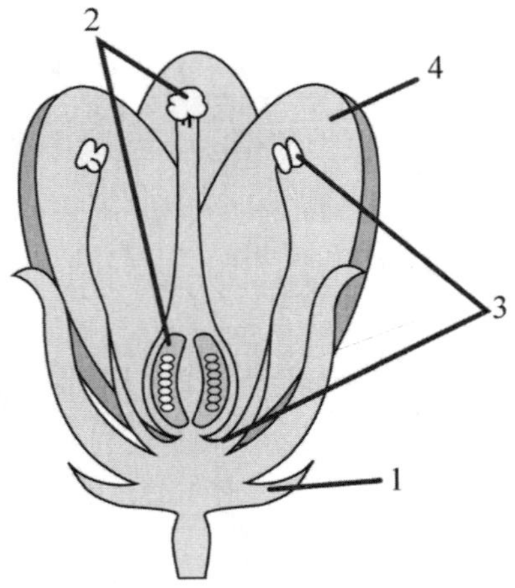

Parts of a flower in a vertical section

28. The female reproductive organ in the given plant diagram is represented by number

A. 1 **B.** 2

C. 3 **D.** 4

29. As a young male enters puberty, his vocal cords lengthen, causing his voice to deepen when he speaks. The two body systems that interact to produce and distribute the hormones responsible for these two changes are, respectively, the

A. endocrine and circulatory systems

B. circulatory and endocrine systems

C. nervous and circulatory systems

D. circulatory and nervous systems

30. Which two systems cooperate to directly regulate both nutrient and toxin levels in the body?

A. Digestive and excretory

B. Circulatory and endocrine

C. Digestive and integumentary

D. Endocrine and integumentary

Answers and Solutions

Biology: Tissues, Organs, and Systems of Living Things

1. A	7. B	13. C	19. A	25. D
2. OR	8. D	14. C	20. D	26. OR
3. A	9. OR	15. OR	21. C	27. 3421
4. OR	10. B	16. A	22. D	28. B
5. A	11. B	17. A	23. B	29. A
6. OR	12. C	18. B	24. C	30. A

1. A

The right to patent a natural compound is a major ethical issue surrounding the development of drugs from natural sources. Pharmaceutical companies spend large quantities of money on the development of new drugs and want to own the sole rights to any compounds they discover. The issue lies in whether a company can claim ownership over a naturally occurring substance they did not create.

2. OR

Some potential ethical issues that could be outlined are the individual's right to privacy, the individual's right to choose if he or she should be screened, the individual's right to protection from discrimination, and the question of who holds the right to access the technology.

- The privacy rights of the individual being screened—ethical concerns revolving around patient privacy may include whether or not the results of the screening should be made available to current or potential employers, insurance companies, or any other individual, group, or organization that might be negatively impacted by health issues the patient may have. The privacy rights of the patient relative to the long-term consequences suffered by those individuals, groups, or organizations may be impacted.

- An individual's right to choose whether he or she is to be screened or not—ethical concerns related to an individual's right to choose may include references to mandatory screening of those individuals genetically predispositioned to a particular condition or disorder in order to determine whether or not these people are at risk of propagating the disease within the population should they decide to have children.

- An individual's right to protection from discrimination—ethical concerns about discrimination of those individuals who have discovered through genetic screening that they are affected by a disorder may include decisions made by employers, insurance companies, and governments about an individual's employability, insurability, and rights to marriage, immigration, emigration, and procreation.

- Access to screening technology—ethical concerns related to an individual's access to DNA screening technology may include whether DNA screening will be covered by health care or made free to all people so that everyone has equal access, or whether it will be a luxury available to only those people that can afford to pay for the testing.

3. A

X-rays are a form of radiation and are part of the electromagnetic spectrum. X-rays can be used to assess dental conditions, bone injuries, lung ailments, and a variety of other medical conditions.

4. OR

Biophotonics is the study of the relationship between biological systems and photons. Photons are particles of light and electromagnetic radiation. All living things emit very low levels of photons. These levels are not enough to be considered true bioluminescence, but are detectable with sensitive electronic equipment.

Biophotonics were used to detect cancer under the Stalin regime, a concept not tested in the West, and regarded for a long time as a pseudoscience. More recently, biophotonics have made advances in microscopy with the advent of the confocal microscope and the florescence microscope.

5. A

The Public Health Agency of Canada's mandate is to prevent and control chronic and infectious diseases and promote public health. This includes raising public awareness of health risks, including screening for cancer, encouraging early cancer detection, and tracking emerging diseases. They do not inspect food. The Canadian Food Inspection Agency is responsible for ensuring the safety of food in Canada.

6. OR

The following are some ways of raising public awareness about the emergence of new strains of the flu:

1. Media-based public education programs, such as radio or television advertisements
2. Informative websites with important techniques and precautions that will help prevent viral exposure and spread
3. Posters or other visual advertisements in public places such as doctors' offices and drug stores
4. School campaigns organized and implemented by school nurses or teachers

7. B

During metaphase, the chromosomes arrange themselves at the cell equator. The following image depicts metaphase:

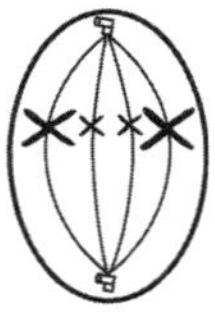

8. D

During prophase, the nucleus enlarges, and the nucleolus and nuclear membrane disappear.

9. OR

Metaphase is the best stage for showing an abnormal number of chromosomes in a cell because the cell's chromosomes have shortened and are easily visible. The chromosomes are arranged at the equator of the cell and are easier to count than in other stages of mitosis.

10. B

Mitosis is the process of cell division in which the parent cell divides once. This creates two daughter cells with the same number of chromosomes as the original parent cell.

11. B

Mitosis maintains the genetic composition of cells. The daughter cells are clones of the parent cell. Mitosis maintains genetic composition, produces identical cells to repair skin wounds, and grows organs. Because the daughter cells are clones, mitosis does not induce variation. Genetic variation occurs during the crossing over stage of meiosis; crossing over does not occur during mitosis.

12. C

The process for making more body cells in order to grow and repair the body involves the creation of daughter cells. Cell division that leads to identical daughter cells is called mitosis.

Meiosis describes a special form of cell division in which the resulting cells have fewer chromosomes than the parent. Mating describes sexual reproduction, and fusion is the process whereby two cells fuse or combine. There are few, if any, examples of fusion happening with normal animal or plant cells.

13. C

Cell walls are found only in plant cells. They give plant cells structural support.

14. C

Both Cell 1 and Cell 2 have common features, such as cytoplasm, a nucleus, and a cell membrane. Cell 1 is a plant cell because it has a rigid cell wall, contains at least one large vacuole, and has chloroplasts. Cell 2 is an animal cell, characterized by a thin cell membrane, an irregular shape, small vacuoles, and no chloroplasts. Both plant and animal cells carry on cellular respiration but only plant cells perform photosynthesis.

15. OR

The labeled organelles are correctly matched with their names in the following table.

Organelle Name	Letter
Vacuole	C
Cell membrane	B
Nucleus	F
Mitochondria	H
Cell wall	A
Endoplasmic reticulum	D
Golgi apparatus	G
Ribosome	E

16. A

Cirrhosis is a chronic liver disease that is characterized by the replacement of normal, healthy liver tissue with scarred, damaged liver tissue. Normal, healthy liver tissue can regenerate new cells when it becomes damaged. However, when the liver tissue is scarred, the cells cannot replace themselves, and the flow of blood through the liver is impeded, which in turn impairs the liver's many functions.

17. A

When a cell differentiates to form a specialized structure, it loses the power to divide again. Some cells, like neurons, are not replaceable and cannot regenerate themselves. Special cells, called stem cells, are undifferentiated and may be able to replace the specialized cells.

18. B

Shoot tips, the actively growing parts of a plant, develop into a flower. The meristematic cells divide actively in the bud.

Ripe fruits and mature leaves are not growing rapidly and are considered permanent tissues, as is xylem, which is dead tissue.

19. A

The only conclusion that can be drawn from the graph is that the rate of division is higher in cancerous cells than in regular cells, since the only information the graph provides is the number of cells over time. While the other statements regarding cancer are accurate, they are not shown by the information in the graph.

20. D

The cell is the basic unit of body structure for an organism. Cells can be grouped and organized to form tissues. Tissues can come together to form organs. Certain organs can be connected to form an organ system, and the body of a complex organism consists of many organ systems.

21. C

The thylakoid of the chloroplast contains chlorophyll that traps solar energy and converts it into chemical energy in the form of glucose.

22. D

Muscle cells require a large portion of the energy (ATP) produced by the body. As a result, cells found in muscles are packed with ATP-generating mitochondria. Relative to the other cell types listed, all of which contain mitochondria, muscle cells would glow most brightly.

23. B

The organelle labelled II is a chloroplast. The chloroplast is the part of the plant cell that is responsible for photosynthesis.

The organelle labelled I is the nucleus. The organelle labelled III is the vacuole. The organelle labelled IV is the cell wall.

24. C

The endocrine system consists of glands that secrete hormones. Hormones are chemical compounds that coordinate and control specific functions within the body.

25. D

The nervous system, acting through the brain, is responsible for coordinating and maintaining all the body's homeostatic activities.

26. OR

The blood vessels belong to the circulatory system, which circulates blood throughout the earthworm's body. The earthworm breathes through its skin, and the oxygen is absorbed into the blood stream and carried to other body tissues.

27. 3421

Vertebrate	Heart Number
Amphibian	3
Mammal	4
Reptile	2
Fish	1

Image 1 is a two-chambered, venous heart and is present in fish. Image 2 is a reptilian heart and is characterized by the incomplete partitioning of the ventricles. This means that while it contains two separate auricles, the ventricles remain partially connected. Image 3 is a three-chambered heart and is present in amphibians and anurans. Image 4 is a four-chambered heart, which is characteristic of mammals.

28. B

There are four types of floral organs: sepal, petal, carpel, and stamen. The carpel (2) and the stamen (3) are essential organs that are directly involved in sexual reproduction. A carpel is a female reproductive organ consisting of a stigma, a style, and an ovary. Stamens, the male reproductive organs of a plant, consist of a slender stalk called a filament and an anther.

The sepal (1) and the petal (4) are non-essential floral organs that do not participate in sexual reproduction. Sepals are green, leaf-like structures that arise at the base of a flower, and mainly protect the flower before it opens. Petals are the whorl of brightly coloured and fragrant appendages that attract insects, and are located inside the sepal.

29. A

The endocrine system is made up of glands that produce and secrete hormones. The hormones are released into the circulatory system, which distributes them throughout the body.

30. A

The digestive system is responsible for the ingestion and absorption of nutrients. The excretory system maintains the body's osmotic balance by filtering the blood and removing water and toxins as needed.

Unit Test

CHALLENGER QUESTION

1. Which of the following scientific developments is **not** related to genetic engineering?
   - **A.** Recombinant DNA
   - **B.** Transgenic animals
   - **C.** Organ transplantation
   - **D.** Plant breeding techniques

Open Response

2. Briefly outline the **main** arguments for and against stem cell research.

3. What is MRI technology used for?
   - **A.** Visualizing soft body tissues
   - **B.** Visualizing functional body processes
   - **C.** Measuring electrical activity of the heart
   - **D.** Measuring electrical impulses in the brain

Open Response

4. Identify an imaging technique that is very commonly used to view a fetus during pregnancy, and explain how this procedure works.

5. All of the following are primary goals of the Public Health Agency of Canada **except**
   - **A.** preventing and controlling injuries and chronic disease
   - **B.** promoting public health and awareness about disease
   - **C.** preventing and controlling infectious disease
   - **D.** providing treatment for acute disease

Use the following information to answer the next question.

The MMR vaccine was introduced as a combination vaccine designed to protect against three common diseases: measles, mumps, and rubella.

Open Response

6. Briefly describe the effect of the nationwide use of the MMR vaccine, and identify who receives it.

7. A vascular bundle in the stem of a plant contains
   - **A.** xylem and phloem
   - **B.** phloem and root hairs
   - **C.** guard cells and xylem
   - **D.** root hairs and stomates

CHALLENGER QUESTION

Use the following information to answer the next question.

The given diagrams show four phases of mitosis.

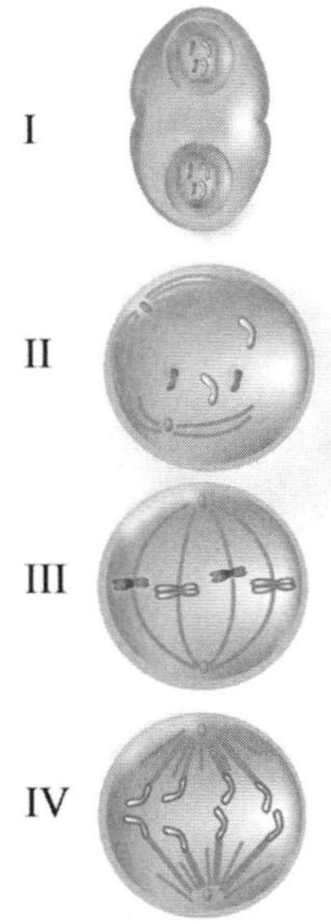

8. Which of the diagrams depicts the anaphase stage of mitosis?

A. Diagram I **B.** Diagram II

C. Diagram III **D.** Diagram IV

Open Response

9. Sketch a diagram of a cell in prophase, and describe the major features of this phase of mitosis.

____

____

____

____

____

10. Which of the following statements about plant cells and animal cells is **true**?

A. Both plant cells and animal cells contain a cell membrane.

B. Both animal cells and plant cells contain chloroplasts.

C. Animal cells contain a cell wall; plant cells do not.

D. Plant cells contain vacuoles; animal cells do not.

Open Response

11. Animals are called heterotrophs because unlike plants, they cannot make their own food. What is the name of the process by which plants make their own food? Sketch and label a diagram of the organelle, unique to plants, that is essential to this process.

____

____

____

____

____

12. Xylem cells in plant stems are elongated and hollow, but the cells in leaves are round or flattened. Which of the following statements describes a reason that xylem and leaf cells differ?

A. Leaf cells receive more sunlight.

B. Leaf cells are rounded or flattened from the wind.

C. Xylem cells and leaf cells receive different nutrients.

D. Xylem cells and leaf cells perform different functions.

13. Which of the following characteristics is **not** associated with malignant tumors?

A. Self-regulation

B. Uncontrolled growth

C. Ability to metastasize

D. Intrusion on other tissues

Use the following information to answer the next question.

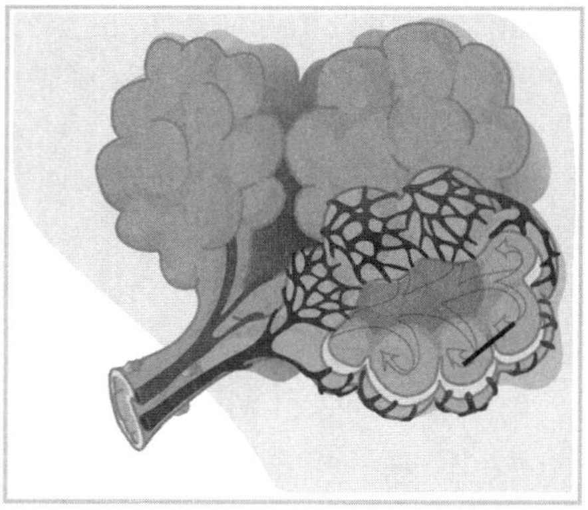

Open Response

14. Identify the **two main** structures depicted in the given diagram. Which **two** internal systems are illustrated by the picture and in what way do they work together?

____
____
____
____
____
____
____

15. The development of heart disease is **most closely** associated with excess intake of

A. proteins

B. saturated fats

C. carbohydrates

D. unsaturated fats

16. Which of the following processes occurs during the S phase of the cell cycle?

A. Mitosis **B.** Cell division

C. Cytokinesis **D.** DNA synthesis

17. The cell process that immediately follows mitosis is

A. prophase **B.** anaphase

C. telekinesis **D.** cytokinesis

CHALLENGER QUESTION

18. Stem cells are undifferentiated primitive cells that have the capacity to mature into many different types of tissue or organ cells. They are becoming very important in scientific research. Which of the following medical applications would be most appropriate for the use of stem cells?

A. Fight off a bacterial infection

B. Cure a body of a cancerous growth

C. Repair a brain that has been damaged by an accident

D. Protect a person from the symptoms of a genetic disorder

19. Which of the following statements explains the importance of stem cells in both, embryonic development and medical research?

A. Stem cells are resistant to harmful viruses and bacteria.

B. Stem cells can differentiate into all specialized embryonic tissue.

C. Stem cells can be extracted in large amounts.

D. Stem cells replicate at an extremely fast rate.

20. An organ is **best** described as a group of

A. similar cells, connected to serve the same purpose

B. different cells, connected to serve the same purpose

C. similar tissues that work together to serve the same function

D. different tissues that work together to serve the same function

Use the following information to answer the next question.

> Stomata are referred to as "the gateways of transpiration" because their behaviour influences the rate of transpiration. This rate is generally very low at night and increases rapidly from early morning until midday.

21. Which of the following plant cells regulate the opening and closing of the stomata?
- **A.** Parenchyma cells
- **B.** Epidermal cells
- **C.** Root hair cells
- **D.** Guard cells

CHALLENGER QUESTION

22. Which of the following functions is **true** of both the integumentary system and the excretory system?
- **A.** Both systems help bring oxygen into the body and help transport nutrients around the body.
- **B.** Both systems help the body get rid of wastes and help transport nutrients to body tissues.
- **C.** Both systems help bring oxygen into the body and regulate water levels in the body.
- **D.** Both systems help the body get rid of wastes and regulate water levels in the body.

23. The body system that functions **primarily** to fight infections is the
- **A.** nervous system
- **B.** immune system
- **C.** digestive system
- **D.** endocrine system

24. Groups of female lions often hunt together, working together to kill large-hoofed mammals. Which of the following pairs of body systems are interacting to coordinate movements as a lioness chases her prey?
- **A.** Integumentary and muscular
- **B.** Endocrine and digestive
- **C.** Nervous and muscular
- **D.** Endocrine and skeletal

25. Which two systems interact to bring oxygen into an athlete's body and carry it to the muscles?
- **A.** Respiratory and circulatory
- **B.** Respiratory and muscular
- **C.** Excretory and circulatory
- **D.** Excretory and muscular

Answers and Solutions – Unit Test

1. C	6. OR	11. OR	16. D	21. D
2. OR	7. A	12. D	17. D	22. D
3. A	8. D	13. A	18. C	23. B
4. OR	9. OR	14. OR	19. B	24. C
5. D	10. A	15. B	20. D	25. A

1. C

Genetic engineering is the use of DNA technology in relation to biological processes. It is useful for obtaining novel materials for agricultural, industrial, domestic, medical, and other purposes.
Organ transplantation does not involve genetic engineering; an organ from a donor is simply placed in a recipient.

Plant breeding techniques, recombinant DNA, and transgenic animals are products of genetic engineering as they involve the use of DNA technology.

2. OR

Stem cell research is a hot topic because it involves the creation, use, and destruction of human embryonic stem cells.

Pro-stem cell arguments (for stem cell research) are focused on the huge medical potential of the technology. It may offer treatment hope for degenerative conditions, physical trauma, and genetic disorders. People with this view argue that since many zygotes do not end up implanting and blastocysts are balls of cells with no human-like form, the use of stem cells is not destroying a human life.

Anti-stem cell arguments (against stem cell research) consist of the belief that a zygote is human from the moment of fertilization, and that life should not be destroyed. Additionally, arguments against stem cell research often consider creation of human zygotes for research purposes a slippery slope toward human cloning, which is itself a hot topic of ethical debate.

3. A

MRI stands for magnetic resonance imaging, a process that uses powerful magnetic fields to create an image of the body. The image is created using the magnetic field generated by the hydrogen atoms in the water molecules in the human body. The image is rotatable and provides contrast between the different soft-tissue layers of the body.

PET scans visualize functional body processes, ECGs measure electrical activity of the heart, and EEGs measure electrical impulses in the brain.

4. OR

Pregnant women often go for ultrasound tests. These are also known as medical sonographs. Ultrasound is a sound with a frequency much higher than what can be detected by the human ear.
By projecting ultrasound through a medium, the reflections can be measured, creating an image of the medium. Ultrasound is sent through the mother's stomach, and the differing reflection signatures create a live image of the fetus.

5. D

The Public Health Agency of Canada (PHAC) is a federal health program. Its mandate is to promote public health and prevent and control chronic and infectious diseases.

Providing treatment for disease is not one of the PHAC's main goals.

6. OR

The widespread implementation of the MMR vaccine has almost completely reduced the incidence of measles, mumps, and rubella in populations that receive it as a part of their regular vaccination regime. Children receive their first MMR shot around the age of one and their second shot when they reach school age.

7. A

Vascular tissue transports materials composed of xylem and phloem. Xylem and phloem both exist as tubes. Tiny tubes have a greater surface area relative to their diameter than large tubes do. A vascular bundle is a bundle of tiny xylem and phloem tubes. In a leaf, vascular bundles appear as veins.

8. D

During the anaphase stage of mitosis, the sister chromatids of the paired chromosomes separate and migrate toward opposite poles. Prior to separating during the anaphase stage, the chromotids assemble and come together in the centre of the cell in the prophase and metaphase stages.

9. OR

Prophase is the first stage in mitosis. The diagram should show condensing, visible chromosomes with identical sister chromatids, the nuclear membrane dissolving, and early formation of the spindle apparatus.

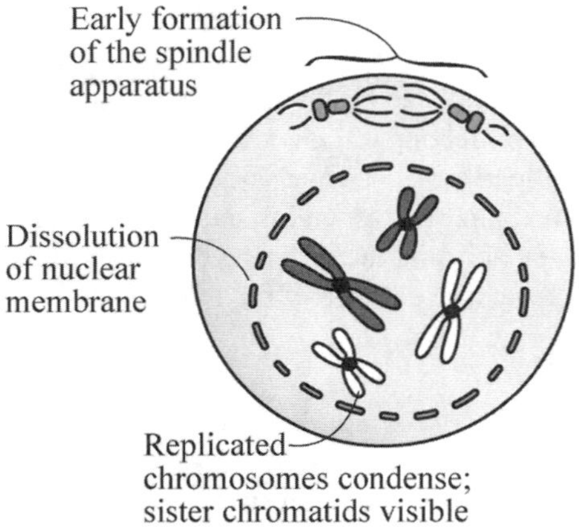

10. A

Both plant and animal cells have a cell membrane. This membrane acts as a barrier between the outside environment and the inside environment. Vacuoles are found in both plant and animal cells. Cell walls and chloroplasts are characteristic of plant cells only.

11. OR

Plants use a process called photosynthesis to make their own food. Specialized organelles, called chloroplasts, contain pigments in the thylakoid membrane that allow plant cells to capture energy from the sun's rays and convert it into sugars.

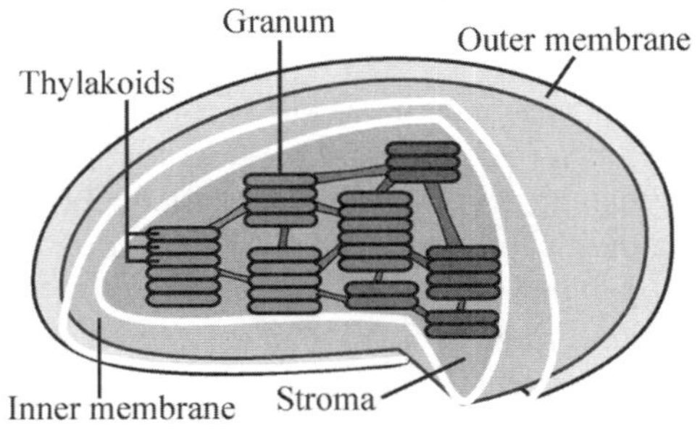

A chloroplast labelled with some key structures

12. D

Xylem cells are elongated and hollow so they can conduct water to various plant parts. Leaf cells perform photosynthesis, so they are round and flattened to expose as much surface area as possible for the exchange of gases. The cells are different from each other because they perform different functions.

13. A

Malignant tumors are harmful. The three main characteristics of malignant tumors are uncontrolled growth, ability to metastasize (break apart and spread through the body), and the tendency to invade and intrude on other tissues. Tumors that do not have any of these characteristics are called benign.

14. OR

The structures in the diagram are *alveoli* and their associated *capillaries*. The two internal systems illustrated are the *respiratory* and *circulatory*. These two systems work together to exchange respiratory gases such as carbon dioxide and oxygen between the external environment and the internal tissues.

15. B

Saturated fats accumulate in the arteries near the heart, minimizing the space blood has to flow. This means that the heart has to work harder to pump blood. This results in an increased risk of heart disease.

16. D

The S phase is the period in the cell cycle between the G_1 and G_2 phases. After leaving the G_1 phase, the cell enters S phase. DNA synthesis occurs during this phase. This results in the duplication of the genetic material in the cell that will ultimately be divided in two during mitosis.

17. D

Mitosis is usually followed immediately by cytokinesis, in which the cytoplasm and cell membrane divide. This results in two identical daughter cells with a roughly equal distribution of organelles and other cellular components. Mitosis and cytokinesis together are defined as the mitotic (M) phase of the cell cycle.

18. C

The most useful aspect of stem cells is their ability to specialize as needed. That is, they have the ability to become a certain kind of cell. If there has been brain damage, stem cells placed in the brain could become the kind of cell that has been lost or damaged.

19. B

Stem cells begin as a blank slate, but become specialized in the early embryonic stage and develop into specific cells, tissue, and organs.

20. D

An organ is a group of different tissues that work together to serve the same function. A tissue is a group of similar cells connected to serve the same purpose.

21. D

Each stomata is surrounded by two guard cells that control its opening and closing by changing the turgidity. The guard cells become turgid when they absorb water from the surrounding cells. When the guard cells become turgid, the outer elastic walls become convex in shape. As the guard cells take this shape, they draw the inner walls apart, resulting in a larger opening or aperture. When the turgor pressure decreases, the reverse situation occurs and the stomata opening becomes smaller.

22. D

The excretory system gets rid of body wastes by filtering the blood and eliminating any wastes through urination. The integumentary system gets rid of small amounts of wastes by sweating.
The excretory system controls water levels in the body by eliminating water that the body does not require through urination. The skin controls water levels in the body by offering a barrier between the dry environment and the moist internal organs.

23. B

The immune system, in conjunction with the lymphatic and circulatory systems, functions to fight infections.

The nervous system coordinates and conducts the activities of different organs and tissues.
The digestive system consists of the alimentary canal and its associated glands. Through this system, large organic molecules are hydrolyzed into smaller molecules, which are absorbed by the body.
The endocrine system consists of glands that secrete hormones into the blood.

24. C

All body systems work together, but the coordination of movements is caused by an interaction between the nervous system and muscular system. As a lioness chases her prey, the nervous system sends instructions to the muscular system to contract the muscle fibres.

25. A

Oxygen is brought into the athlete's body via the respiratory system. It is then carried by the blood cells, which are part of the circulatory system, to the muscle tissues. The heart is a muscle that aids in increasing the rate of circulation, but the red blood cells themselves actually carry the oxygen molecules.

NOTES

Chemistry

Chemistry: Chemical Reactions

Table of Correlations

Specific Expectation		Practice Questions	Unit Test Questions	Practice Test 1	Practice Test 2
10.3.C1	analyse a variety of safety and environmental issues associated with chemical reactions, including the ways in which chemical reactions can be applied to address environmental challenges				
10.3.C1.1	*analyse, on the basis of research, various safety and environmental issues associated with chemical reactions and their reactants and/or product(s) (e.g., chemical reactions related to the use of cyanide in gold mining, the corrosion of metal supports on bridges, the use of different antibacterial agents such as chlorine and bromine in recreational pools)*	1	1, 2	11	
10.3.C1.2	*analyse how an understanding of the properties of chemical substances and their reactions can be applied to solve environmental challenges (e.g., renewing the Great Lakes, neutralizing acid spills, scrubbing smokestack emissions)*	2, 3	3		11
10.3.C2	investigate, through inquiry, the characteristics of chemical reactions				
10.3.C2.1	*use appropriate terminology related to chemical reactions, including, but not limited to: compounds, product, and reactant*	27	4	12	
10.3.C2.2	*construct molecular models to illustrate the structure of molecules in simple chemical reactions (e.g., $C + O_2 \rightarrow CO_2$; $2H_2 + O_2 \rightarrow 2H_2O$)), and produce diagrams of these models*	16, 17, 18	5, 6		12
10.3.C2.3	*investigate simple chemical reactions, including synthesis, decomposition, and displacement reactions, and represent them using a variety of formats (e.g., molecular models, word equations, balanced chemical equations)*	21, 22, 23	7	13a, 13b, 13c	
10.3.C2.4	*use an inquiry process to investigate the law of conservation of mass in a chemical reaction (e.g., compare the values before and after the reaction), and account for any discrepancies*	7, 8	8		13
10.3.C2.5	*plan and conduct an inquiry to identify the evidence of chemical change (e.g., the formation of a gas or precipitate, a change in colour or odour, a change in temperature)*	11	9	14	
10.3.C2.6	*plan and conduct an inquiry to classify some common substances as acidic, basic, or neutral (e.g., use acid-base indicators or pH test strips to classify common household substances)*	26	10		14
10.3.C3	demonstrate an understanding of the general principles of chemical reactions, and various ways to represent them				
10.3.C3.1	*describe the relationships between chemical formulae, composition, and names of binary compounds (e.g., carbon dioxide, CO_2, has two oxygen atoms and one carbon atom)*	4, 5	11, 12	15	
10.3.C3.2	*explain, using the law of conservation of mass and atomic theory, the rationale for balancing chemical equations*	6			15
10.3.C3.3	*describe the types of evidence that indicate chemical change (e.g., changes in colour, the production of a gas, the formation of a precipitate, the production or absorption of heat, the production of light)*	9, 10	13	16	
10.3.C3.4	*write word equations and balanced chemical equations for simple chemical reactions (e.g., $2H_2 + O_2 \rightarrow 2H_2O$)*	12, 13, 14, 15	14, 15, 16	17, 18	16, 17

Table of Correlations

Specific Expectation		Practice Questions	Unit Test Questions	Practice Test 1	Practice Test 2
10.3.C3.5	*describe, on the basis of observation, the reactants in and products of a variety of chemical reactions, including synthesis, decomposition, and displacement reactions (e.g., reactions occurring when magnesium burns or in the production of oxygen from hydrogen peroxide; the reaction of iron and copper sulphate; reactions occurring when fossil fuels burn)*	19, 20	17, 18		18
10.3.C3.6	*describe the process of acid-base neutralization (i.e., an acid reacts with a base to form a salt and often water)*	24	19, 20	19	
10.3.C3.7	*describe how the pH scale is used to classify solutions as acidic, basic, or neutral (e.g., a solution with a pH of 1 is highly acidic; a solution with a pH of 7 is neutral)*	25	21, 22		19
10.3.C3.8	*identify simple ionic compounds (e.g., NaCl), simple compounds involving polyatomic ions (e.g., KNO3, NaOH), molecular compounds (e.g., CO2, H2O, NH3), and acids (e.g., HCl(aq), H2SO4(aq)), using the periodic table and a list of the most common polyatomic ions (e.g., OH-, SO 4 -2), and write the formulae*	28, 29, 30	23, 24, 25	20	20

10.3.C1.1 *analyse, on the basis of research, various safety and environmental issues associated with chemical reactions and their reactants and/or product(s) (e.g., chemical reactions related to the use of cyanide in gold mining, the corrosion of metal supports on bridges, the use of different antibacterial agents such as chlorine and bromine in recreational pools)*

Chemical Reactions: Safety and Environmental Issues

Chemical reactions provide many benefits for society; they are used in the creation of useful compounds and the processing of many different materials. A solid understanding of the reactions involved is required to avoid and minimize the potential safety and environmental issues.
For example, both ammonia and chlorine bleach are used as household cleaning agents. When the two substances are mixed, however, they produce a highly toxic chlorine gas. WHMIS and MSDS are two systems created to reduce the safety concerns and environmental issues that can arise as a result of chemical reactions.

WHMIS and Laboratory Safety

The Workplace Hazardous Materials Information System (WHMIS) provides information to help people recognize certain hazardous materials.

There are eight standard symbols that have been designed to advise people that they must be careful when handling certain materials. You must be able to recognize each symbol and know its meaning.

Compressed Gas

Flammable and Combustible Material

Oxidizing Material

Poisonous and Infectious Material Materials Causing Immediate and Serious Toxic Effects

Poisonous and Infectious Material Materials Causing Other Toxic Effects

Biohazardous Infectious Material

Corrosive Material

Dangerously Reactive Material

Material Safety Data Sheets

In Canada, all chemicals must have a material safety data sheet (MSDS) attached that identifies the chemical and its physical properties, as well as any dangers the chemical may present to the person handling it.

In addition to the appropriate WHMIS symbol or symbols, each sheet gives the melting point, the boiling point, and the toxicity of the material, as well as first aid, spill, and cleanup procedures. Material safety data sheets also list chemical combinations that should be avoided.

Material Safety Data Sheet

Section 1 – Product Information				
Product Name			Product ID #	
Product Use				
Manufacturer's Name			Supplier's Name	
Street Address			Street Address	
City	Prov.		City	Prov.
Postal code	Emergency telephone		Postal code	Emergency telephone
Section 2 – Hazardous Ingredients				
Hazardous Ingredients	%	CAS #	LC50	LD50
Section 3 – Physical Data				
Physical state	Odour and Appearance			Odour Threshold
Vapour pressure	Vapour density		Evaporation rate	Boiling point
Freezing point	pH	Specific gravity	Coefficient of water/oil distribution	
Section 4 – Fire and Explosion Data				
Flammability yes☐ no ☐ if yes, what conditions?				
Means of extinction		Flash point and method of determination		
Upper flammable limit	Lower flammable limit		Auto-ignition temperature	
Hazardous combustion products				
Explosion data – mechanical impact		Explosion data – static discharge		

Your knowledge of these warning symbols and their meanings and your awareness of the safety precautions that should be followed will contribute to your confidence, comfort, and safety in your home, workplace, and school laboratory.

Use the following information to answer the next question.

Household products, such as those listed below, can be dangerous even though they are used on a daily basis.

1. Pet-care products
2. Cooking products
3. Paint and paint products
4. Cleaning products
5. Personal hygiene products

1. Which of the given household products are considered hazardous household chemicals and usually have special disposal instructions?

A. 1 and 3 **B.** 1 and 4

C. 3 and 4 **D.** 3 and 5

10.3.C1.2 *analyse how an understanding of the properties of chemical substances and their reactions can be applied to solve environmental challenges (e.g., renewing the Great Lakes, neutralizing acid spills, scrubbing smokestack emissions)*

Using Chemistry to Solve Environmental Challenges

A solid understanding of chemistry and chemical reactions can be used to solve environmental challenges. Calcium oxide, commonly called lime, can be added to lakes that have been affected by acid rain. The lime neutralizes the acid, renewing the pH of the lake water and improving water quality. Similarly, acid spills can be cleaned up using a variety of bases. Oil spills, which are very toxic to marine and terrestrial wildlife, can be mediated using chemicals that react with and break up the oil particles. Catalytic converters in car exhaust systems use chemical reactions to turn the toxic byproducts of vehicle exhaust into less toxic compounds.

Use the following information to answer the next question.

Smokestacks are large chimneys used in industrial plants to provide oxygen for combustion reactions. In the process, they vent the byproducts of combustion. During the Industrial Revolution, citizens realized that the smokestacks were spewing noxious chemicals into the air around the plants.

2. Which of the following courses of action would be the **best** solution when considering both the environment and the economy?

A. Install scrubbers on the smokestacks

B. Make the smokestacks taller

C. Stop using smokestacks

D. Close down the plants

Use the following information to answer the next question.

When dangerous chemical materials are shipped across Canada, they must always be accompanied by a detailed shipping document. When shipped by truck, the document must be in a pocket mounted on the driver's side door. When shipped by rail, the document must be in the first locomotive. On a ship, the document must be kept on the bridge.

Open Response

3. What type of information should be contained within the document, and why is it so important to have it in a set place?

10.3.C3.1 *describe the relationships between chemical formulae, composition, and names of binary compounds (e.g., carbon dioxide, CO_2, has two oxygen atoms and one carbon atom)*

Chemical Formula, Composition, and Naming

Chemicals, many of which are potentially hazardous, are used all around the world, so it is important to have a clear, consistent way of describing and identifying them. The International Union of Pure and Applied Chemistry (IUPAC) standardized the relationships between chemical formula, composition, and names, so it is now easier for chemists on either side of the globe to communicate about their research or for consumers anywhere in the world to understand information about the chemicals they are buying.

The composition of a chemical refers to the number of each type of atom it contains. For example, water, shown on the left, is a chemical compound. It is composed of two hydrogen atoms and one oxygen atom, shown on the right. This arrangement of atoms is its composition.

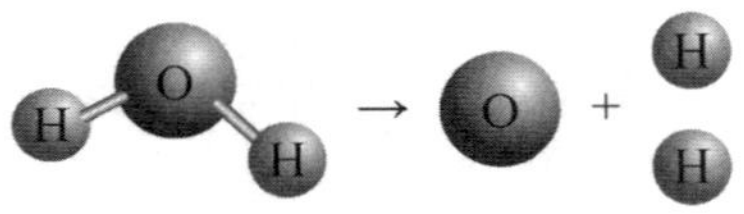

The chemical formula of a compound indicates the number of each type of atom in the compound. The formula of water is H_2O. Each atom is identified using its symbol from the periodic table. The number of that type of atom in the chemical is represented by the subscript number following the atom.

Naming is also standardized and is done using the rules discussed later in this unit. Water is the common name for H_2O. The real chemical name for this compound is dihydrogen monoxide. Notice that the name also indicates the type of atoms found and the number of each type of atom.

CHALLENGER QUESTION

Use the following information to answer the next question.

An iron ion can have a charge of 3+. An oxygen ion has a charge of 2−. Iron and oxygen readily combine to form a compound commonly known as rust.

$Fe^{3+}O^{2-}$

4. Which of the following charts identifies the correct formula and IUPAC name for rust?

A.

Chemical Formula	IUPAC Name
Fe_3O_2	Iron (III) oxide

B.

Chemical Formula	IUPAC Name
Fe_3O_2	Iron (II) oxide

C.

Chemical Formula	IUPAC Name
Fe_2O_3	Iron (III) oxide

D.

Chemical Formula	IUPAC Name
Fe_2O_3	Iron (II) oxide

Use the following information to answer the next question.

The composition of a compound is represented by its molecular formula, which indicates a compound's constituent elements and the proportion in which they are present in the compound.

5. The molecular formula of carbon dioxide is

A. C_2H_2 **B.** CH_4
C. CO_2 **D.** CO

10.3.C3.2 *explain, using the law of conservation of mass and atomic theory, the rationale for balancing chemical equations*

10.3.C2.4 *use an inquiry process to investigate the law of conservation of mass in a chemical reaction (e.g., compare the values before and after the reaction), and account for any discrepancies*

The Law of Conservation of Mass

Chemical changes occur when a chemical reaction takes place, creating new substances. In the late 1700s, a scientist named Lavoisier did an experiment in which he sealed some tin and air inside a glass vessel. He weighed the vessel, heated it, and watched as the tin reacted with the oxygen to form tin oxide. When he weighed the vessel at the end of the reaction, he found that even though the compounds in the vessel had changed, the mass of the vessel was the same as when he began the experiment. Similar experiments led to the development of the law of conservation of mass: the total mass of the substances present after a chemical reaction is the same as the total mass of the substances present before the reaction.
This means that the total number of atoms of each element will be the same before and after the reaction.

The law of conservation of mass is modelled in chemical reactions. For example, when a molecule of water is separated into oxygen and hydrogen, there is one oxygen atom before the reaction, or in the reactants. After the reaction, there is still one atom of oxygen in the products. There are two hydrogen atoms before the reaction occurs, and two hydrogen atoms following the reaction. The mass is conserved during the reaction.

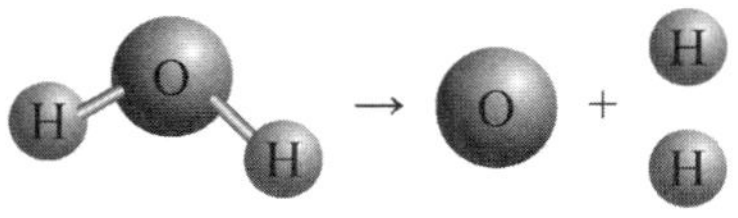

Water broken into constituent elements retains equal numbers of atoms on both sides of the reaction.

6. The law of conservation of mass is applicable to all chemical reactions

A. whose products are solids

B. whose reactants are solids

C. where both the reactants and products are solids

D. regardless of whether or not the reactants or products are solids

Use the following information to answer the next question.

> Titanium dioxide is used as a white pigment in paints, rubbers, plastics, and paper. Titanium dioxide is formed in this reaction.
> $TiCl_{4(g)} + O_{2(g)} \rightarrow TiO_{2(s)} + 2Cl_{2(g)}$

7. Which of the following statements is **true**?

A. The mass of chlorine is exactly twice the mass of titanium dioxide.

B. The masses of the products outweigh the masses of the reactants.

C. The masses of the reactants outweigh the masses of the products.

D. The combined mass of the products equals the combined mass of the reactants.

Use the following information to answer the next question.

> According to the law of conservation of mass, in all physical and chemical changes, the total mass of the reactants is equal to the total mass of the products. This law is also called the law of indestructibility of matter.

8. The law of conservation of mass was proposed by the French chemist

A. Lavoisier

B. Ritcher

C. Proust

D. Dalton

10.3.C3.3 *describe the types of evidence that indicate chemical change (e.g., changes in colour, the production of a gas, the formation of a precipitate, the production or absorption of heat, the production of light)*

10.3.C2.5 *plan and conduct an inquiry to identify the evidence of chemical change (e.g., the formation of a gas or precipitate, a change in colour or odour, a change in temperature)*

Evidence of Chemical Change

A chemical change is a change in matter that produces one or more new substances. These new substances have properties that are different from the properties of the reactants. For example, fire is created when oxygen and wood react in the presence of heat.

Indicators that a chemical change has occurred include the following:

- A gas is produced
- The temperature changes
- A substance disappears
- A solid (precipitate) is formed
- Heat is given off
- A smell is produced
- A color change occurs

9. Production of a gas, colour change, and formation of a precipitate are all evidence of

A. a temperature change

B. a chemical change

C. condensation

D. sublimation

10. Which of the following events is an example of a chemical change?

A. Fog formation

B. Sugar fermentation

C. Water changing into steam

D. Preparation of a sugar solution

Use the following information to answer the next question.

Mrs. Lam, the chemistry teacher, had run out of litmus paper, so boiled some purple cabbage. Mrs. Lam then used a small dropper to put some of the purple cabbage juice into a glass of vinegar. The purple juice turned red in the vinegar.

11. Which change that occured during this experiment was a chemical change?

A. The colour of the juice changed in the vinegar.

B. Steam from the cabbage juice condensed.

C. A gas was produced in the boiling pot.

D. The cabbage juice evaporated.

10.3.C3.4 *write word equations and balanced chemical equations for simple chemical reactions (e.g., $2H_2 + O_2 \rightarrow 2H_2O$)*

10.3.C2.2 *construct molecular models to illustrate the structure of molecules in simple chemical reactions (e.g., $C + O_2 \rightarrow CO_2$; $2H_2 + O_2 \rightarrow 2H_2O$)), and produce diagrams of these models*

Molecular Models and Chemical Equations

There are several methods for representing chemical compounds and equations. One method is to build or draw molecules to show their shape and constituent atoms. Another method is to write chemical equations either using words or formulas for the compounds. Chemical equations communicate what the reactants and products are in a reaction.

Molecular Models

Many of the common substances you use every day are made up of simple compounds. To get a better understanding of these compounds, scientists build models of them. These models are useful because they represent what a molecule would look like if you were able to see it. The model can reveal useful information about a molecule by showing how many atoms of each element are present and how they are arranged.

For example, the chemical formula for water is H_2O. The letters represent elements found on the periodic table. The subscript number after the letter indicates how many atoms of that particular element are present in the compound. If no number is found after an element, it means there is only one atom of that element present. For water, the first letter, H, represents hydrogen. The subscript, two, that comes after indicates there are two hydrogen atoms present. The O represents oxygen. Because no number is found after the oxygen, it indicates that only one atom of oxygen is present.

To draw a molecule of water, simply place the oxygen in the centre and attach the two hydrogen molecules to it.

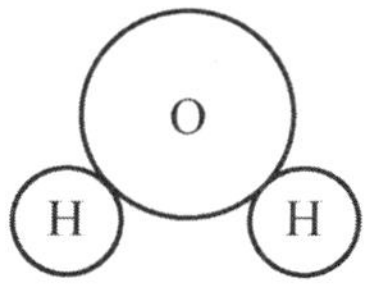

Oxygen is simply O_2, two oxygen molecules. They are represented below.

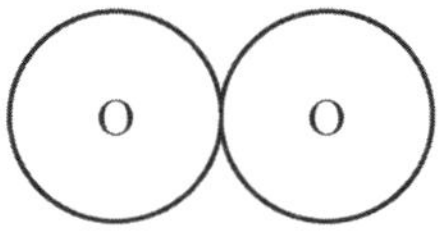

Ammonia has the chemical formula NH_3. There is one nitrogen atom surrounded by three hydrogen atoms.

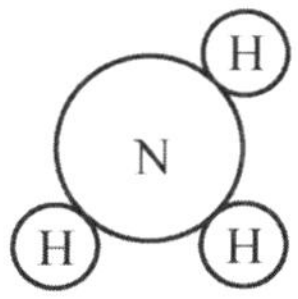

Methane, CH_4, is composed of one carbon atom surrounded by four hydrogen atoms.

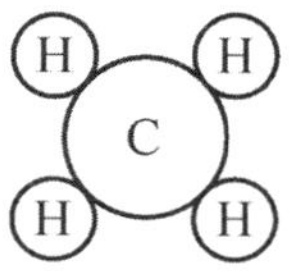

Carbon Dioxide, CO_2, can be drawn in the following manner.

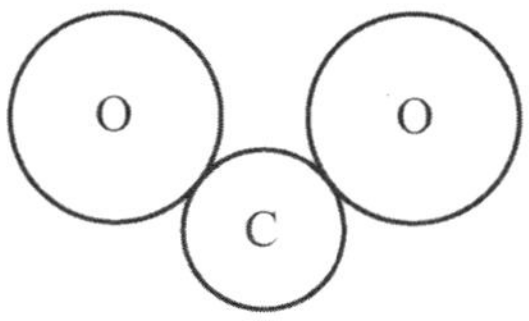

Writing Chemical Equations

A word equation or formula can be used to describe a chemical reaction. A formula equation uses the chemical symbols and formulas for the reactants and products. According to the law of conservation of mass,the number of each type of atom should be the same in the reactants as it is in the products. Numbers, called coefficients, are placed in front of a chemical symbol or chemical formula to indicate the number of molecules involved in the reaction. This is called balancing the equation.

Example

The reaction between stomach acid and baking soda can be described with the following word equation: "Hydrochloric acid and sodium bicarbonate react to form sodium chloride, water, and carbon dioxide gas."

Or it can be described by the formula equation:
$HCl_{(aq)} + Na_2CO_{3(s)} \rightarrow NaCl_{(s)} + H_2O_{(l)} + CO_{2(g)}$

Counting the number of each type of atom, it is seen that the above reaction is not balanced.
For example, there is one atom of hydrogen in the products, but two atoms of hydrogen in the products. This reaction can be balanced by adding coefficients as follows:
$2HCl_{(aq)} + 1Na_2CO_{3(s)}$
$\rightarrow 2NaCl_{(s)} + 1H_2O_{(l)} + 1CO_{2(g)}$
Note that the numbers of chlorine, carbon and sodium atoms are also balanced. A balanced equation must have the same number of each atom on the reactant side as the product side.

By convention, a coefficient of 1 is not usually written in formula equations.

Open Response

12. Predict the reaction products, and write a balanced chemical equation for the reaction $HCl_{(aq)} + Ca(OH)_{2(aq)} \rightarrow$.

____

____

Open Response

13. Balance the chemical equation $C_{10}H_{8(s)} + O_{2(g)} \rightarrow CO_{2(g)} + H_2O_{(l)}$.

____

____

Use the following information to answer the next question.

A chemical equation is a symbolic notation that uses formula instead of words to represent a chemical reaction. A balanced chemical equation must satisfy mass balance.

14. Which of the following chemical equations is balanced?
A. $Fe_{(s)} + H_2O_{(l)} \rightarrow Fe_2O_{3(s)} + H_{2(g)}$
B. $CH_{4(g)} + 4Cl_{2(g)} \rightarrow CCl_{4(l)} + 4HCl_{(g)}$
C. $Zn_{(s)} + AgCN_{(s)} \rightarrow Ag_{(s)} + Zn(CN)_{2(s)}$
D. $2Zn_{(s)} + 2H_2SO_{4(aq)}$
$\rightarrow 2ZnSO_{4(s)} + H_{2(g)}$

15. The combustion of hydrogen gas with oxygen gas produces water. What is the correct balanced equation to represent this reaction?
A. $H_{2(g)} + O_{2(g)} \rightarrow H_2O_{(l)}$
B. $2H_{2(g)} + O_{2(g)} \rightarrow 2H_2O_{(l)}$
C. $H_{2(g)} + O_{2(g)} \rightarrow 2H_2O_{(l)}$
D. $2H_{2(g)} + 2O_{2(g)} \rightarrow H_2O_{(l)}$

16. Which of the following molecular models represents the molecular structure of CO_2?
A.
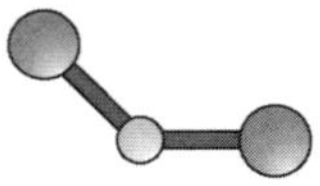
B.
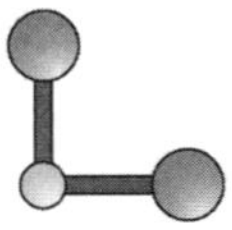
C.
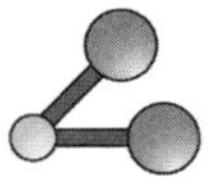
D.

Use the following information to answer the next question.

The given illustration represents the model of a molecule. The balls represent the atoms, and the sticks represent the bonds between the atoms.

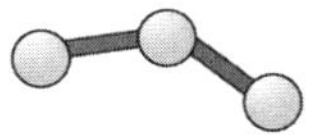

17. The given illustrated model represents a

A. linear, diatomic molecule

B. linear, triatomic molecule

C. non-linear, diatomic molecule

D. non-linear, triatomic molecule

Open Response

18. Draw a ball and stick model to represent the balanced equation for the combustion of methane (CH_4).

____

____

____

____

____

____

____

10.3.C3.5 *describe, on the basis of observation, the reactants in and products of a variety of chemical reactions, including synthesis, decomposition, and displacement reactions (e.g., reactions occurring when magnesium burns or in the production of oxygen from hydrogen peroxide; the reaction of iron and copper sulphate; reactions occurring when fossil fuels burn)*

10.3.C2.3 *investigate simple chemical reactions, including synthesis, decomposition, and displacement reactions, and represent them using a variety of formats (e.g., molecular models, word equations, balanced chemical equations)*

Classifying Chemical Reactions

There are six types of chemical reactions that you should understand. Reactions can be classified as follows:

1. **Synthesis**—two reactants are elements that combine to form a product that is a compound.
   $A + B \rightarrow AB$
   $2H_2 + O_2 \rightarrow 2H_2O$
2. **Decomposition**—a reactant is broken down into products that are elements.
   $AB \rightarrow A + B$
   $2CaO \rightarrow 2Ca + O_2$
3. **Single Replacement**—the reactants are an element and a compound, and the products are a new compound and element.
   $AB + C \rightarrow A + BC$
   $Cu + 2AgNO_3 \rightarrow Cu(NO_3)_2 + 2Ag$
4. **Double Replacement**—the reactants and the compounds are both compounds. Elements "switch partners," but there will always be a metal with a non-metal.
   $AB + CD \rightarrow AD + BC$
   $Pb(NO_3)_2 + 2KI \rightarrow PbI_2 + 2KNO_3$
5. **Combustion**—an element or compound combines with oxygen to form the most common oxide or oxides.
   Element: $2Mg + O_2 \rightarrow 2MgO$
   Compound: $CH_4 + 2O_2 \rightarrow 2H_2O + CO_2$
6. **Neutralization**—an acid and a base are combined to form a salt and water.
   $HCl + NaOH \rightarrow H_2O + NaCl$

19. Methyl orange turns from red to yellow in a solution during the course of a reaction. This reaction is classified as a

A. synthesis reaction

B. hydrolysis reaction

C. neutralization reaction

D. decomposition reaction

20. The reaction of the hydrogen ions from an acid and the hydroxide ions from a base to produce salt and water is known as

A. neutralization **B.** precipitation

C. desalination **D.** dissociation

21. The reaction in which CH_4 is burned in the presence of air is given as $CH_4 + O_2 \rightarrow X + Y$. In this reaction, $X + Y$ represent

A. $CO + H_2O$

B. $C + H_2O$

C. $CO_2 + H_2O$

D. $C + H_2$

22. A chemical reaction is written as $Zn + H_2SO_4 \rightarrow ZnSO_4 + X$. Which substance is represented by X in this reaction?

A. H **B.** 2H

C. H_2 **D.** $2H_2$

Open Response

23. Complete the following table.

Type of Reaction	Generalized Reaction
	$A + B \rightarrow AB$
Decomposition	
	$AB + C \rightarrow AC + B$
Double replacement	
	$CH_4 + O_2 \rightarrow H_2O + CO_2$

10.3.C3.6 *describe the process of acid-base neutralization (i.e., an acid reacts with a base to form a salt and often water)*

ACID-BASE NEUTRALIZATION

One of the most important properties of both acids and bases is their ability to neutralize, or cancel, the properties of the other. Reactions in which an acid and a base react are called neutralization reactions. The products of an acid-base neutralization are water and an ionic compound called a salt.

Example

Hydrochloric acid, HCl, is a strong acid similar to that found in your stomach. Sodium hydroxide, NaOH, is a powerful base. When the two react, the sodium and chloride ions join to form a salt called sodium chloride, while the remaining atoms form water. The following equation summarizes this reaction: $HCl_{(aq)} + NaOH_{(aq)} \rightarrow NaCl_{(aq)} + H_2O_{(l)}$.

24. A first-aid manual suggests that vinegar should be used to neutralize the pain of wasp stings, indicating that wasp stings are

A. basic **B.** acidic

C. neutral **D.** amphoteric

10.3.C2.6 *plan and conduct an inquiry to classify some common substances as acidic, basic, or neutral (e.g., use acid-base indicators or pH test strips to classify common household substances)*

10.3.C3.7 *describe how the pH scale is used to classify solutions as acidic, basic, or neutral (e.g., a solution with a pH of 1 is highly acidic; a solution with a pH of 7 is neutral)*

10.3.C2.1 *use appropriate terminology related to chemical reactions, including, but not limited to: compounds, product, and reactant*

Acids, Bases, and the pH Scale

Solutions are typically classified as either acidic, basic, or neutral, and the pH scale is used to determine this classification. If the pH of a solution is exactly 7, it is considered neutral. If the pH is less than 7, it is considered an acid, and if the pH is more than 7, it is considered a base.

Acids

Acids are chemicals that turn litmus paper from blue to red and taste sour. According to the simplest definition of an acid, the compound must contain one or more hydrogen ions (H^+). It is these hydrogen ions that give the compound its acidic qualities.

Bases

Bases turn litmus paper from red to blue. They taste bitter and feel slippery. Bases contain one or more hydroxide ions (OH^-) that give them their basic properties.

The pH Scale

Not all acids and bases are equally strong. The relative acidity of an acid or alkalinity of a base is measured using a 14-point scale called the pH scale. A pH measurement of 7 indicates a neutral compound: a compound that is neither an acid nor a base. Distilled water is an example of a neutral compound. A pH measurement of less than 7 indicates an acid. The lower the value, the stronger the acid. For example, tomato juice has a pH measurement of around 4. It is a much weaker acid than stomach acid, which is a very strong acid and has a pH of around 2. A pH measurement greater than 7 indicates a basic compound. The higher the pH, the stronger the base. Baking soda, for example, has a pH of around 9. It is a much weaker base than oven cleaner, which has a pH around 13. In some cases, the pH value of a solution may be below 0 and actually be negative. A negative pH value represents a highly concentrated, strongly acidic solution. By the same token, extremely concentrated strong bases may form solutions with a pH above 14. Any solution with a pH outside of the 14-point scale should be handled with extreme caution, since it will likely be very reactive and potentially dangerous to people and property.

Use the following information to answer the next question.

> Linda's teacher has three beakers containing three different solutions that are basic, acidic, and neutral. The teacher asks Linda to differentiate the three solutions.

25. The chemical that can be used to differentiate the three solutions is

A. litmus

B. thymol blue

C. methyl orange

D. phenolphthalein

Use the following information to answer the next question.

Lemon juice has a pH of 2. Milk has a pH of 6.

26. How many times more acidic is lemon juice than milk?

A. 4 **B.** 400

C. 1000 **D.** 10000

27. Which of the following rows correctly identifies the reactants and the products of the general reaction $A + B \rightarrow C + D$?

A.

Reactants	Products
A and *B*	*C* and *D*

B.

Reactants	Products
C and *D*	*A* and *B*

C.

Reactants	Products
A and *C*	*B* and *D*

D.

Reactants	Products
A and *D*	*B* and *C*

10.3.C3.8 *identify simple ionic compounds (e.g., NaCl), simple compounds involving polyatomic ions (e.g., KNO3, NaOH), molecular compounds (e.g., CO2, H2O, NH3), and acids (e.g., HCl(aq), H2SO4(aq)), using the periodic table and a list of the most common polyatomic ions (e.g., OH-, SO 4 -2), and write the formulae*

Naming Compounds and Writing Their Formulas

The International Union of Pure and Applied Chemists, IUPAC, has developed a system for naming chemical compounds. Depending on whether the compound is ionic or molecular, these rules differ.

Naming Binary Ionic Compounds

When naming binary ionic compounds, different rules apply if the compound is formed between two elements only, a metal and a non-metal, or a metal and a polyatomic ion (more than two elements).

Binary Ionic Compounds Involving a Metal and a Non-Metal

The IUPAC rules state that for the names of binary ionic compounds, the metal is named first, and the non-metal is written second. The name of the non-metal is changed so that it ends in *-ide*.

Transition metals appear in the periodic table from Group 3 to the staircase-shaped line that indicates the non-metals. Most transition metals have more than one possible charge for their ions. An element that can have different charges is said to be multivalent. The periodic table indicates the ion's most common charge, as well as the ion's other possible charges. When writing the name of an ionic compound that contains a transition metal, roman numerals are used to indicate the charge.
For example, a copper ion with a charge of 1+ (Cu^{+}) would be named copper(I).

Name	Formula
Copper(I) chloride	$CuCl$
Copper(II) chloride	$CuCl_2$
Iron(II) oxide	FeO
Iron(III) oxide	Fe_2O_3

Binary Ionic Compounds Involving a Metal and a Polyatomic Ion

Sometimes two or more non-metals are combined to form a polyatomic ion. When a metal combines with a polyatomic ion, the polyatomic ion's name is left unchanged. Some examples include cyanide (CN^{-}), hydroxide (OH^{-}), sulfate (SO_4^{2-}), phosphate (PO_4^{3-}), and nitrate (NO_3^{-}).

Naming Molecular Compounds

Molecular compounds are named using prefixes with each of the elements involved.

Number	Prefix
1	*mono*
2	*di*
3	*tri*
4	*tetra*
5	*penta*
6	*hexa*
7	*hepta*
8	*octa*
9	*nona*
10	*deca*

By convention, *mono* is not used for the first element named, and the ending of the first element is not changed. The ending of the second element is changed to *-ide*. Some examples are given in the following table:

Formula	IUPAC Name
CO_2	Carbon dioxide
P_2O_3	Diphosphorous trioxide
P_4O_{10}	Tetraphosphorous decaoxide
CCl_4	Carbon tetrachloride

CHALLENGER QUESTION

28. NH_3 is the formula for a compound that is commonly used in fertilizers. Which of the following tables **correctly** identifies the compound's common name, scientific (IUPAC) name, and the number of atoms present in one molecule?

A.

Common Name	IUPAC Name	Number of Atoms
Ammonia	Nitrogen trihydride	3

B.

Common Name	IUPAC Name	Number of Atoms
Ammonium	Nitrogen hydride	4

C.

Common Name	IUPAC Name	Number of Atoms
Ammonium	Nitrogen hydride	3

D.

Common Name	IUPAC Name	Number of Atoms
Ammonia	Nitrogen trihydride	4

29. Fertilizer contains NH_4^+ ions and SO_4^{2-} ions.

The compound formed when these ions come together would have the formula

A. $NH_4(II)SO_{4(s)}$ **B.** $NH_4SO_{4(s)}$
C. $NH_4(SO_4)_{2(s)}$ **D.** $(NH_4)_2SO_{4(s)}$

Open Response

30. Name the following compounds and classify them as an acid, base, ionic compound, or molecular compound. The first row is completed as an example.

Compound Formula	Compound Name	Type of Compound
$Ca(NO_3)_{2(s)}$	calcium nitrate	ionic compound
$H_2SO_{4(aq)}$		
$(NH_4)_2SO_{3(s)}$		
$NaCl_{(s)}$		
$P_2O_{5(s)}$		
$KOH_{(aq)}$		

Answers and Solutions
Chemistry: Chemical Reactions

1. C	7. D	13. OR	19. C	25. A
2. A	8. A	14. B	20. A	26. D
3. OR	9. B	15. B	21. C	27. A
4. C	10. B	16. D	22. C	28. D
5. C	11. A	17. D	23. OR	29. D
6. D	12. OR	18. OR	24. A	30. OR

1. C

Paint products and cleaning products often contain harsh chemicals. These products are considered hazardous waste and could cause environmental damage if sent to a landfill. They should be take to an ecocentre for proper disposal.

2. A

Industrial processes and plants are important to society. Shutting them down is likely not good for the economy. The plants need to vent their combustion reactions, so people cannot simply stop using the smokestacks. Building the smokestacks higher does not solve the environmental problem; it just spreads the pollution out. Scrubbers can remove most of the byproducts of the combustion reactions.

Installing scrubbers is the best choice when considering both the economy and the environment.

3. OR

The document contains information such as the type and class of chemicals being transported, the hazards associated with them, the amount of chemicals being transported, and 24-hour emergency numbers. This information is critical in case of an emergency situation, including leaks and spills. Keeping the document in a set place makes it easy for anyone to access the document in case of emergency.

4. C

The charges must balance when forming a compound, so the correct formula is Fe_2O_3.

The compound is named after the ion involved. The ion is 3+, so the compound is named iron (III) oxide.

5. C

Carbon dioxide is made up of two elements: carbon (C) and oxygen (O). It contains one atom of carbon and two atoms of oxygen. Hence, the molecular formula for carbon dioxide is CO_2.

C_2H_2 is the molecular formula for ethane.

CH_4 is the molecular formula for methane.

CO is the molecular formula for carbon monoxide.

6. D

The law of conservation of mass is applicable to all chemical reactions, regardless of the phases of the reactants and products.

7. D

The law of conservation of mass states that the mass of the products of a chemical reaction equals the mass of the reactants. When you balance a chemical reaction by ensuring equal numbers of atoms are on both sides of a chemical equation, you are applying the law of conservation of mass.

8. A

Lavoiser was key in solidifying the law of conservation of mass, through his experiments in closed systems.

9. B

Production of a gas, colour change, and formation of a precipitate are all evidence that a chemical change has occurred.

10. B

Sugar fermentation is an example of a chemical change. During fermentation, sugar changes into alcohol.

11. A

A chemical change was evident because the cabbage juice changed colour in the vinegar. A colour change is evidence of a chemical change. The water boiling in the pot is a physical change. It is changing from a liquid to a gas. Evaporation and condensation are both physical changes.

12. OR

The balanced chemical equation for the reaction is $2HCl_{(aq)} + Ca(OH)_{2(aq)} \rightarrow 2H_2O_{(l)} + CaCl_{2(aq)}$.

Because this is a neutralization reaction between a strong acid and a strong base, the products will most likely be an ionic salt and water. The products of the neutralization reaction between hydrochloric acid and calcium hydroxide will be calcium chloride and water.

13. OR

In order to balance this chemical equation, the total number of each type of molecule on the reactant side of the equation must equal the total number of each type of molecule on the product side of the equation. $C_{10}H_{8(s)} + 12O_{2(g)} \rightarrow 10CO_{2(g)} + 4H_2O_{(l)}$

14. B

In a balanced chemical equation, the number of molecules present on both sides of the equation must be equal. In the equation representing the reaction between methane and chlorine, the number of atoms of all three elements, carbon, hydrogen, and chlorine, is equal.

On the left side: carbon $= 1$, hydrogen $= 4$, chlorine $= 8$.

On the right side: carbon $= 1$, hydrogen $= 4$, chlorine $= 8$.

15. B

The standard form of a complete balanced equation is one that contains an equal number of atoms on both the reactant and the product sides.

Hence, the correct balanced chemical equation for the production of water by hydrogen and oxygen is represented by $2H_{2(g)} + O_{2(g)} \rightarrow 2H_2O_{(l)}$

16. D

Carbon dioxide (CO_2) is tri-atomic molecule made up of two atoms of oxygen and one atom of carbon. It is linear in shape with a bond angle of 180°. There are no pairs of electrons out of the 180° plane.

17. D

The illustrated model contains three atoms (triatomic) and has a bent (non-linear) structure. Hence, the model represents a non-linear, triatomic molecule.

18. OR

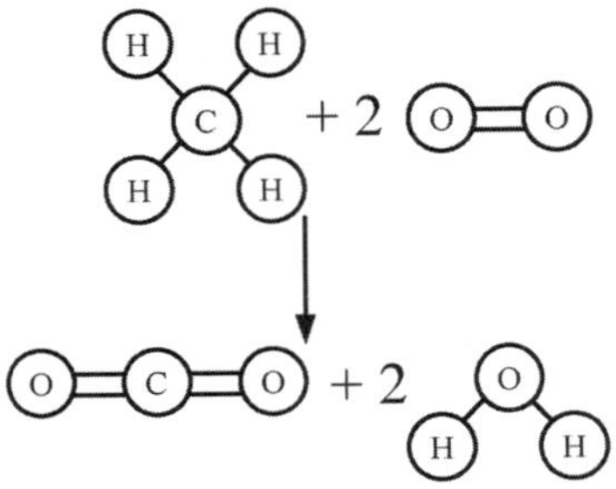

One molecule of methane will react with two molecules of oxygen to produce one molecule of carbon dioxide and two molecules of water.

19. C

Methyl orange is an indicator used in acid-base neutralization reactions to determine the nature of the resulting solution. The colour of methyl orange changes from red to yellow as the pH increases and the solution becomes less acidic. Therefore, the given reaction is classified as a neutralization reaction.

20. A

A neutralization reaction produces salt and water when an acid and a base are combined in solution. Acids dissociate in aqueous solution to create hydrogen or hydronium ions, while bases dissociate and create hydroxide ions. The hydrogen or hydronium ions combine with the hydroxide ions to form water, and the remaining ions in the solution combine to form a salt. This reaction of acids and bases results in a solution with a pH that is more neutral than either the original acid or base reactants.

21. C

Complete combustion reactions with a carbon reactant always produce carbon dioxide and water. When compounds other than carbon are burned, they will produce the most common oxide for that reactant.

22. C

The law of conservation of mass states that the atoms on the reactant side must be present on the product side. This reaction is a single replacement reaction, with the Zn displacing the H_2. The equation is balanced with a single molecule of H_2; there is no coefficient required.

23. OR

Type of Reaction	Generalized Reaction
Synthesis	$A + B \rightarrow AB$
Decomposition	$AB \rightarrow A + B$
Single replacement	$AB + C \rightarrow AC + B$
Double replacement	$AB + CD \rightarrow AD + BC$
Combustion	$CH_4 + O_2 \rightarrow H_2O + CO_2$

24. A

Vinegar is an acid with a pH of 3. Treating wasp stings with vinegar will neutralize the basic injected chemicals and reduce the pain.

25. A

In order to answer this question correctly, the student must know the range of various acid-base indicators. Litmus produces a red colour on reacting with acids and a blue colour on reacting with bases. In neutral conditions, it produces an intermediate colour. Therefore, litmus can be used to differentiate the three solutions. Phenolphthalein produces a pink colour when it reacts with bases, but when $pH < 8.2$, it remains colourless. Hence, it cannot be used to differentiate between water and acid. Methyl orange produces a red colour on reaction with acid, but above pH 4.4, it produces a yellow colour. Hence, it cannot be used to differentiate between water and bases. Thymol blue produces a blue colour on reaction with bases, but below pH 8.0, it produces a yellow colour.

26. D

The pH scale is a logarithmic scale, meaning that each unit on the scale is ten times stronger than the last. So a difference of 4 units on the pH scale is the same as $10 \times 10 \times 10 \times 10$, or 10000 times as acidic.

27. A

A and *B* are called reactants. During the reaction, *A* and *B* are converted into *C* and *D*. *C* and *D* are the products.

28. D

NH_3 has a total of four atoms: one nitrogen atom and three hydrogen atoms. The IUPAC name is nitrogen trihydride, and the common name is ammonia. Ammonium, NH_4^+, is a related compound.

29. D

Ammonium (NH_4^+) is a polyatomic ion that has a charge of +1. Sulfate (SO_4^{2-}) is a polyatomic ion with a charge of –2. It takes two ammonium ions (total charge +2) to balance one sulfate ion. The brackets are needed to indicate that the 2 refers to both the nitrogen and the hydrogens of the ammonium. Roman numerals, such as II, are used in Stock's system. They are used for the transition metals, such as iron and copper, which are multivalent. This means that they can have different charges. Roman numerals are used to indicate the charge on the ion. This system would not be used for ammonium, which is not multivalent, and always has a charge of +1.

30. OR

Compound Formula	Compound Name	Type of Compound
$Ca(NO_3)_{2(s)}$	Calcium nitrate	Ionic compound
$H_2SO_{4(aq)}$	Sulfuric acid	Acid
$(NH_4)_2SO_{3(s)}$	Ammonium sulfite	Ionic compound
$NaCl_{(s)}$	Sodium chloride	Ionic compound
$P_2O_{5(s)}$	Diphosphorous pentoxide	Molecular compound
$KOH_{(aq)}$	Potassium hydroxide	Base

Unit Test

1. A career that requires extensive knowledge of the physical and chemical properties of elements and compounds and their effect on natural processes is
   A. an environmental engineer
   B. a weather forecaster
   C. an x-ray technician
   D. a field biologist

Use the following information to answer the next question.

> Cyanide is often used to help extract gold from its ore in gold mining. The use of cyanide is controversial because of its toxicity. When cyanide is used to process gold ores, it must be carefully collected, stored, and chemically neutralized to minimize its toxic effects on the environment.

Open Response

2. If a small town with little employment has just discovered a gold mine nearby, what are some of the issues the town should consider before allowing the gold mine to open?

Use the following information to answer the next question.

> Acid rain occurs when emissions from coal-burning plants, smelters, cars, factories, and other human sources enter the atmosphere and combine with moisture to become sulfuric and nitric acid. The acid is deposited on Earth in the form of rain, sleet, snow, or fog. Acid precipitation damages buildings by eating at their surfaces. Companies are developing paints that protect buildings from the acidity.

Open Response

3. Given the nature of chemical reactions, how could a layer of paint protect a building from acid rain?

4. Which scientific law states that the total mass of the products of a chemical reaction will be equal to the total mass of the reactants in a closed system?
   A. The law of constant proportions
   B. The law of reciprocal proportions
   C. The law of conservation of matter
   D. The law of conservation of momentum

5. Which of the following molecular models represents the balanced chemical equation for the combustion of methane?

A.

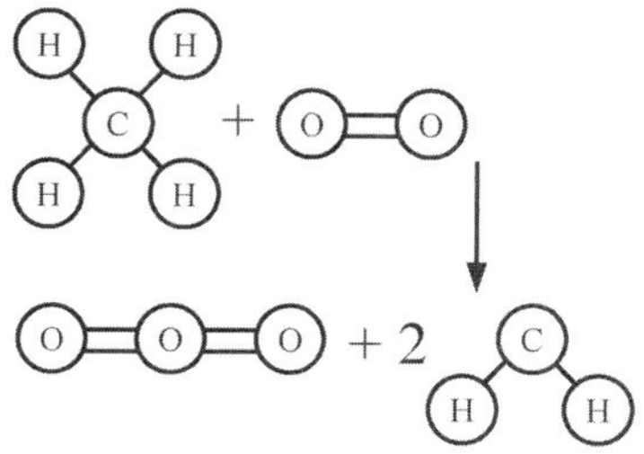

B.

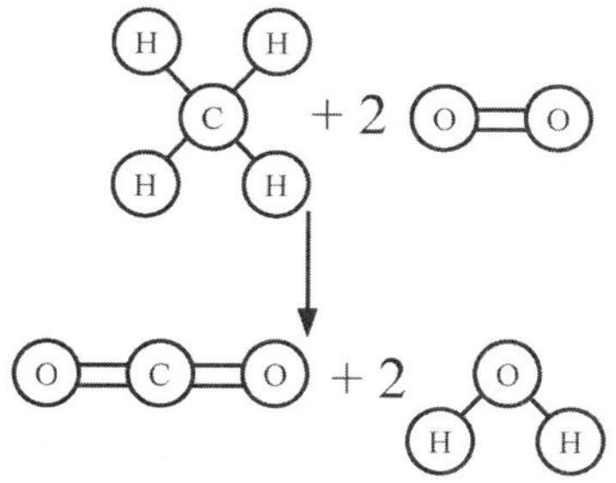

C.

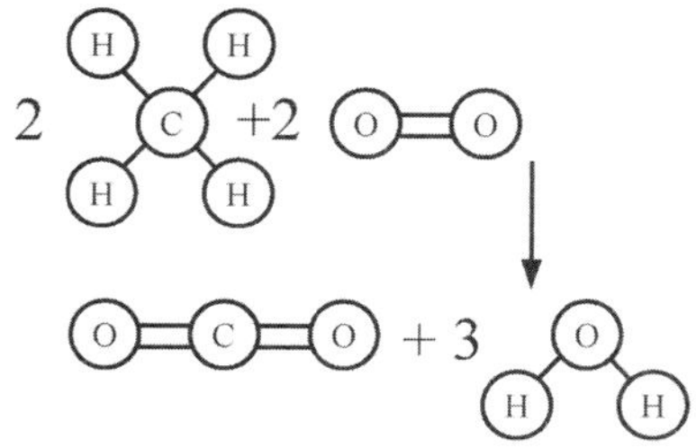

D.

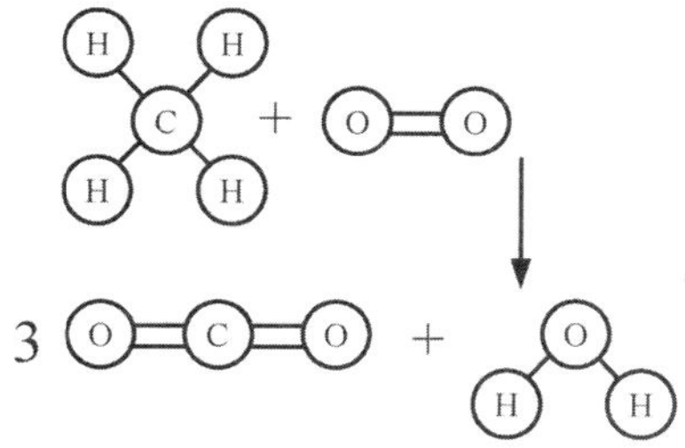

Use the following information to answer the next question.

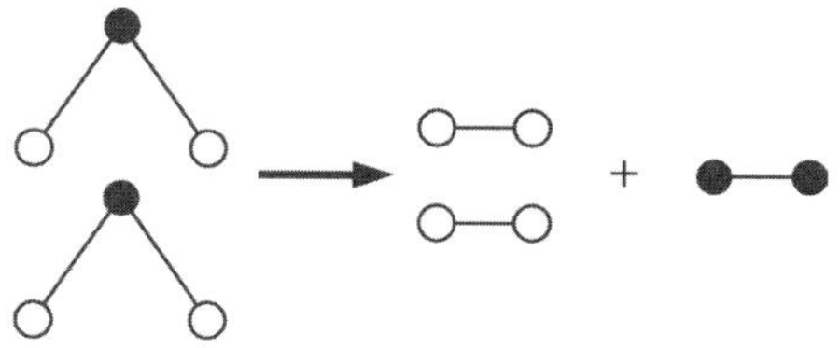

A structural model of an equation

6. Which of the following chemical equations is represented by the given structural model?
   A. $2CaC_2 \rightarrow 2Ca + C$
   B. $H_2O \rightarrow H_2 + O_2$
   C. $2H_2O \rightarrow 2H_2 + O_2$
   D. $H_2O \rightarrow H^+ + O^{2-}$

7. The type of chemical reaction in which one element displaces another element from a compound and takes its place is known as what type of reaction?
   A. Double replacement
   B. Single replacement
   C. Decomposition
   D. Synthesis

Use the following information to answer the next question.

Milo placed 3 g of calcium into a test tube containing 49.8 g of water. He expected the mass of the products from this reaction to be 52.8 g. Instead, the products had a mass of 51.2 g.

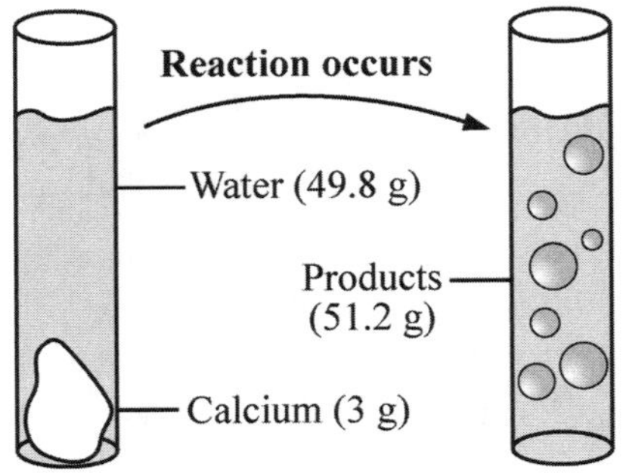

8. Milo explained the loss of 1.6 g of mass by inferring that the gas formed

A. was absorbed by the test tube

B. dissolved into the other product

C. escaped from the open test tube

D. burned up from the heat created by the reaction

Use the following information to answer the next question.

Observed changes to materials can be classified as physical changes or chemical changes.

9. Which of the following events is **not** an example of a chemical change?

A. A popsicle melting

B. A metal bar rusting

C. A firecracker exploding

D. A car motor converting gasoline

10. If the pH value of NaOH is 14, then it is

A. highly basic

B. highly acidic

C. slightly basic

D. slightly acidic

11. Which of the following statements about chemical formulas is **false**?

A. A chemical formula indicates the fixed proportion in which atoms combine.

B. A chemical formula is the symbolic representation of a molecule within a compound.

C. A chemical formula is the symbolic representation of the reactants and products in a reaction.

D. A chemical formula denotes the number of atoms of each element that are present in a compound.

12. Carbon monoxide is a toxic substance that is produced during the combustion of natural gas. The chemical formula for carbon monoxide is

A. C **B.** CO

C. CO_2 **D.** CH_4

Use the following information to answer the next question.

Water decomposes into two products. This reaction is illustrated by the following chemical equation.

$2H_2O_{(l)} \rightarrow 2H_{2(g)} + O_{2(g)}$

13. The clearest evidence that a chemical change occurs in this reaction is

A. a colour change

B. the formation of a gas

C. the formation of a solid

D. the release of heat energy

Use the following information to answer the next question.

A chemist receives a sample of an unlabelled solution that could possibly be lead(II) nitrate. She uses a potassium iodide solution to test for the presence of lead(II) ions. If lead(II) ions are present in the sample, a yellow precipitate, lead(II) iodide, will form when potassium iodide solution is added. The reaction, expressed as an unbalanced chemical equation, is

$Pb(NO_3)_{2(aq)} + KI_{(aq)}$
$\rightarrow PbI_{2(s)} + KNO_{3(aq)}$.

Numerical Response

14. From left to right, the coefficients of the balanced equation are __________. (Record your answer as a four-digit number.)

Open Response

15. Write out the standard balanced equation for the burning of aluminum in the presence of oxygen.

____

____

Use the following information to answer the next question.

The combustion of methane is represented in the following reaction:
$CH_4 + xO_2 \rightarrow 2H_2O + CO_2$

16. What is the number of moles of oxygen gas (x) required to balance the given chemical equation?

A. 1 **B.** 2
C. 3 **D.** 4

17. Water is one of the products in a reaction between an acid and a base. This reaction is **best** classified as a

A. combustion reaction
B. replacement reaction
C. neutralization reaction
D. double replacement reaction

Use the following information to answer the next question.

The mantle of a camping lantern is covered in thorium hydroxide and ceramic nitrate. They burn when the mantle is ignited and provide a catalytic surface for the pressurized fuel-air combustion. The equation for this reaction involving thorium hydroxide is:
$Th(OH)_{4(s)} \rightarrow ThO_{2(s)} + 2H_2O_{(g)}$

18. This reaction is **best** classified as

A. formation
B. decomposition
C. single replacement
D. double replacement

Use the following information to answer the next question.

$KOH_{(aq)} + HNO_{3(aq)} \rightarrow KNO_{3(aq)} + H_2O_{(l)}$

19. Which of the following species is the salt in the given neutralization reaction?

A. $KNO_{3(aq)}$ **B.** $KOH_{(aq)}$
C. $HNO_{3(aq)}$ **D.** $H_2O_{(l)}$

Use the following information to answer the next question.

Sophie has to present a chemistry project to her class. She fills a beaker with baking soda and adds several drops of red food colouring. Then, she forms a volcanic shape with a hole at the top out of modeling clay and places it over the beaker. When it is her turn to present, Sophie pours a small amount of vinegar through the hole into the volcano. After a couple of seconds, the volcano starts to hiss and red bubbles begin foaming out.

20. Which of the following terms **best** describes the reaction occurring in Sophie's chemistry project?

A. Decomposition reaction

B. Neutralization reaction

C. Synthesis reaction

D. Nuclear reaction

Use the following information to answer the next question.

This figure shows a pH scale with common substances.

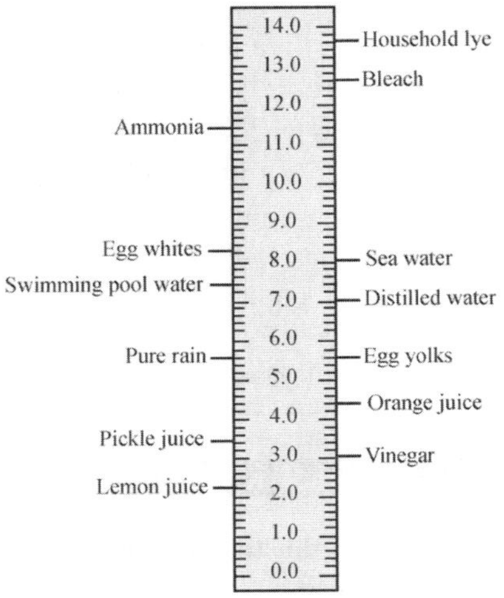

21. Which of the following substances is a base?

A. Vinegar **B.** Ammonia

C. Lemon juice **D.** Orange juice

22. Which of the following properties is a characteristic of bases?

A. Sour taste

B. pH greater than 7

C. Turns blue litmus red

D. Forms H^+ ions when dissolved in water

23. The IUPAC name of SO_2 is

A. sulfur oxide

B. sulfur dioxide

C. monosulfur oxide

D. monosulfur dioxide

24. The chemical formula for diiodine hexachloride is

A. ICl_2

B. I_2Cl

C. ICl_6

D. I_2Cl_6

Open Response

25. What are the formulas for chromium(II) bromide, manganese(II) oxide, chromium(III) bromide, and manganese(IV) oxide?

____

____

Answers and Solutions – Unit Test

1. A	6. C	11. C	16. B	21. B
2. OR	7. B	12. B	17. C	22. B
3. OR	8. C	13. B	18. B	23. B
4. C	9. A	14. 1212	19. A	24. D
5. B	10. A	15. OR	20. B	25. OR

1. A

Environmental engineers are responsible for minimizing the environmental impacts of many human activities. They must have an extensive understanding of chemistry to repair damage that has been done to the environment and prevent further damage by human activities.

2. OR

The following are some of the issues the town should consider:

- What kind of alternative methods could be used to process gold ore instead of using cyanide?
- What is the environmental track record of the company that wants to open and run the mine?
- If cyanide is used, what types of precautions will need to be taken? It will need to be stored in specially designed secure containers that cannot overflow into local ecosystems.

3. OR

Acids can be neutralized by bases. If the paint layer contained basic compounds, the acid would be neutralized on contact with the paint, preventing the acid from wearing away at the building.

4. C

The law of conservation of matter (or law of conservation of mass) states that matter can neither be created nor destroyed, it can only be redistributed. The atoms making up the reactants are rearranged to form the products, but they are not lost; therefore, in a closed system, the mass of the reactants and the products should be equal.

5. B

The balanced chemical equation for the combustion reaction of methane is as follows:
$CH_{4(g)} + 2O_{2(g)} \rightarrow CO_{2(g)} + 2H_2O_{(l)}$

This equation is represented by the given image.

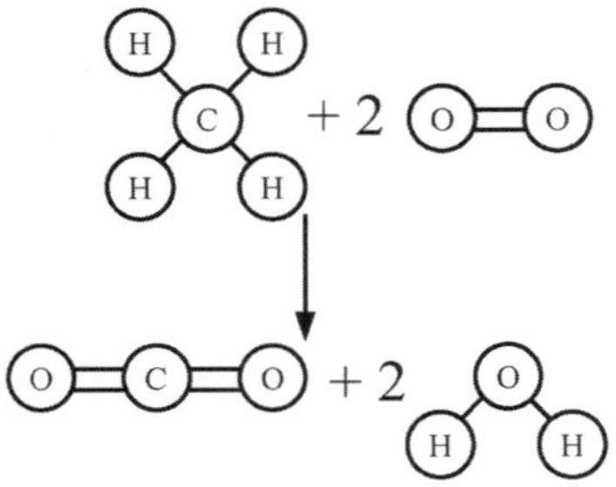

6. C

The structural models are illustrating the hydrolysis, or splitting, of water molecules. There are two molecules on the reactant side of the model, therefore there must be two molecules on the reactant side of the equation. The products of the model show two molecules (each with two atoms) of one element and one molecule with two atoms of the second element. Therefore there must be two of one type of molecule and one of another type of molecule on the product side of the equation.

7. B

In a single replacement reaction, one element displaces another element from the compound.

Example: $Zn_{(aq)} + CuSO_{4(aq)}$
$\rightarrow Cu_{(aq)} + ZnSO_{4(aq)}$

$Zn_{(aq)}$ displaces $Cu_{(aq)}$ from $CuSO_{4(aq)}$ and takes its place.

8. C

Mass cannot be created or destroyed and is conserved in chemical reactions. Because the test tube did not have a stopper in it, it was not a closed system. The gas bubbles are less dense than the water and will rise to the top and escape from the open system.

9. A

In a physical change, no new substances are formed. When a popsicle melts, water is changed from a solid to a liquid, but no new substances are formed. When a metal rusts, a chemical reaction (oxidation) that creates a new substance (rust) occurs. A firecracker gives off light, heat, and sound energy, indicating a chemical change has occures. A car's engine converts chemical energy in gasoline into heat, sound, and mechanical energy.

10. A

On the pH scale, pH values from 7.1 to 14.0 are considered basic. A solution having a pH of 14 is a highly basic solution

11. C

A chemical formula is the symbolic representation of a molecule in a compound, while a chemical equation is the symbolic representation of the reactants and products in a reaction.

12. B

Carbon monoxide is a molecular compound. By convention, there is no *mono-* prefix added to the first atom in the compound if it is singular. The formula indicates there is one atom of carbon. *Monoxide* indicates there is one atom of oxygen. The formula for carbon monoxide is CO.

13. B

Hydrogen gas and oxygen gas are produced. When this happens in water, the gas bubbles rise through the water. This is clear evidence that a chemical change is taking place.

14. 1212

When balancing equations that contain compounds with common polyatomic ions where an identical polyatomic ion appears in compounds on both sides of the equation, it saves time by counting the atoms in the polyatomic ion as a group rather than as individual atoms.
In the equation in this example, the nitrate ion, NO_3^-, is present in both $Pb(NO_3)_2$ and KNO_3.
The group of atoms in the nitrate ion, NO_3, can be counted as a single entity when balancing an equation like this.

The balanced chemical equation for the reaction is $Pb(NO_3)_{2(aq)} + 2KI_{(aq)} \rightarrow PbI_{2(s)} + 2KNO_{3(aq)}$.

The coefficients are 1, 2, 1, and 2.

15. OR

A balanced chemical equation must contain an equal number of atoms on the reactant side and the product side. The standard balanced equation must contain the smallest whole number of coefficients.

The balanced equation for the burning of aluminum in the presence of oxygen is as follows:
$4Al_{(s)} + 3O_{2(g)} \rightarrow 2Al_2O_{3(s)}$

16. B

The complete balanced chemical equation is as follows:
$CH_4 + 2O_2 \rightarrow 2H_2O + CO_2$

There are four oxygen atoms on the product side. Thus, to balance the given chemical equation, the reactant side should also have four oxygen atoms, which is possible only if the value of x is 2. Hence, two moles of oxygen gas are required to balance the given chemical equation.

17. C

In a neutralization reaction, an acid reacts with a base to form salt and water by the mutual exchange of ions.

Therefore, water is one of the products of a neutralization reaction.

18. B

When a compound is broken down into elements or simpler compounds, a decomposition has taken place.

19. A

An acid reacts with a base to form salt and water by the mutual exchange of ions in a neutralization reaction.

Therefore, in a neutralization reaction
Base + Acid → Salt + Water.

$KNO_{3(aq)}$ is the salt formed in the given reaction.

20. B

Baking soda is a base, and vinegar is an acid. When a base and an acid are combined, they form a salt and water in a neutralization reaction. The baking soda and vinegar in Sophie's project are reacting in a neutralization reaction. The gas and bubbles are evidence that a chemical reaction is occurring.

21. B

Substances with pH values less than 7 are acids, whereas those with pH values greater than 7 are bases. Among the given substances, only ammonia has a pH value greater than 7. Hence, ammonia is a base.

22. B

Bases are compounds with pHs greater than 7. Bases taste bitter, turn red litmus blue, and form ions OH^- when dissolved in water. The remaining alternatives are characteristics of acids.

23. B

By convention, a prefix is not used when there is a single atom of the first element. Because there are two oxygen atoms, the correct name is sulfur dioxide.

24. D

The chemical formula for diiodine hexachloride is I_2Cl_6.

25. OR

The compounds listed are ionic compounds.
The formula for chromium(II) bromide is $CrBr_2$.
The formula for manganese(II) oxide is MnO.
The formula for chromium(III) bromide is $CrBr_3$, and the formula for manganese(IV) oxide is MnO_2.

Earth and Space Sciences

EARTH AND SPACE SCIENCE: CLIMATE CHANGE

Table of Correlations

Specific Expectation		Practice Questions	Unit Test Questions	Practice Test 1	Practice Test 2
10.4.D1	analyse some of the effects of climate change around the world, and assess the effectiveness of initiatives that attempt to address the issue of climate change				
10.4.D1.1	*analyse current and/or potential effects, both positive and negative, of climate change on human activity and natural systems (e.g., loss of habitat for Arctic mammals such as polar bears and loss of traditional lifestyles for Inuit as Arctic ice shrinks; famine as arable land is lost to desertification; an increase in water-borne disease and human resettlement as coastal lands are flooded; expansion of the growing season in some regions)*	1, 2	1, 2, 3		21
10.4.D1.2	*assess, on the basis of research, the effectiveness of some current individual, regional, national, or international initiatives that address the issue of climate change (e.g., Drive Clean, ENERGY STAR, federal and provincial government rebates for retrofitting older buildings to be more energy efficient, carbon offset programs, community tree-planting programs, municipal recycling programs, Intergovernmental Panel on Climate Change [IPCC]), and propose a further course of action related to one of these initiatives*	3, 4	4, 5	21	
10.4.D2	investigate various natural and human factors that influence Earth's climate and climate change				
10.4.D2.1	*use appropriate terminology related to climate change, including, but not limited to: albedo, anthropogenic, atmosphere, cycles, heat sinks, and hydrosphere*	9, 10	6		22
10.4.D2.2	*design and build a model to illustrate the natural greenhouse effect, and use the model to explain the anthropogenic greenhouse effect*	19	7		
10.4.D2.3	*analyse different sources of scientific data (e.g., lake cores, tree rings, fossils and preserved organisms, ice cores) for evidence of natural climate change and climate change influenced by human activity*	30	8	22	
10.4.D2.4	*investigate a popular hypothesis on a cause-and-effect relationship having to do with climate change (e.g., the combustion of fossil fuels is responsible for rising global temperatures; the concentration of atmospheric CO2 is responsible for rising global temperatures; global temperatures have been on the increase since the industrial revolution; the severity of cyclones, hurricanes, and tornadoes increases as atmospheric temperatures increase), using simulations and/or time-trend data that model climate profiles (e.g., data from Statistics Canada and Environment Canada)*	22	9		23
10.4.D2.5	*investigate, through laboratory inquiry or simulations, the effects of heat transfer within the hydrosphere and atmosphere*	14		23	
10.4.D2.6	*investigate, through laboratory inquiry or simulations, how water in its various states influences climate patterns (e.g., water bodies moderate climate, water vapour is a greenhouse gas, ice increases the albedo of Earth's surface)*	15		24	
10.4.D2.7	*investigate, through research or simulations, the influence of ocean currents on local and global heat transfer and precipitation patterns*	16		25	

Table of Correlations

	Specific Expectation	Practice Questions	Unit Test Questions	Practice Test 1	Practice Test 2
10.4.D2.8	*classify the climate of their local region using various tools or systems (e.g., Ecoregions of Canada, bioclimate profiles), and compare their region to other regions in Ontario, Canada, and the world*	5			24
10.4.D2.9	*compare different perspectives and/or biases evident in discussions of climate change in scientific and non-scientific media (e.g., with reference to knowledge, beliefs, and values)*	6	10, 11	26	
10.4.D3	demonstrate an understanding of natural and human factors, including the greenhouse effect, that influence Earth's climate and contribute to climate change				
10.4.D3.1	*describe the principal components of Earth's climate system (e.g., the sun, oceans, and atmosphere; the topography and configuration of land masses) and how the system works*	7, 8	12, 13, 14		25
10.4.D3.2	*describe and explain heat transfer in the hydrosphere and atmosphere and its effects on air and water currents*	11, 12, 13		27	
10.4.D3.3	*describe the natural greenhouse effect, explain its importance for life, and distinguish it from the anthropogenic greenhouse effect*	17, 18	15, 16		26
10.4.D3.4	*identify natural phenomena (e.g., plate tectonics, uplift and weathering, solar radiance, cosmic ray cycles) and human activities (e.g., forest fires, deforestation, the burning of fossil fuels, industrial emissions) known to affect climate, and describe the role of both in Canada's contribution to climate change*	20, 21	17, 18	28	27
10.4.D3.5	*describe the principal sources and sinks, both natural and/or anthropogenic, of greenhouse gases (e.g., carbon dioxide, methane, nitrous oxide, halocarbons, water vapour)*	23, 24	19, 20		28
10.4.D3.6	*describe how different carbon and nitrogen compounds (e.g., carbon dioxide, methane, nitrous oxide) influence the trapping of heat in the atmosphere and hydrosphere*	25	21	29	
10.4.D3.7	*describe, in general terms, the causes and effects of the anthropogenic greenhouse effect, the depletion of stratospheric and tropospheric ozone, and the formation of ground-level ozone and smog*	26, 27	22, 23	30	29
10.4.D3.8	*identify and describe indicators of global climate change (e.g., changes in: glacial and polar ice, sea levels, wind patterns, global carbon budget assessments)*	28, 29	24, 25		30

10.4.D1.1 *analyse current and/or potential effects, both positive and negative, of climate change on human activity and natural systems (e.g., loss of habitat for Arctic mammals such as polar bears and loss of traditional lifestyles for Inuit as Arctic ice shrinks; famine as arable land is lost to desertification; an increase in water-borne disease and human resettlement as coastal lands are flooded; expansion of the growing season in some regions)*

Climate Change

Climate change has many effects on natural systems. While a relatively small increase in annual temperature might seem unimportant, climate change has been linked to many environmental problems. The increasing temperature results in increasing evaporation from freshwater sources. In areas already facing freshwater shortages, increased evaporation often means devastating droughts. Some areas of the world, such as China, are experiencing desertification as a result of climate change. Desertification is the conversion of previously diverse and biologically productive land to inhospitable dry land. At the same time that freshwater sources are decreasing, the sea level is rising as polar ice shelves, caps, and glaciers break apart and melt. Much of the world's population lives on coastlines, which face increasing flooding problems as the sea level rises. Permafrost regions in the Canadian Arctic are shrinking in size as they are being affected by climate change.
Striking pictures of polar bears standing on shrinking ice sheets show evidence of climate change's impact in the North.

As the temperature increases in the Northern Hemisphere, many animal and plant species that were unable to survive in the cold temperatures are expanding their range and moving northward. This is a major concern, as invasive species are taking over the habitats of native species. There is also the possibility of diseases moving northward as their host insects expand their ranges.
The increasing frequency of natural disasters including hurricanes, floods, and big storms also contributes to the spread of disease, as the destruction left behind provides breeding grounds for many infectious agents.

One small benefit of climate change is the lengthened growing season in temperate regions. The positive effects of an increased growing season, however, are likely to be offset by the changes in hydrology and decreases in productivity caused by climate change.

Use the following information to answer the next question.

> Recent droughts in Ontario, brought on by higher than normal temperatures, have negative impacts on the environment. It is believed that these droughts may be directly linked to human-caused climate change.

1. Which of the following scenarios is **not** an environmental concern associated with droughts?

A. Increased fire risk

B. Hot and humid weather

C. Soil erosion and dust storms

D. Increased pressure on fish habitats

Use the following information to answer the next question.

> The polar bear has developed adaptions for life in the Arctic. Polar bears have white fur to blend into their snowy background when hunting for food. They have a thick layer of blubber, or fat, and two layers of fur to keep warm. They have black skin underneath their fur to help absorb the sun's energy.
> Polar bears hunt by swimming out onto sea ice, and seals are their main food source.

Open Response

2. Explain how a warmer climate could affect the polar bear.

10.4.D1.2 *assess, on the basis of research, the effectiveness of some current individual, regional, national, or international initiatives that address the issue of climate change (e.g., Drive Clean, ENERGY STAR, federal and provincial government rebates for retrofitting older buildings to be more energy efficient, carbon offset programs, community tree-planting programs, municipal recycling programs, Intergovernmental Panel on Climate Change [IPCC]), and propose a further course of action related to one of these initiatives*

Climate Change Initiatives

The world is beginning to accept climate change as a reality. Many initiatives are being put in place to slow the causes of climate change and reduce its impacts. These initiatives include the Drive Clean and ENERGY STAR programs, municipal recycling programs, and the Intergovernmental Panel on Climate Change. More information can be found on these and other environmental protection programs on the Internet.

The ENERGY STAR Program

The ENERGY STAR program began in 1992 as a program developed by the United States Environmental Protection Agency. It was started as a voluntary labelling program, in which energy-efficient computers and monitors were marked by the ENERGY STAR label. Consumers were encouraged to buy ENERGY STAR products to save both money and energy, thereby reducing greenhouse gases. Since then, the program has expanded to include thousands of different products for both household and commercial consumers. Each product must meet efficiency standards set by the Environmental Protection Agency to receive an ENERGY STAR label. ENERGY STAR estimates that customers, organizations, and businesses saved $17 billion dollars in 2009 alone, just by using ENERGY STAR appliances. More information on the program can be found on their website, www.energystar.gov.

The Intergovernmental Panel on Climate Change

The Intergovernmental Panel on Climate Change (IPCC) is the biggest international initiative on climate change. Composed of governmental representatives and scientists from all over the world, the IPCC endeavors to bring together objective, high-quality science and information on climate change. They assemble a huge amount of information and produce comprehensive reports that can be used by policy-makers.
More information on the IPCC can be found on their website, www.ipcc.ch.

Use the following information to answer the next question.

> In order to become carbon neutral, people need to balance out the amount of greenhouse gases they produce.
> Some strategies for balancing out greenhouse gases are reducing the amount of $CO_{2(g)}$ and other greenhouse gases produced and purchasing carbon offset credits. Buying credits allows people to support projects such as those fuelled by renewable resources that produce less $CO_{2(g)}$ than would otherwise be produced.

3. Which of the following locations produces the **most** carbon neutral energy resources?

A. Natural gas well

B. Wind farm

C. Coal mine

D. Oil well

CHALLENGER QUESTION

Use the following information to answer the next question.

Compact fluorescent lamps (CFLs) are used as an alternative to conventional incandescent light bulbs.

Open Response

4. List three advantages of using CFLs instead of incandescent bulbs.

____

____

____

____

____

____

____

10.4.D2.8 *classify the climate of their local region using various tools or systems (e.g., Ecoregions of Canada, bioclimate profiles), and compare their region to other regions in Ontario, Canada, and the world*

Classifying Ontario's Climate

Climate is defined as the long-term average conditions (temperature, precipitation, wind speed and direction, etc.) for a given area. In contrast, weather describes the day-to-day variation in the same conditions.

Climate plays an important role in determining the type and distribution of species in an area. Because of this, many classification schemes use variables such as topography, hydrology, and vegetation when classifying a region's climate. These variables serve as indicators of climate, and areas with similar climates will tend to have similar characteristics. Two climate classification systems used in Canada are bioclimate profiles and ecoregions.

Bioclimate profiles (BCPs) were first developed by the Ontario Ministry of Natural Resources to provide an overview of recent and current climate conditions. BCPs use information including minimum, maximum, and mean temperature and precipitation, frost-free days, and water surplus or deficit to define local climate. Information is available from 112 climate stations across Canada for the years 1951 to 2000. This data can be used as a baseline, or normal, climate, and can be compared to predictions of future climate profiles. The change in minimum, maximum, and extreme values gives an idea of the effect of future climate change. Bioclimate profiles can also be used to compare different regions.

Another tool used to classify climate is an ecoregion (or ecological region). Ecoregions, which are smaller than ecozones, are areas that have a characteristic topography, hydrology, soil, temperature, and moisture regime.

Most of Ontario falls in the Boreal Shield ecozone. The Hudson Plains ecozone is located in northern Ontario, extending from the shore of Hudson Bay, and the Mixed Wood Plains ecozone in southern Ontario covers the Great Lakes-St. Lawrence river valley.

Each of these areas is divided into smaller areas called ecoregions. For example, the Mixed Wood Plains ecozone in southern Ontario is divided into the Manitoulin-Lake Simcoe ecoregion and the Lake Erie Lowland ecoregion. These ecoregions generally have similar climate conditions, but the Lake Erie Lowland ecoregion is distinguished by less forest cover and different soil types.

Other parts of Canada are classified as different ecozones and ecoregions. The Prairies ecozone, which covers the southern parts of Alberta, Saskatchewan, and Manitoba, is divided into nine ecoregions characterized by hot, short summers, long, cold winters, and grassland vegetation. The Pacific Maritime ecozone along the west coast of British Columbia is divided into 14 ecoregions, characterized by warm temperatures and high precipitation. In total, there are 15 terrestrial ecozones in Canada.

5. Which of the following ecozones is **not** found in Ontario?
   A. Taiga Shield
   B. Boreal Shield
   C. Hudson Plains
   D. Mixedwood Plains

10.4.D2.9 *compare different perspectives and/or biases evident in discussions of climate change in scientific and non-scientific media (e.g., with reference to knowledge, beliefs, and values)*

Perspectives on Climate Change

There is a great deal of controversy over the validity of the data regarding climate change and how it is interpreted. Critics of climate-change theories argue that the predictions made by scientists about future warming trends are exaggerated or unlikely to come true. Scientists and others respond that critics are motivated by personal interests to downplay the potential consequences of climate change.

How people interpret climate-change data depends on their pre-existing biases or beliefs. In order to have a balanced understanding of the issue, it is necessary to review the data in an objective way. The reliability of the source should be considered along with the data or facts that are presented. For example, information from a peer-reviewed scientific journal is more reliable than information learned through hearsay.

Different perspectives on climate change are also reflected in the potential responses to and mechanisms for dealing with climate change. Many environmentalists think that everything possible should be done to stop and reverse global climate change. This reflects the belief that ecosystems and other species have an intrinsic value that people should respect. Economists generally believe that market tools, such as taxes or incentives, should be adopted to deal with climate change. Some believe the most efficient policy is not necessarily to try and control the climate, the interrelated parts of which are not fully understood, but to have mechanisms in place to deal with the consequences. Politicians often have to consider many different views, including the economy and jobs, public health, and agreements with other countries. Because of this, they often try to get as much information as possible on large-scale issues like climate change, and they proceed slowly with decisions.

These viewpoints all reflect what each person or group thinks are the most important issues pertaining to climate change. Understanding the biases underlying different perspectives allows a more balanced assessment of different sources of information.

Use the following information to answer the next question.

> A series of advertisements about climate change were published on the Internet with the message "Carbon dioxide: you call it toxin, we call it life."
> The advertisements were making the argument that carbon dioxide is essential for photosynthesis and is therefore needed by plants, so it should not be considered a pollutant. These advertisements were released just before governments were set to discuss the Kyoto protocol.

6. The advertisements **most likely** represent the perspective of a
   A. plant biologist
   B. car manufacturer
   C. climate change scientist
   D. developing nation's citizen

10.4.D3.1 *describe the principal components of Earth's climate system (e.g., the sun, oceans, and atmosphere; the topography and configuration of land masses) and how the system works*

10.4.D2.1 *use appropriate terminology related to climate change, including, but not limited to: albedo, anthropogenic, atmosphere, cycles, heat sinks, and hydrosphere*

THE REGIONS OF THE BIOSPHERE

The area in which living things can survive on Earth is called the biosphere. The biosphere has regions within each of Earth's three main spheres.
The following list provides the main characteristics of each of these spheres:

- Hydrosphere (oceans, lakes, rivers, wetlands, and water vapour)
- Lithosphere (beginning at Earth's crust and extending from the surface to approximately 85 km to 100 km)
- Atmosphere (the gaseous area above Earth's surface extending to about 300 km)

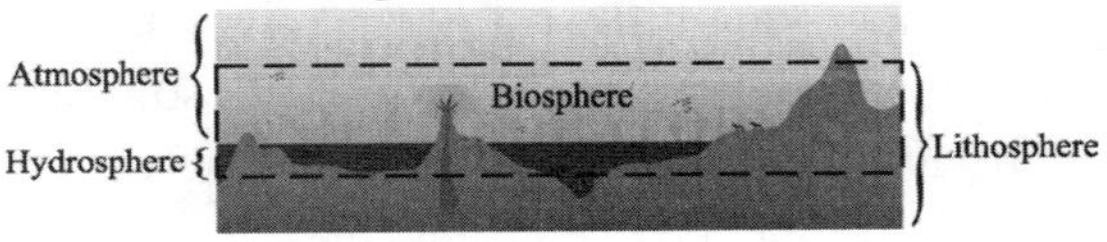

THE ATMOSPHERE

The atmosphere extends 300 km into outer space. It is denser near Earth because gravity holds the molecules of a gas more tightly together.
The atmosphere is composed of the following gases:

- 78% nitrogen
- 21% oxygen
- 0.93% argon
- 0.04% carbon dioxide
- Other gases in very tiny amounts

The given composition includes dry percentages and does not include water vapour, which makes up about 4% of the atmosphere overall.

The atmosphere is made up of the following layers:

- Troposphere (up to 10 km in altitude)—contains 80% of the gases in the atmosphere.
- Stratosphere (up to 60 km in altitude)—contains the protective ozone (O_3) layer. Gets warmer at higher altitudes.
- Mesosphere (up to 80 km in altitude)
- Thermosphere (up to 300 km in altitude)—can reach temperatures of 1500°C.

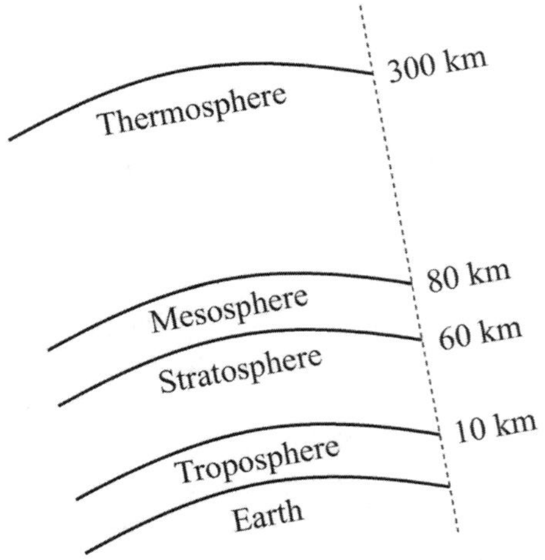

The biosphere extends into the first few kilometres of the atmosphere.

THE LITHOSPHERE

The lithosphere extends through Earth's crust (which is 40 km thick) into the semisolid mantle to a depth of 85 km to 100 km. The mantle extends down even farther to Earth's core. The greater the depth, the hotter the temperature. The region in which terrestrial organisms can live within the lithosphere extends from the surface down through the soil and rock to a depth of no more than 5 km.

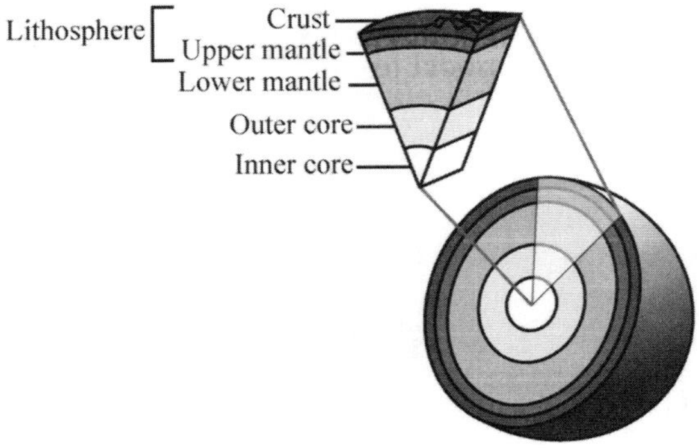

Organisms that live deep inside Earth have to be adapted to darkness. They are not able to use photosynthesis to make food—only chemosynthesis is possible at these depths. There is little or no oxygen present, so organisms have to use anaerobic respiration. High heat and high pressure are present in this region. Most of the organisms that live here are bacteria.

THE HYDROSPHERE

Water covers 80% of Earth's surface. More living things live in the hydrosphere than in either of the other two regions of the biosphere. Organisms that live in the hydrosphere have to be adapted to the specific characteristics of water: high density, high heat capacity, lower oxygen concentrations, and high surface tension. Organisms that live in water are either marine (live in salt water) or aquatic (live in fresh water).

Water's high specific heat capacity makes it the major moderator of temperatures on Earth. Water stores large amounts of heat and acts as a heat sink when air temperatures are high, preventing air temperatures from becoming too unbearable. When air temperatures are low, water gives off its stored heat back to the atmosphere, helping to maintain a livable temperature on Earth. The heat absorbed and released by water is responsible for ocean and air currents, which are in turn responsible for weather and climate.

7. Atmospheric winds are caused by

A. differential heating

B. the moon's tidal effect

C. the gravitational force of Earth

D. convection currents in Earth's mantle

Use the following information to answer the next question.

> Steven spent his summer holiday at a beachfront cottage near the ocean. He observed that the wind blew in one direction during the day and in the opposite direction during the night. He inferred that the reason for this change in wind direction had something to do with the nearby ocean.

8. What is the reason for the winds changing direction near the ocean over the course of a day?

A. High and low tides occur.

B. Ocean currents reverse direction.

C. Land and water heat up unevenly.

D. Oceans reflect air off their surfaces.

9. Which of the following pairs of processes describes the transfer and use of thermal energy from sunlight?

A. Conduction and absorption

B. Conduction and reflection

C. Radiation and absorption

D. Radiation and reflection

CHALLENGER QUESTION

Use the following information to answer the next question.

Polar sea ice has an important function in moderating the global energy balance. Sea ice has an albedo of 0.8; that is, it reflects 80% of the solar radiation it receives. Melted sea ice is, of course, water, which has an albedo of 0.2.

10. Which of the following statements about the absorption of solar radiation and albedo is **true**?

A. Sea ice, which absorbs 20% of solar radiation, has a lower albedo than water.

B. Sea ice, which absorbs 80% of solar radiation, has a lower albedo than water.

C. Sea water, which absorbs 80% of solar radiation, has a lower albedo than ice.

D. Sea water, which absorbs 20% of solar radiation, has a lower albedo than ice.

10.4.D3.2 *describe and explain heat transfer in the hydrosphere and atmosphere and its effects on air and water currents*

10.4.D2.5 *investigate, through laboratory inquiry or simulations, the effects of heat transfer within the hydrosphere and atmosphere*

10.4.D2.6 *investigate, through laboratory inquiry or simulations, how water in its various states influences climate patterns (e.g., water bodies moderate climate, water vapour is a greenhouse gas, ice increases the albedo of Earth's surface)*

10.4.D2.7 *investigate, through research or simulations, the influence of ocean currents on local and global heat transfer and precipitation patterns*

Heat Transfer and Climate

Heat transfers strongly influence climate and atmospheric conditions. Air and water are fluids, so they can undergo convection. Recall that in convection, warmer particles flow to cooler areas and are replaced by cooler particles, creating circular flows. The flow of air particles creates winds. Water has a higher heat capacity than land does, meaning that the sun's rays will heat the land faster than the water. When the difference between the temperatures of the land and water is great, such as in the summer, the air over the land becomes less dense, rises, and moves toward the sea. This creates a convection air current as air that was above the water moves over the land to fill the space. This results in a sea breeze.

Just as the land heats up more quickly than the sea, it also cools more quickly. In the evenings, the air over the sea is warmer than the air over the land, so the air over the sea rises and moves toward the lands, creating a convection current in which the denser air covering the land moves out toward the sea, creating a land breeze.

Wind and Ocean Currents

Earth's atmosphere and oceans play a significant role in redistributing the energy that is received from the sun. As the air above Earth's surface is warmed, it begins to rise. The warm air becomes wind as it moves horizontally toward low-pressure areas, and as the air cools, it begins to sink. The circles of rising, moving, and sinking air are called convection currents or convection cells. The uneven solar heating of Earth's atmosphere causes three major bands of convection currents or wind belts to develop in each hemisphere. The Coriolis force bends the winds of the convection currents.
The wind in these particular bands around Earth is generally in one direction, called the **prevailing** wind direction. For example, the prevailing winds in Ontario are toward the northeast.

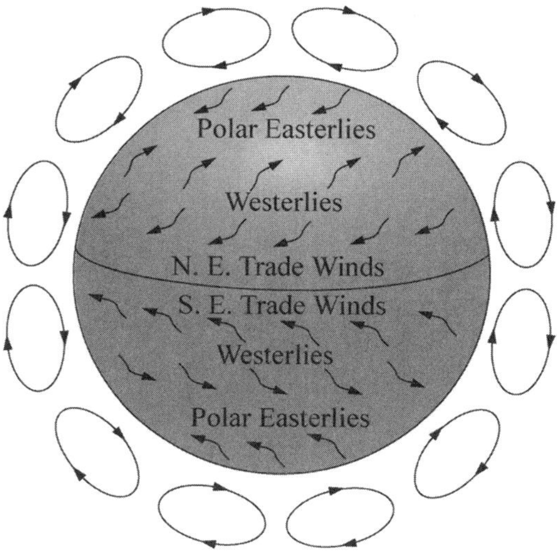

Most of the thermal energy created at Earth's surface is stored in the water of the oceans. Water has a high specific heat capacity, which means that water can hold a lot of energy compared to other substances. The reason water regulates and stabilizes Earth's temperature is that the enormous amount of water on Earth's surface gains and loses energy relatively slowly.

Ocean water surrounding the equator receives much more solar energy than other parts of the ocean, and the water near the poles receives much less solar energy than other parts of the ocean. Atmospheric wind currents help to redistribute the warm water of the equator and the cold water of the poles around the ocean. Ocean currents follow the general pattern of the atmospheric wind currents but are also influenced by land masses, the Coriolis force, and tides.

The combined effects of oceanic and atmospheric convection currents are responsible for weather, precipitation, and general climatic patterns.

The Impact of Varying States of Water on Climate

The state of water can have an impact on the climate surrounding it. In areas where water is primarily found as snow or ice, such as at the poles, Earth has a high albedo (reflectivity). When sunlight reaches Earth's surface in these areas, much of it is reflected back into the atmosphere and into space. As a result, these areas are typically much colder than areas where there is little or no snow and ice.
When sunlight hits areas of the surface where there is lots of bare land and rock exposed, much of the sunlight is absorbed and released at the surface as heat.

The impact of large bodies of water on neighboring cities provides another example of how the state of water can have an impact on the climate surrounding it. Cities like Toronto and Vancouver, which are quite close to large bodies of water like the Great Lakes and the Pacific Ocean, respectively, tend to experience much less dramatic temperature variations than cities like Edmonton or Saskatoon, which are not located close to large bodies of water. This is because of the high specific heat capacity of water. Water holds much more heat than the surrounding air, so when the air around the water drops to a lower temperature, some of the heat in the water is transferred to the air. Likewise, when the temperature of the air heats up beyond the temperature of the neighboring body of water, some of that heat is transferred back to the water. In this manner a large body of water has a moderating effect on the temperature of the air surrounding it.

Water vapor in the atmosphere also dramatically impacts climate because it functions as a greenhouse gas. When sunlight enters the atmosphere and reaches Earth's surface, some of it is reflected back toward space. Greenhouses gases function to trap that reflected solar radiation in the atmosphere, promoting a warming effect on climate.

11. In coastal areas, wind blows from

A. sea to land during the night and land to sea during the day

B. land to sea during the night and sea to land during the day

C. sea to land all the time

D. land to sea all the time

12. Heat is a transfer of thermal energy. When heat is transferred, the thermal energy of the substance increases as the

A. motion of the particles in the substance increases

B. motion of the particles near the substance increases

C. temperature of the particles in the substance decreases

D. temperature of the particles near the substance increases

Open Response

13. **Complete** the following table which compares how heat energy is distributed in the atmosphere with how heat energy is distributed in the hydrosphere. List the similarities and the differences in the two processes.

Comparison of Heat Energy Distribution in the Atmosphere and the Hydrosphere

Similarities	Differences

14. Which of the following effects of sunlight reaching Earth does **not** represent a conversion of solar energy to thermal energy?

A. It drives winds and water currents

B. It is captured by photosynthesis

C. It is reflected back into space

D. It drives the water cycle

CHALLENGER QUESTION

15. Newfoundland is surrounded by water, so there is always lots of moisture there, both on the ground and in fogs.
The temperature never gets very high in the summer because heat energy is removed from the air by the

A. water's specific heat capacity and its heat of fusion

B. water's specific heat capacity and its heat of vaporization

C. albedo effect and the heat of fusion from Newfoundland's surface

D. albedo effect and the heat of vapourization from Newfoundland's surface

16. In the ocean, heat is transferred vertically through

A. convection currents

B. ocean currents

C. waves

D. tides

10.4.D3.3 *describe the natural greenhouse effect, explain its importance for life, and distinguish it from the anthropogenic greenhouse effect*

10.4.D2.2 *design and build a model to illustrate the natural greenhouse effect, and use the model to explain the anthropogenic greenhouse effect*

THE GREENHOUSE EFFECT

When the sun's rays reach Earth, some are reflected back toward space. However, gases in the atmosphere, such as carbon dioxide, methane, water vapour, and nitrous oxide, trap some rays around Earth, preventing them from leaving the atmosphere. This natural phenomenon is known as the greenhouse effect. Without the greenhouse effect keeping the planet warm, Earth's temperature would be below zero, which would be too cold to sustain life.

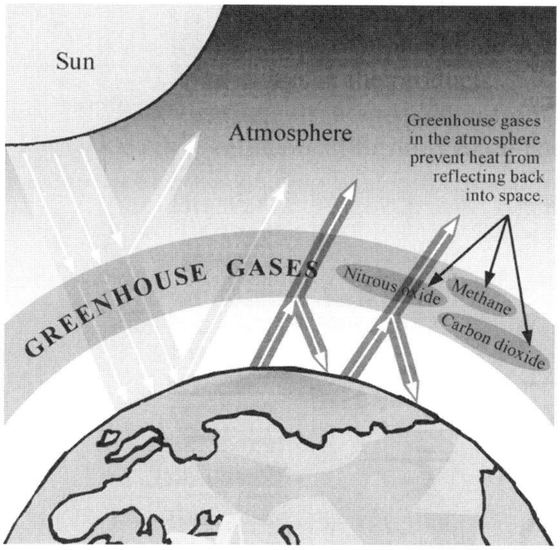

The greenhouse effect

The natural greenhouse effect, however, is being amplified by human activities. Since the industrial and agricultural revolutions, the production of greenhouse gases has increased dramatically. Two of the main greenhouse gases are carbon dioxide and methane. Carbon dioxide is produced by fossil fuels that power factories, homes, and vehicles. Methane is produced in large quantities by big farming operations, including cattle yards and rice paddies. The rising levels of greenhouse gases are contributing to an increase in the average global temperature. As climate and weather patterns are driven by thermal-energy transfers, the effects of the increasing global temperature can be dramatic.

Use the following information to answer the next question.

> In the centuries before the Industrial Revolution, the greenhouse effect was **primarily**____*i*____ and its effects were ____*ii*____.

17. Which pair of terms accurately completes the given statement?

A.

i	*ii*
natural	insignificant

B.

i	*ii*
natural	significant

C.

i	*ii*
anthropogenic	insignificant

D.

i	*ii*
anthropogenic	significant

Open Response

18. Distinguish between the natural and anthropogenic greenhouse effects.

____

____

____

____

____

Use the following information to answer the next question.

> The greenhouse effect is named for the similarities between the heat trapping effects of Earth's atmosphere and those of an actual greenhouse.

19. In this analogy, the function of the atmosphere is **most similar** to the function of which part of a greenhouse?

A. The frame that supports the greenhouse walls

B. The air trapped within the greenhouse walls

C. The glass composing the greenhouse walls

D. The vents perforating the greenhouse walls

10.4.D3.4 *identify natural phenomena (e.g., plate tectonics, uplift and weathering, solar radiance, cosmic ray cycles) and human activities (e.g., forest fires, deforestation, the burning of fossil fuels, industrial emissions) known to affect climate, and describe the role of both in Canada's contribution to climate change*

10.4.D2.4 *investigate a popular hypothesis on a cause-and-effect relationship having to do with climate change (e.g., the combustion of fossil fuels is responsible for rising global temperatures; the concentration of atmospheric CO2 is responsible for rising global temperatures; global temperatures have been on the increase since the industrial revolution; the severity of cyclones, hurricanes, and tornadoes increases as atmospheric temperatures increase), using simulations and/or time-trend data that model climate profiles (e.g., data from Statistics Canada and Environment Canada)*

Phenomena Affecting Climate

There are a number of natural and anthropogenic, or human-caused, phenomena that can affect climate. These phenomena are contributing to what is now considered climate change.

Natural Contributors to Climate Change

Earth's climate has always varied over the course of geological time, alternating between periods of glaciation and thaw. The last ice age was approximately 10000 years ago. One of the main theories behind this variation in global climate is that Earth's movement patterns also vary. Earth's orbit around the sun is not perfectly circular; it can also be slightly elliptical, so that Earth actually travels closer to the sun at times. Earth's tilt also varies. Together, these changes are thought to bring on ice ages and thaws.

Plate tectonics are also thought to contribute to climate change. As the plates of Earth's crust shift, volcanic activity increases. Volcanic eruptions contribute significant amounts of carbon dioxide to the atmosphere. Carbon dioxide is also released by the weathering of sedimentary rocks, which act as traps for carbon dioxide.

Anthropogenic Contributors to Climate Change

Information provided by Environment and Statistics Canada and other sources gives very solid evidence that human activities also contribute to climate change. Carbon dioxide levels have increased dramatically since the Industrial Revolution, and the burning of fossil fuels is thought to be one of the largest contributors to the increase. Industrial processing and agricultural activities also emit carbon dioxide and other greenhouse gases.

As well as increasing the level of greenhouse gases in the atmosphere, humans have deforested much of Earth's surface. Trees and plants are major carbon dioxide sinks. Through the process of photosynthesis, they capture carbon dioxide and produce oxygen. The removal of so many trees and rainforest plants means that carbon dioxide, which would normally be removed from the air, is being left in the atmosphere, and the carbon dioxide already trapped in the tissues of the plants is being released back into the air.

Canada's Contributions to Climate Change

Canadians are dependent on fossil fuel technologies for transportation, electricity, and heat. Canada is also a major source of the world's oil and gas supply. As oil and gas deposits become scarcer, more energy is needed to extract them. Alberta's tarsands are major contributors to greenhouse gas emissions. Along with personal transportation, Canadians create greenhouse gases through consumer choices. Much of the food and goods Canadians rely on is made in other countries, meaning it has to be transported to Canada. Many of Canadians' favorite products are grown on land that used to be rainforest, and many of Canada's forests are used to supply pulp, paper, and lumber.

Not all of Canada's contributions to climate change are anthropogenic. The mountain pine beetle epidemic in western Canada is contributing to climate change in several ways. Pine trees being killed by the infestation are no longer able to photosynthesize, reducing the amount of carbon dioxide being recycled, and the standing dead timber is a fire risk. British Columbia is predicted to experience more major forest fires as the climate becomes drier and hotter. Burning plant matter is another major contributor to greenhouse gas emissions.

Use the following information to answer the next question.

> The average surface temperature of Earth is increasing because of the effect of greenhouse gases. Increasing levels of greenhouse gases are associated with global climate change.

20. Which of the following human activities is **most directly** associated with global climate change?

A. Capturing solar energy

B. Burning fossil fuels

C. Building dams

D. Planting trees

21. Why is deforestation directly linked with climate change?
    A. Deforestation causes soil erosion.
    B. Deforestation reduces the amount of rainfall.
    C. The process of getting lumber releases toxic gases.
    D. The amount of carbon dioxide in the air increases as a result of deforestation.

Use the following information to answer the next question.

There are many cause-and-effect theories regarding anthropogenic climate change.

22. One such theory is that the increase in global temperatures has resulted in an increase in
    A. atmospheric carbon dioxide
    B. combustion of fossil fuels
    C. severe weather events
    D. ozone depletion

10.4.D3.5 *describe the principal sources and sinks, both natural and/or anthropogenic, of greenhouse gases (e.g., carbon dioxide, methane, nitrous oxide, halocarbons, water vapour)*

Sources and Sinks of Greenhouse Gases

Greenhouse gases can be discussed in terms of sources and sinks. Any process or object that releases greenhouse gases into the atmosphere is considered a **source**; any process or object that removes carbon dioxide from the atmosphere is considered a **sink**. The three main greenhouse gases are carbon dioxide, methane, and nitrous oxide. Although methane and nitrous oxide are actually more damaging per molecule, carbon dioxide is the most abundant greenhouse gas.

Carbon Dioxide

Carbon dioxide is the most abundant greenhouse gas in Earth's atmosphere. It is affected by the carbon cycle, and has many natural sources: forest fires, volcanic eruptions, weathering of sedimentary rock, natural decomposition of materials, and cellular respiration in plants and animals. Its primary anthropogenic source is the burning of fossil fuels. Environmental sinks for carbon dioxide include photosynthesizing plants, sediments, and the oceans.

Methane

Methane has both natural and anthropogenic sources. Natural sources of methane include wetlands, oceans and bodies of fresh water, certain types of soils, and wildfires. Anthropogenic sources include fossil fuel production, livestock and farming practices, and gases from landfills. Wetlands can act as a sink for methane, although the number of wetlands is declining around the globe.
Methane can also be captured and used as an energy source. It is often referred to as natural gas, and it is a clean-burning fuel.

Nitrous Oxide

Nitrous oxide has several natural and anthropogenic sources. It is emitted from some types of soils, and it can result from the use of fertilizers on crops. Nitrous oxide is also created during industrial processing, and it is produced from the burning of fossil fuels and other organic materials.
Nitrous oxide does not have many natural sinks.

Use the following information to answer the next question.

> Environmental scientists tested the air quality near a coal-fired power plant. They determined that the smoke stacks emitted several different gases into the atmosphere.

23. Which of the following gases detected by the scientists is **not** a greenhouse gas?

A. Methane

B. Nitrous oxide

C. Sulfur dioxide

D. Carbon monoxide

Use the following information to answer the next question.

> Gas X is a major greenhouse gas. Environment Canada estimates its atmospheric concentration has increased 145% since the mid-1700s. Anthropogenic sources include livestock production, rice cultivation, combustion of biomass, landfills, and energy production and delivery.

24. From the description, greenhouse gas X is

A. methane **B.** water vapour

C. nitrous oxide **D.** carbon dioxide

10.4.D3.6 *describe how different carbon and nitrogen compounds (e.g., carbon dioxide, methane, nitrous oxide) influence the trapping of heat in the atmosphere and hydrosphere*

How Greenhouse Gases Trap Heat

Molecules of greenhouse gases trap the sun's rays by absorbing radiation. The atoms in the molecule can absorb this energy and store it as vibrations. Different molecules can absorb different amounts of energy. For example, methane and nitrous oxide are the two most damaging greenhouse gases because they are able to absorb the most energy—even more than carbon dioxide. However, carbon dioxide is much more abundant in Earth's atmosphere than methane and nitrous oxide, so it is often seen as the main culprit behind the anthropogenic greenhouse effect.

25. Carbon dioxide contributes to the greenhouse effect because it allows

A. light but not heat to pass through it

B. heat but not light to pass through it

C. both heat and light to pass through it

D. neither heat nor light to pass through it

10.4.D3.7 *describe, in general terms, the causes and effects of the anthropogenic greenhouse effect, the depletion of stratospheric and tropospheric ozone, and the formation of ground-level ozone and smog*

Other Anthropogenic Atmosphere and Climate Problems

Along with climate change and the anthropogenic greenhouse effect, humans have created other atmospheric and climate-related problems, such as the depletion of the stratospheric and tropospheric ozone layer and the formation of smog and ground-level ozone.

Depletion of the ozone layer

When solar energy reaches the ozone layer, the rays can be divided into three categories: UV-A, UV-B, and UV-C. These rays, listed in order from least to most potentially dangerous, have the potential to mutate DNA, causing harm to life on Earth. The ozone layer forms a protective shield between the most harmful of the sun's rays and Earth's surface. The ozone layer is an area of the Earth's atmosphere that has a high density of ozone molecules, O_3. These molecules absorb all of the sun's UV-C rays and most of the UV-B rays.

Human activities, however, have resulted in a thinning of the ozone layer in certain places. Molecules called chlorofluorocarbons, or CFCs, which used to be commonly used in refrigeration and cooling systems and aerosol devices, reach the ozone layer and destroy ozone molecules, depleting the ozone layer. The chlorine atom of a CFC molecule essentially steals one of the oxygen atoms from the ozone molecule. This stolen oxygen molecule is then combined with another stolen oxygen atom to create O_2, freeing up the chlorine atom to destroy another molecule of ozone. One chlorine atom is able to destroy ozone for up to two years before it is removed from the ozone layer through natural processes.

Formation of Smog

The word *smog* is a combination of the words *smoke* and *fog*. Smog is a completely anthropogenic condition caused by emissions from the burning of fossil fuels, coal combustion, and industrial emissions. It can be seen over urban and industrial centers as a brownish haze that accumulates, particularly in hot conditions. Smog is also known as ground-level ozone.

Smog impacts ecosystems by reducing photosynthesis and clogging the stomata of plants, preventing the intake of CO_2 and reducing productivity. This has the potential to decrease food supplies and the ability of plants to remove CO_2 from the air, making the greenhouse effect more extreme. Animals, including humans, can suffer from respiratory problems such as asthma and other chronic breathing difficulties as a result of smog. Burning eyes and skin damage are other problems caused by smog. The elderly, those with other health problems, and children can be strongly affected by breathing difficulties. In many cities, particularly in southern Asia, it is common to see people wearing masks to prevent the inhalation of smog. In some places school is canceled on bad smog days, citizens are told not to drive, and it is recommended that people remain indoors.

Use the following information to answer the next question.

The use of chlorofluorocarbon (CFCs) compounds was phased out after the signing and implementation of the Montreal Protocol in the late 1980s.

26. The Montreal Protocol was concerned with the depletion of ozone in the

A. troposphere **B.** mesosphere

C. stratosphere **D.** thermosphere

CHALLENGER QUESTION

27. Nitrogen oxide, sulfur dioxide, carbon monoxide, and hydrocarbons contribute to smog, acid rain, global warming, and certain illnesses, such as heart disease and respiratory problems. These pollutants can be found in

A. automobile exhaust

B. uncooked food

C. pesticides

D. garbage

10.4.D3.8 *identify and describe indicators of global climate change (e.g., changes in: glacial and polar ice, sea levels, wind patterns, global carbon budget assessments)*

10.4.D2.3 *analyse different sources of scientific data (e.g., lake cores, tree rings, fossils and preserved organisms, ice cores) for evidence of natural climate change and climate change influenced by human activity*

Evidence and Indicators of Climate Change

There are many sources of information available that enable scientists to gather information about Earth's climate. Earth-orbiting satellites, ice-core and tree-ring samples, coral reef building, and atmosphere-monitoring stations provide different types of data. Scientists use this data to study global climate change, and have identified several indicators of changes in the climate including changes in glacier and polar ice, sea levels, wind patterns, and global carbon budget assessments.

Information from the Gravity Recovery and Climate Experiment shows that the Greenland and Antarctic ice sheets decreased in both area and mass between 2002 and 2006. Mountain glaciers are also retreating in many areas of the world, such as Canada and Europe. As snow cover disappears, the dark soil underneath is uncovered. Dark soil is able to absorb more solar energy than snow, and this heats up the ground more quickly, speeding up the rate of snow melt.

The melting of glaciers increases the amount of water flowing into the oceans. Over the last 100 years, there has been a 17-centimeter rise in global sea levels, and the rate of this rise has increased in the past 10 years. This means that sea levels are now rising faster than before, which may create an increased danger of flooding in many coastal and low-lying areas of the world.

In addition to rising sea levels, patterns of precipitation and evaporation over the oceans have changed. Melting polar sea ice leaves more surface area available for the evaporation of water. Oceans are now more saline near the equator and less saline at higher latitudes (farther away from the equator) because of the increased freshwater run-off from the melting glaciers. This change in salinity can disrupt ocean current patterns.

Wind patterns are partly determined by the oceans' surface temperatures. Changes in wind patterns result in temperature and precipitation pattern changes. This means that some areas will experience longer and more severe droughts, while other areas will experience flooding.

The global carbon budget is the balance of carbon released from and stored in the environment. Carbon is stored in four major reservoirs: plants, the terrestrial biosphere, sediment, and the ocean. Carbon is released through combustion, respiration, and other biological and chemical reactions. Burning fossil fuels has increased the amount of carbon dioxide released into the atmosphere, while deforestation has decreased the amount of carbon removed from the atmosphere and stored in plant tissues. Many other processes are involved in carbon additions and removals, and these processes include complex feedback mechanisms. However, it is generally accepted that more carbon is being released than can be removed, and it is building up in the atmosphere as carbon dioxide.
The concentration of atmospheric CO_2 is higher now than it has been for thousands of years.

28. Global warming is directly responsible for which of the following environmental occurrences?

- **A.** Erosion of mountains
- **B.** Rising sea levels
- **C.** Earthquakes
- **D.** Landslides

29. Scientists predict that if current climate change trends continue, average global temperatures will

- **A.** decrease and ocean water levels will decrease
- **B.** decrease and ocean water levels will increase
- **C.** increase and ocean water levels will decrease
- **D.** increase and ocean water levels will increase

CHALLENGER QUESTION

30. Scientists can measure historic levels of carbon dioxide from all of the following sources **except**

- **A.** ice cores
- **B.** tree rings
- **C.** lake water
- **D.** coral reefs

Answers and Solutions

Earth and Space Science: Climate Change

1. B	7. A	13. OR	19. C	25. A
2. OR	8. C	14. C	20. B	26. C
3. B	9. C	15. B	21. D	27. A
4. OR	10. C	16. A	22. C	28. B
5. A	11. B	17. B	23. D	29. D
6. B	12. A	18. OR	24. A	30. C

1. B

Hot and humid weather is not associated with droughts because humid weather implies that there is moisture in the air.

Increased fire risk, soil erosion, and increased pressure on fish habitats are all scenarios that are associated with droughts.

2. OR

Because the polar bear is adapted to a cold climate, it would not do well in a warmer climate. It would overheat because of its thick layers of insulation, and would have less camouflage if the snow melted. Subsequently, it would have difficulty hunting its prey. As the sea ice melts because of warmer temperatures, the hunting habitat of the bear would diminish, and it would be difficult for the bear to hunt its favourite prey, seals. Climate change will have drastic consequences for the polar bear. This is supported by research indicating global declines in polar bear population numbers.

3. B

A resource that is carbon neutral does not produce products that create significant greenhouse gas emissions. A wind farm does not produce fossil fuels or significant amounts of greenhouse gases.

A natural gas well, a coal mine, and an oil well all produce products that release large amounts of carbon dioxide when burned.

4. OR

The advantages of CFLs over incandescent bulbs could include any of the following important benefits:

- CFLs use less energy.
- CFLs have a longer life span.
- CFLs provide more natural light.
- CFLs burn much cooler.

5. A

The Taiga Shield ecozone is not found in Ontario, although it is found on either side of Ontario, in the northern parts of Quebec and Manitoba.

The Hudson Plains, Boreal Shield, and Mixedwood Plains ecozones are all found in Ontario. Each of these ecozones encompasses many smaller ecoregions.

6. B

The advertisements are meant to combat the labelling of carbon dioxide as a pollutant. If carbon dioxide were not considered a pollutant, governments would have no reason to place limitations on carbon dioxide emissions.
These limits and restrictions would have a negative impact on a car manufacturer, who would be responsible for carbon dioxide emissions both from the manufacturing plant and from the cars that were made at the plant.

Plant biologists and climate change scientists recognize that carbon dioxide is a part of the carbon cycle, but also recognize that anthropogenic carbon contributions are too much for the plants to process and are resulting in climate change. A citizen in a developing nation is unlikely to share the given perspective, since many developing nations are suffering from the consequences of climate change, yet contributing very little to the greenhouse effect.

7. A

The differential heating of Earth's atmosphere causes a change in the density of air in different places. It is for this reason that air flows from a region of higher density to a region of lower density, thereby creating winds.

The tidal effect of the moon causes tides to rise at night. It does not lead to the formation of winds.

Earth's gravitational force attracts objects toward its centre. It does not lead to the formation of winds.

The convection currents from the mantle lead to the heating of Earth's surface. They do not lead to the formation of winds.

8. C

The land heats up more quickly during the day than the ocean does. The warm air above the land rises. Cooler air from the ocean moves in to take its place. This creates a sea breeze. During the night, the land has cooled off, but the ocean is still warm. The air above the ocean now rises. The cooler air from the land moves toward the ocean, creating a land breeze.

9. C

Sunlight is radiated towards the Earth, where it must be absorbed to be used. Some sunlight is reflected back towards the atmosphere, and is not used. Conduction is a method of heat transfer by direct contact of the particles involved.

10. C

If ice has an albedo of 0.8, meaning that it reflects 80% of the solar radiation it absorbs, and water has an albedo of 0.2, this would indicate that water reflects 20% of the solar radiation it absorbs. If water reflects 20%, it must absorb and hold on to 80%. Since albedo is the ability to reflect solar radiation, water has a lower albedo than ice.

11. B

Compared to land, water cools down and heats up rather slowly. During the day, the sea is much cooler than the land surface, which creates a high-pressure zone of relatively cold air in the atmosphere over the sea. On the other hand, land surface, which heats quickly, creates a low-pressure zone. Winds flow from a high pressure zone over the sea to a low pressure zone over the land. At night, the land surface releases heat much faster than the water, so the land cools faster than the sea. This creates a high-pressure zone over the land surface and a low-pressure zone over the sea. At night, winds flow from land to sea.

In coastal areas, winds do not flow from sea to land during the night and from land to sea during the day.

In coastal areas, winds do not always flow from sea to land.

In coastal areas, winds do not always flow from land to sea.

12. A

As heat is transferred, the particles inside the substance start vibrating more vigorously. The energy of motion of the particles in the substance is the substance's thermal energy. As the thermal energy of the substance increases, the thermal energy of the surroundings will decrease.

13. OR

Comparison of Heat Energy Distribution in the Atmosphere and the Hydrosphere

Similarities	Differences
– convection currents are produced in both processes – uneven heating produces both types of convection currents – both are affected by the Coriolis forces	– occurs in water and one occurs in air – global wind currents are more uniform than ocean currents – wind currents influence the direction of oceanic currents, but not necessarily vice versa – water's high specific heat capacity stabilizes Earth's temperature more than the atmosphere – land masses interfere more directly with ocean current pathways – ocean salinity can cause ocean currents to work in the opposite direction of temperature gradients

14. C

During photosynthesis, light energy is converted to chemical energy; however, some energy is converted to heat because no energy transfer is 100% efficient. The water cycle involves light energy heating Earth's surface and causing water to evaporate. Wind and water currents require more light to be converted to heat in some areas than in others. However, if light is reflected back to space, there is no conversion to heat.

15. B

The high specific heat capacity of water means that a lot of heat energy is required to increase the temperature of air that is laden with moisture. The heat of vapourization is the amount of heat energy required to change liquid water to water vapour. Adding this energy changes the state of water without increasing the temperature. The heat of fusion is the energy required to melt snow or ice. A high albedo would keep temperatures from getting too high, but during the summer, the albedo of Newfoundland would not be high. A covering of snow and ice would have a high albedo, but Newfoundland would not have that during the summer.

16. A

In the ocean, the temperature of the surface varies from the temperature at the bottom. A vertical temperature gradient is created within the body of water. Generally, the temperature of the water at the bottom is greater than that at the surface. This causes a convection current within the ocean water. Heat is transferred vertically in the ocean through this convection current.

17. B

People tend to think of the greenhouse effect as a modern-day problem, but the greenhouse effect is actually necessary for life and has been present on Earth since the atmosphere first developed. Without the greenhouse effect promoting warming of the atmosphere, Earth's surface would be too cold for life of any kind. The concern among many scientists now is the rate at which the greenhouse effect is increasing as a result of anthropogenic emissions from the burning of fossil fuels and various other industrial and agricultural practices. In previous centuries, there was less pollution than there is now, so the greenhouse effect was primarily natural, but it was still significant because it was, and still is, one of the main reasons that the planet is warm enough to sustain life.

18. OR

The natural greenhouse effect is what allows life to exist on Earth. It is caused by a layer of gases that traps the heat from the sun's rays against Earth, keeping it warm. The term *anthropogenic* means "caused by humans." The anthropogenic greenhouse effect amplifies the natural greenhouse effect through the gases human activities have added to the atmosphere. The combustion of fossil fuels is the biggest contributor to the anthropogenic greenhouse effect.

19. C

The atmosphere traps heat against Earth's surface. This is similar to the way the glass of a greenhouse traps heat inside the greenhouse, keeping it warm.

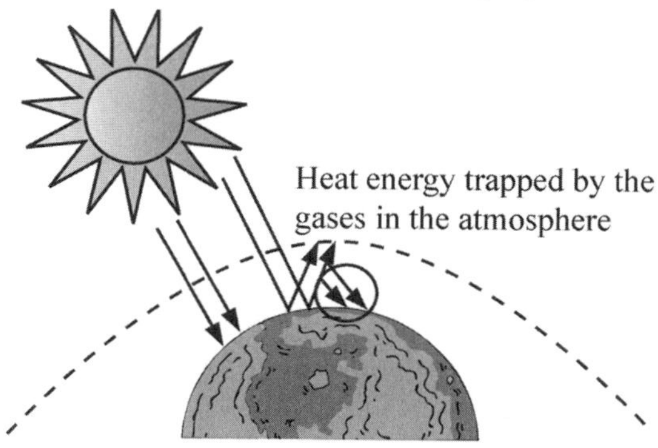

20. B

When fossil fuels are burned, they produce carbon dioxide. Carbon dioxide is a major greenhouse gas, trapping Earth's heat and increasing the temperature.

Solar energy comes directly from sunlight, so it is a non-polluting fuel. The building of dams keeps floods and droughts in check and does not have a direct association with climate change. Planting trees actually reduces the amount of greenhouse gases in the atmosphere by absorbing water and carbon dioxide.

21. D

Carbon dioxide is one of the gases thought to contribute to global warming and climate change. Trees take carbon dioxide from the air to manufacture food. Carbon dioxide is released into the air by animals and pollutants such as motor vehicles. Therefore, trees reduce pollution by using carbon dioxide. When the number of trees declines because of deforestation, less carbon dioxide can be taken from the air.

22. C

The increase in global annual temperatures has caused an increase in severe weather events, such as hurricanes, cyclones, and tornadoes.

The increased combustion of fossil fuels has caused an increase in carbon dioxide. The increase in atmospheric carbon dioxide has caused an increase in the global annual temperature. Increasing global temperatures do not contribute to ozone depletion.

23. D

Burning coal releases a significant portion of carbon dioxide, methane, nitrous oxide, and sulfur dioxide gases into the atmosphere. Methane, nitrous oxide, and sulfur dioxide are all greenhouse gases. Carbon monoxide is released in small quantities, and it is not a greenhouse gas.

24. A

Methane is a major greenhouse gas, anthropogenically produced by livestock production, rice cultivation, combustion of biomass, landfills, and energy production and delivery. Methane is sometimes referred to as natural gas.

25. A

Carbon dioxide contributes to the greenhouse effect because it allows light but not heat to pass through it. This prevents the loss of heat from Earth's atmosphere and contributes to the overall warming of Earth.

26. C

The major depletion of ozone was occurring in the stratosphere. The stratospheric ozone layer acts as a filter for the sun's rays, filtering out the harmful UVA and UVB rays.

27. A

Automobile emissions are very harmful and contribute to negative, long-term effects, such as global warming.

28. B

Global warming is causing global temperatures to rise. As this occurs, the polar ice caps are melting, adding huge amounts of water to the oceans. This, in turn, causes the water levels in the seas and oceans to rise.

Although there is some evidence to indicate that global warming may indirectly influence the other environmental occurrences through shifts in precipitation patterns and oceanic currents, of the occurrences listed, it is only directly responsible for rising sea levels. Mountain erosion is primarily a natural process, exacerbated by deforestation. Earthquakes and landslides are mainly caused by the movements of tectonic plates.

29. D

Current climate change trends indicate that global temperatures are rising. Warmer temperatures are expected to cause rising sea levels as a result of the melting of polar ice.

30. C

Lake water does not give any information as to past carbon dioxide levels since its chemical composition is constantly changing and does not store any information.

Ice cores, tree rings, and coral reefs are all sources of data about historic carbon dioxide levels.

UNIT TEST

1. Rapid climate change will **most likely** have the greatest effect on

A. developed nations at low elevations

B. developed nations at high elevations

C. developing nations at low elevations

D. developing nations at high elevations

Open Response

2. Name at least **three** potential consequences of climate change that result in the heating of the Earth. At least one consequence should deal with terrestrial ecosystems and one with aquatic ecosystems.

Use the following information to answer the next question.

> British Columbia is home to five different species of salmon, all with similar life cycles. Salmon are born in freshwater streams and rivers. They follow these river systems to the ocean, where they mature into adults. When they are ready to reproduce, salmon return to the freshwater systems, swimming upstream to the area where they were born.
> After they spawn, they die, and their carcasses return valuable nutrients to the ecosystem.

Open Response

3. How might the lowered precipitation associated with climate change affect salmon populations?

4. The **main** purpose of afforestation programs is to

A. increase soil fertility of forests

B. protect wildlife in forests

C. protect forest resources

D. increase forest area

Use the following information to answer the next question.

Ontario's Ministry of Transportation has recently added over 450 km of new High-Occupancy Vehicle (HOV) lanes along some of the province's most congested highways. HOV lanes are designed for use by vehicles carrying at least two passengers, including carpool vehicles, buses, and taxis with customers.

Open Response

5. How might HOV lanes contribute to climate change action? Name two ways the HOV lanes would benefit the communities they are built in and two benefits to the users of HOV lanes.

6. Which of the following substances is considered to be a carbon sink?
   A. Exposed limestone
   B. Marine sediment
   C. Detergent
   D. Fertilizer

Open Response

7. What is the greenhouse effect, and why is it essential for all life on Earth? You may use a diagram to help explain the greenhouse effect.

CHALLENGER QUESTION

8. Which of the following statements regarding the data that climate change scientists have gathered from ice cores and tree rings is **true**?
   A. Average global temperatures are changing much more quickly than they have historically.
   B. Average global temperatures are higher now than they have been in the last 650000 years.
   C. Atmospheric carbon dioxide levels are decreasing much more quickly than they have historically.
   D. Atmospheric carbon dioxide levels are much higher now than they have been in the last 650000 years.

CHALLENGER QUESTION

Use the following information to answer the next question.

A science class is studying climate change. A student has been asked to present visual evidence that global temperatures have been on the rise since the Industrial Revolution.

Open Response

9. Explain the type of display that would provide the strongest evidence of climate change since the Industrial Revolution, and suggest a good source for this information.

Use the following information to answer the next question.

Erica has been asked to present a report on the evidence of climate change to her class. When Erica began her research, she found information from these sources:

1. An article on Wikipedia
2. A report from the Intergovernmental Panel on Climate Change (IPCC) website
3. An article in a national newspaper
4. A report in a scientific journal

10. Which of Erica's sources is **most likely** to present an objective perspective on climate change?

A. Newspaper article

B. Wikipedia article

C. Journal report

D. IPCC report

Open Response

11. In terms of developed and developing nations, what does the phrase "the great irony of climate change" refer to?

CHALLENGER QUESTION

Use the following information to answer the next question.

A group of students tried to identify why Earth's surface is heated unevenly. They speculated that the following factors contributed to the climatic variations between tropical and arctic regions.

I. Latitude
II. Longitude
III. Tilt of Earth's axis
IV. Amount of solar radiation received

12. Which of the given factors is the **least responsible** for the given climatic differences?

A. I **B.** II

C. III **D.** IV

CHALLENGER QUESTION

13. Which of the following statements about the effect of latitude on climate is **true**?

A. At lower latitudes, the sun's radiation hits straight on, causing cool temperatures.

B. At higher latitudes, the sun's radiation hits at an angle, causing cool temperatures.

C. At lower latitudes, the sun's radiation hits at an angle, causing warm temperatures.

D. At higher latitudes, the sun's radiation hits straight on, causing warm temperatures.

Open Response

14. How does the hydrosphere act as a heat sink? Is it a good or poor heat sink?

Use the following information to answer the next question.

> "To stop climate change we must get rid of the greenhouse effect."

15. The reason that the given statement about climate change is **inaccurate** is that

A. Earth's climate is not changing

B. eliminating the greenhouse effect would make Earth much warmer

C. scientists have already reduced the greenhouse effect over the poles

D. without the greenhouse effect Earth would be much too cold to support life

16. Which of the following statements about the greenhouse effect is **true**?

A. The greenhouse effect is essential for life.

B. Global warming is not related to the greenhouse effect.

C. The enhanced greenhouse effect decreases Earth's temperature.

D. A decrease in atmospheric carbon dioxide causes the greenhouse effect.

17. Which of the following conditions is a result of the Coriolis effect?

A. The deflection of winds in both hemispheres

B. Moisture-laden winds moving rain clouds

C. The seasonal occurrence of winds

D. Local winds that reverse daily

Use the following information to answer the next question.

> Canada has received international attention because of the greenhouse gas emissions resulting from the mining of deep reserves of fossil fuels called the tar sands.

18. The tar sands are located in which province?

A. British Columbia

B. Saskatchewan

C. Manitoba

D. Alberta

Use the following information to answer the next question.

> The levels of two nitrogen oxides, nitrous oxide (N_2O) and nitrogen dioxide (NO_2), have increased in the atmosphere as a result of human activities. N_2O is used as a spray propellant in whipped cream and cooking spray containers, an anesthetic in dentistry, and a preservative in bags of potato chips and other snack foods. NO_2 is produced by internal combustion engines when nitrogen combines with oxygen in the intense heat of the engine's cylinders.

19. Which of the following statements **most accurately** describes the environmental effects of N_2O and NO_2?

A. N_2O contributes to acid rain, and NO_2 acts as a greenhouse gas.

B. N_2O acts as a greenhouse gas, and NO_2 contributes to acid rain.

C. Both N_2O and NO_2 act as greenhouse gases.

D. Both N_2O and NO_2 contribute to acid rain.

Use the following information to answer the next question.

In a bog, acidity prevents decay. Because of this, the surface of a bog is covered by thousands of years of non-decomposed sphagnum moss. When a dam is built and bogs are flooded, the acidity is rinsed away, and the sphagnum moss is killed. Methane, an important greenhouse gas, is released when sphagnum moss decays.

20. From the given information, it can be concluded that the flooding of bogs contributes to

A. climate change **B.** soil erosion

C. skin cancer **D.** ozone loss

CHALLENGER QUESTION

21. Which of the following statements **best** describes how heat is trapped by greenhouse gases?

A. Greenhouse gas molecules absorb the sun's rays in the form of vibrational energy and convert it to infrared energy.

B. Greenhouse gas molecules absorb the sun's rays in the form of infrared energy and convert it to vibrational energy.

C. Greenhouse gas molecules absorb the sun's rays in the form of vibrational energy and convert it to ultraviolet energy.

D. Greenhouse gas molecules absorb the sun's rays in the form of ultraviolet energy and convert it to vibrational energy.

Use the following information to answer the next question.

Andrea attended a conference concerning the greenhouse effect. At the conference, she learned that the average temperature of Earth is 20 to 30°C warmer than it would be without the greenhouse effect. She also learned that various modes of transportation have led to an increase in the greenhouse effect.

22. Which of the following modes of transportation has the **greatest** impact on the greenhouse effect?

A. Bicycle **B.** Airplane

C. Horse cart **D.** Electric train

CHALLENGER QUESTION

23. Which of the following substances is **not** a constituent of photochemical smog?

A. Volatile Organic Compounds

B. Peroxyacetyl nitrates

C. Chlorofluorocarbons

D. Ozone

24. Satellites stationed over Earth's polar and high-altitude regions show direct evidence of a warming climate by providing

A. maps of greenhouse gas emissions

B. images of declining glacial ice cover

C. measurements of changes in sea level

D. measurements of changes in ozone layer thickness

CHALLENGER QUESTION

25. The Surface Heat Budget of the Arctic Ocean project (SHEBA) was undertaken with the goal of enhancing scientific understanding of arctic energy dynamics. This project seeks to investigate all of the following uncertainties **except** the

A. degree and rate at which arctic sea ice and ice sheets are melting

B. impact of alterations to arctic energy dynamics on global climate change

C. limitations of climate modeling scenarios involving arctic ice-albedo feedback systems

D. significant discrepancies between climate models simulating present and future climates in the arctic

Answers and Solutions – Unit Test

1. C	6. B	11. OR	16. A	21. B
2. OR	7. OR	12. B	17. A	22. B
3. OR	8. D	13. B	18. D	23. C
4. D	9. OR	14. OR	19. B	24. B
5. OR	10. D	15. D	20. A	25. A

1. C

For nations at lower elevations, there is a greater risk of coastal flooding caused by melting polar ice. Developing nations have fewer resources and less technology to deal with this impact of climate change. This is in contrast to developed countries at low elevations, such as the Netherlands, that use resources and technologies, like dikes and ocean barriers, to prevent flooding. These same resources and technologies are not readily available to developing nations.

2. OR

Many potential consequences are possible.

1. Aquatic ecosystems will be severely impacted as the heating of Earth causes the melting of mountain glaciers, icecaps, and icebergs.
2. All of these factors will increase sea levels and threaten low-lying coastal areas.
3. Floods will also increase, which will have devastating effects on nations around the world.
4. Increases in water temperatures would be detrimental to a variety of aquatic species, leading to the extinction of some.
5. In terrestrial ecosystems, there will be an increase in desertification and a loss of vital cropland. Likewise, increased summer dryness would lead to crop failure which, in turn, would result in food shortages.
6. The melting of permafrost in such biomes as the tundra would alter the distribution and function of these ecosystems.
7. More extreme weather conditions would also be observed, increasing the incidence of fires, hurricanes, tornadoes, and drought—all of which alter the function and structure of an ecosystem. Consequently, while some species would be able to tolerate, adapt, or flourish with the changes brought about by the global warming, others would be unable to cope and would become extinct.

3. OR

Salmon depend on healthy streams and rivers to make their long journeys. Lower precipitation might dry up some bodies of water, making them impassible. If droughts interrupt spawning routes, salmon populations are likely to **decline**.

4. D

Afforestation programs involve planting trees in order to increase forest area. Afforestation programs are necessary because extensive deforestation leads to the depletion of these important natural resources.

5. OR

HOV lanes encourage car pooling, reducing the amount of carbon emissions from commuter traffic. Users of the HOV lanes are able to enjoy a faster ride to work. They also save money on gas by sharing rides and reduce stress by sharing driving responsibilities. Community benefits from HOV lanes include improved air quality as a result of decreased vehicle traffic, reduced congestion, and better traffic management.

6. B

A carbon sink is a natural or man-made process that stores carbon, keeping it out of the atmosphere. Marine sediment traps carbon on the bottom of the ocean, so it is considered to be a carbon sink.

A carbon source releases carbon dioxide into the atmosphere. Limestone exposed to the air and rain is a carbon source, as it releases carbon dioxide during erosion.

Detergent and fertilizer are neither carbon sinks nor sources, but the use of these products can lead indirectly to increased carbon dioxide production.

7. OR

The greenhouse effect occurs when rays of sunlight that are radiated towards Earth reflect off its surface and head back towards space. A layer of greenhouse gases, like methane, carbon dioxide, and nitrous oxide, trap most of the reflected rays against the planet, keeping it warm. Without some level of greenhouse effect, it would be too cold for any life to exist on Earth. Diagram should look similar to the one below:

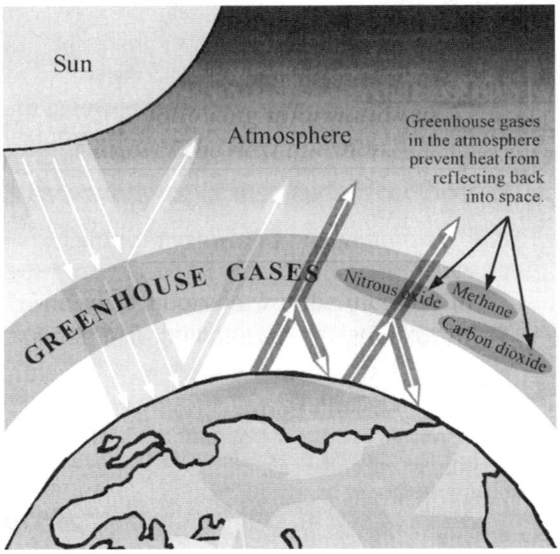

8. D

Ice cores and tree rings are able to provide information on the amount of atmospheric carbon dioxide. The current amount of carbon dioxide is 380 ppm. In the last 650000 years, the atmospheric carbon dioxide level has never risen above 310 ppm.

9. OR

The strongest piece of visual evidence would be a graph showing the average global temperatures from before and since the Industrial Revolution.
The average global temperature should be on the left side of the graph, the y-axis. The year would be placed on the bottom of the graph, the x-axis.

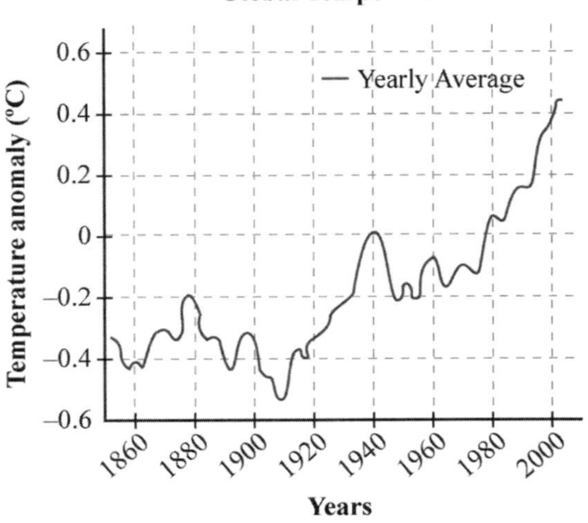

Sample graph of global temperature change versus time.

Data for the graph would be strongest if it came from an unbiased source, such as Environment Canada.

10. D

The Intergovernmental Panel on Climate Change (IPCC) is a scientific body. It is a collaboration between thousands of scientists, and it strives to present objective scientific perspectives.
Where there is more than one scientific perspective, the IPCC will present both in its report. Wikipedia is written by many anonymous people, so there is undoubtedly bias in the articles. Both newspaper articles and journal reports can be good sources of information, but both are usually written by a single person. It is likely that there is some bias in these articles, whether from the writers or the publishers.

11. OR

"The great irony of climate change" refers to the relationship between climate change and developing and developed nations. Developed nations generally have much smaller populations than developing nations, but developed nations are responsible for most of the greenhouse gas emissions. The irony is that most of the effects of climate change, such as droughts, floods, lowered crop production, and extreme weather events, will be felt by the people of developing nations. Most developing nations are close to the equator, and many high-density settlements are in the coastal regions of these nations. Additionally, developing nations are comparatively poor and may have unstable governments. This makes dealing with and recovering from the effects of climate change extremely difficult.

Two major exceptions to this trend are the countries of China and India. These extremely large developing nations are major contributors to the impact of global climate change, primarily as a result of their immense population sizes. These countries combined have around 2.5 billion people (which is over 30% of the global population), and the shear size of these countries combined with their rigorous industrialized efforts towards development make them major contributors to global climate change, regardless of the fact that they have yet to reach developed country designation.

12. B

Variations in longitude cannot explain the uneven heating of Earth because noticeable changes in heating occur as you move from north to south, not east to west. Lines of longitude extend from north to south dividing Earth into wedges. Lines of latitude run from east to west. Latitude determines the amount and intensity of the solar energy received at different points on Earth. The tilt of Earth's axis also causes uneven heating as the sun's rays strike different areas of Earth at different angles. At an area such as the equator, the sun's rays strike Earth more directly. As you move toward the poles, the sun's rays strike less directly. The more direct the sun's rays, the greater the amount of solar energy absorbed and the lower the amount of radiation deflected back into the atmosphere. Therefore, the latitude (I), Earth's axial rotation (III), and the amount of solar radiation (IV), all are responsible for climatic differences. The factor that does not contribute to climatic differences is the longitude (II).

13. B

At higher latitudes, which are farther from the equator, the sun's radiation hits at an angle, so the rays are spread across a large area and the temperatures are relatively cool. At lower latitudes, which are closer to the equator, the sun's radiation hits straight on. The rays are concentrated in a smaller area, and the temperatures are relatively warm, or tropical.

14. OR

The term heat sink is used to refer to any objects that can hold heat energy. Water is an excellent heat sink due to its high specific heat. On Earth, the hydrosphere is responsible for regulating Earth's temperature.

15. D

Although the climate is changing, the greenhouse effect is not causing climate change. The greenhouse effect is necessary to keep Earth warm enough for life to exist. Although, the enhanced greenhouse effect caused by human activities is believed to be contributing to climate change, removing the greenhouse effect is not possible, nor would it be the solution to climate change.

16. A

Earth would be frozen and lifeless if not for the greenhouse effect. The greenhouse effect is essential for life.

17. A

The Coriolis effect leads to the deflection of winds in the hemispheres. Deflection refers to a change in path taken by the wind. In the Northern Hemisphere, the winds deflect to the right, while in the Southern Hemisphere, the winds deflect to the left.

18. D

The tar sands are located in northern Alberta.

19. B

Nitrous oxide (N_2O) is the fourth most abundant greenhouse gas in the atmosphere.

When nitrogen dioxide (NO_2) dissolves in rainwater, it produces a dilute solution of both nitrous acid (HNO_2) and nitric acid (HNO_3).

$$2NO_{2(g)} + H_2O_{(l)} \rightarrow HNO_{2(aq)} + HNO_{3(aq)}$$

20. A

Greenhouse gases, like methane, are responsible for the greenhouse effect. The greenhouse effect is a name given to the general increase in temperatures at Earth's surface because of the insulating properties of greenhouse gases in the atmosphere. When bogs are flooded, the decay leads to the production of more methane, and more heat is trapped by the greenhouse effect. As a result, Earth's atmosphere becomes warmer. This global warming effect is referred to as climate change.

Depletion of ozone in the upper atmosphere (where an ozone layer protects Earth from the harmful and cancer-causing rays of the sun) is an environmental concern, but it does not result from the flooding of bogs. In part, ozone depletion is caused by chlorofluorocarbons (CFCs), which are released into the atmosphere from aerosol sprays, refrigerator and air-conditioner coolant, and during plastic production. The major cause of soil erosion is mass deforestation.

21. B

Infrared energy is heat energy. Greenhouse gas molecules absorb the heat energy by converting it to vibrational energy.

22. B

The emission of greenhouse gases causes an increase in the greenhouse effect. Greenhouse gases include water vapour, carbon dioxide, methane, nitrous oxide, and ozone. Among the given modes of transportation, airplanes emit the greatest amount of gases into the atmosphere. Thus, airplanes have the greatest impact on the greenhouse effect.

A bicycle does not emit any greenhouse gases, but its rider does emit carbon dioxide with each breath. A horse cart releases a small amount of carbon dioxide when the horse breathes. An electric train does not directly emit any gases into the atmosphere, but it does impact the greenhouse effect if the electricity used to power the train comes from power plants that use fossil fuels to generate electricity.

23. C

Photochemical smog occurs when sunlight reacts with pollutants in the air to create a thick layer of chemicals that is hazardous to human health. Volatile Organic Compounds (VOCs), Peroxyacetyl nitrates (PANs), ozone, aldehydes, and nitrogen oxides can all be found in the chemical mix. Chlorofluorocarbons (CFCs) are not a constituent of photochemical smog. CFCs do not often remain in the troposphere. Instead, they migrate to the stratosphere, where they react with stratospheric ozone, depleting the ozone layer.

24. B

Satellites are becoming increasingly advanced, and as such, they are able to measure and record data on all the alternatives provided; however, since the question refers to satellites stationed over polar and high-altitude regions and requests direct evidence of a warming climate, the best alternative is that they provide images of declining glacial ice cover.

Measurements of changes in sea level and greenhouse gas emissions are indirect indicators of global warming. There has yet to be any direct link made between ozone layer depletion and global warming.

25. A

Scientific research and new climate study technologies such as satellite imagery provide ample data regarding the rate and degree of arctic sea ice and ice sheet decline. In other words, there is little to no uncertainty regarding this information, and it is therefore not one of the uncertainties currently being investigated by the SHEBA project.

Physics

PHYSICS: LIGHT AND GEOMETRIC OPTICS

Table of Correlations

Specific Expectation		Practice Questions	Unit Test Questions	Practice Test 1	Practice Test 2
10.5.E1	evaluate the effectiveness of technological devices and procedures designed to make use of light, and assess their social benefits				
10.5.E1.1	*analyse a technological device or procedure related to human perception of light (e.g., eyeglasses, contact lenses, infrared or low light vision sensors, laser surgery), and evaluate its effectiveness*	1, 2	1, 2	31	
10.5.E1.2	*analyse a technological device that uses the properties of light (e.g., microscope, retroreflector, solar oven, camera), and explain how it has enhanced society*	3, 4	3, 4		31
10.5.E2	investigate, through inquiry, the properties of light, and predict its behaviour, particularly with respect to reflection in plane and curved mirrors and refraction in converging lenses				
10.5.E2.1	*use appropriate terminology related to light and optics, including, but not limited to: angle of incidence, angle of reflection, angle of refraction, focal point, luminescence, magnification, mirage, and virtual image*	7		32	32
10.5.E2.2	*use an inquiry process to investigate the laws of reflection, using plane and curved mirrors, and draw ray diagrams to summarize their findings*	11	5		33
10.5.E2.3	*predict the qualitative characteristics of images formed by plane and curved mirrors (e.g., location, relative distance, orientation, and size in plane mirrors; location, orientation, size, type in curved mirrors), test their predictions through inquiry, and summarize their findings*	12, 13		33	
10.5.E2.4	*use an inquiry process to investigate the refraction of light as it passes through media of different refractive indices, compile data on their findings, and analyse the data to determine if there is a trend (e.g., the amount by which the angle of refraction changes as the angle of incidence increases varies for media of different refractive indices*	15		34	34
10.5.E2.5	*predict, using ray diagrams and algebraic equations, the position and characteristics of an image produced by a converging lens, and test their predictions through inquiry*	19, 20, 21, 22	6, 7, 8, 9	35	
10.5.E2.6	*calculate, using the indices of refraction, the velocity of light as it passes through a variety of media, and explain the angles of refraction with reference to the variations in velocity*	25, 26, 27, 28	10, 11, 12, 13	36	35
10.5.E3	demonstrate an understanding of various characteristics and properties of light, particularly with respect to reflection in mirrors and reflection and refraction in lenses				
10.5.E3.1	*describe and explain various types of light emissions (e.g., chemiluminescence, bioluminescence, incandescence, fluorescence, phosphorescence, triboluminescence; from an electric discharge or light-emitting diode [LED])*	5, 6		37	
10.5.E3.2	*identify and label the visible and invisible regions of the electromagnetic spectrum*	8	14, 15		36
10.5.E3.3	*describe, on the basis of observation, the characteristics and positions of images formed by plane and curved mirrors (e.g., location, orientation, size, type), with the aid of ray diagrams and algebraic equations, where appropriate*	9, 10	16	38	

Table of Correlations

Specific Expectation		Practice Questions	Unit Test Questions	Practice Test 1	Practice Test 2
10.5.E3.4	*explain the conditions required for partial reflection/refraction and for total internal reflection in lenses, and describe the reflection/refraction using labelled ray diagrams*	14	17, 18		37
10.5.E3.5	*describe the characteristics and positions of images formed by converging lenses (e.g., orientation, size, type), with the aid of ray diagrams*	18	19	39	38
10.5.E3.6	*identify ways in which the properties of mirrors and lenses (both converging and diverging) determine their use in optical instruments (e.g., cameras, telescopes, binoculars, microscopes)*	23, 24	20, 21		39
10.5.E3.7	*identify the factors, in qualitative and quantitative terms, that affect the refraction of light as it passes from one medium to another*	16, 17	22, 23		40
10.5.E3.8	*describe properties of light, and use them to explain naturally occurring optical phenomena (e.g., apparent depth, shimmering, a mirage, a rainbow)*	29, 30	24, 25	40	

10.5.E1.1 *analyse a technological device or procedure related to human perception of light (e.g., eyeglasses, contact lenses, infrared or low light vision sensors, laser surgery), and evaluate its effectiveness*

The Human Perception of Light

Humans are naturally able to detect light of certain wavelengths. An increased understanding of electromagnetic radiation and the properties of light has led to many developments that modify, and often improve, the human perception of light.

Corrective Lenses

Many people suffer from myopia, also called nearsightedness. People with myopia can see near objects clearly, but distant objects appear blurred. This occurs because their eyeballs are too long and images are focused on the fluid in front of the retina rather than on the retina itself. Contact lenses and eyeglasses correct this problem by refocusing the image on the retina.

Laser Eye Surgery

Laser eye surgery can correct certain types of vision problems. During this type of surgery, a laser is used to cut a small flap into the cornea of the eye. The flap is lifted, the laser reshapes the cornea, and the flap is then replaced. The entire surgery is performed while the patient is awake, and the recovery time is very short. Although the surgery is usually very successful and is usually able to permanently correct myopia, there are still some possible side effects, including permanently dry eyes, poor night vision, and halo-type glares around objects at night.

Infrared Vision

Infrared vision equipment, sometimes called thermal imaging, creates images using infrared radiation that is invisible to the human eye. Infrared waves are longer than visible-light waves, and most objects emit some infrared radiation. The amount of radiation emitted depends on the object's temperature: the warmer the object, the more radiation emitted. The difference between the temperatures of objects is detected by specialized receptors and used to create an image. A person sitting on the floor in complete darkness, for example, could be seen using infrared vision, since the person is much warmer than the floor. Infrared technology is one type of technology used in night-vision goggles.

1. During laser eye surgery, which part of the eye needs to be reshaped to improve vision?

A. Lens **B.** Pupil

C. Retina **D.** Cornea

Use the following information to answer the next question.

Scientists often use infrared sensors when observing animals at night. Infrared sensors are much better for observing mammals and birds than for observing reptiles.

Open Response

2. How do infrared sensors work?
Why would they be more effective for observing mammals and birds than for observing reptiles?

10.5.E1.2 *analyse a technological device that uses the properties of light (e.g., microscope, retroreflector, solar oven, camera), and explain how it has enhanced society*

Light Technology

There have been many advances in technological devices that use the properties of light. For example, cameras are smaller, more powerful, and more accessible than ever, and they allow people to capture important moments as they occur. Cameras are also invaluable tools for research because they keep a permanent and accurate record of the events occurring during any given moment in time. Understanding how light rays refract through lenses has allowed for the precise positioning of images being photographed on the sensor or film of the camera, permitting for capture of the clearest and truest images possible.

Another example of technology that uses light is the microscope. Microscopes have revolutionized both the life sciences and medicine by providing people with a tool that can be used to examine the smallest components of matter, including matter that comprises living things. Again, an understanding of the way light rays reflect through lenses has helped people to develop this invaluable technology.

Reflective technology is used on vehicles, bicycles, and clothes to keep people safe. An understanding of the direction a path of light will take when reflected from a surface allows for creation of materials that will provide the greatest reflectivity and, subsequently, the greatest amount of protection.

3. What does a simple microscope use to produce an image that is both magnified and erect?

- **A.** Concave mirrors
- **B.** Concave lenses
- **C.** Convex mirrors
- **D.** Convex lenses

Use the following information to answer the next question.

Solar ovens are often used in third world countries.

Open Response

4. Describe the main features of a solar oven that are needed to cook a pot of rice, and list two properties of light that make a solar oven efficient.

____

____

____

____

____

10.5.E3.1 *describe and explain various types of light emissions (e.g., chemiluminescence, bioluminescence, incandescence, fluorescence, phosphorescence, triboluminescence; from an electric discharge or light-emitting diode [LED])*

10.5.E2.1 *use appropriate terminology related to light and optics, including, but not limited to: angle of incidence, angle of reflection, angle of refraction, focal point, luminescence, magnification, mirage, and virtual image*

Types of Light Emissions

The sun provides the light required to power photosynthetic reactions around the world. Although the sun is a major source of light, there are many other sources that also emit light.

Chemiluminescence and Bioluminescence

Chemiluminescence is light that is emitted as a result of a chemical reaction. A simple example of a chemiluminescence reaction is elemental phosphorous oxidizing in air, which creates a green glow. More complicated reactions, occurring in either the gas phase or the liquid phase, can produce a variety of light colors. Glow sticks give off light because of chemical reactions within the stick. Crime scene investigators can detect trace amounts of blood using a chemical called luminol, which reacts with the iron in the blood and gives off a blue glow.

Bioluminescence is chemiluminescence that occurs within a living organism. Many deep-sea creatures exhibit bioluminescence, as do some invertebrates such as lightning bugs and glowworms. There are many theories as to the purpose of bioluminescence, including communicating between organisms, attracting mates, or deterring predators.

Incandescence

Incandescence is the emission of light because of the temperature of an object. For example, molten lava glows because it is so hot that it incandesces.

Incandescence can be seen in certain types of light bulbs. Electricity is passed through the filament of the light bulb, which resists the passage of electrons. This resistance generates heat until the filament becomes so hot it starts to glow. Incandescence causes some types of light bulbs to become hot to the touch when they are left on. Incandescent light bulbs are considered inefficient because much of their electricity is lost as heat.

Fluorescence

Fluorescence is the emission of light when a molecule or atom that has been excited relaxes to its normal energy level. As the atom or molecule relaxes, it releases photons. If the photons emitted are in the visible spectrum, the molecule or atom will glow.

Fluorescent light bulbs have become popular because they are more efficient than incandescent light bulbs. Most fluorescent light bulbs contain mercury and must be handled carefully and disposed of properly. The mercury in the glass tube of the light is excited by the electricity supplied to the light bulb. The mercury then emits photons in the ultraviolet (UV) range of the spectrum. A chemical that lines the glass tube absorbs the UV rays and emits visible photons, providing light.

Light-Emitting Diode (LED)

A light-emitting diode (LED) is an electrical light source. LEDs function when electrons are passed along a semiconducting diode. As the electrons find an "electron hole," or empty space, they jump in, fill the hole, and release a photon, which creates light.

LED lights are very efficient and have much longer life spans than incandescent or fluorescent light sources. They also contain solid-state components, so they are not as fragile as fluorescent light bulbs.

5. Light-emitting diodes (LEDs) are increasingly being used in flashlights and other devices, especially devices that use batteries as a power source. When an LED is operating, electrons produce light as they

A. travel though an ionized gas

B. travel through a semiconductor

C. make the transition to higher energy orbitals in an atom

D. make the transition back to lower energy orbitals following a jump to higher levels caused by heat

Use the following information to answer the next question.

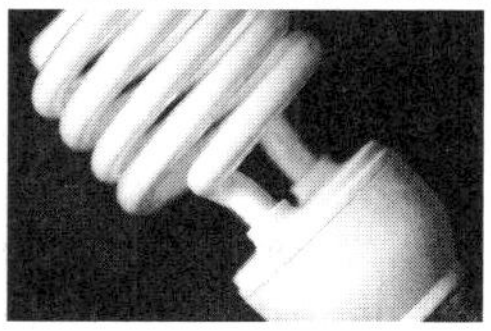

A compact fluorescent light bulb

6. The term fluorescence describes the process during the operation of a fluorescent light bulb in which the

A. gas inside the bulb converts visible light to ultraviolet radiation

B. gas inside the bulb converts ultraviolet radiation to visible light

C. coating on the inside surface of the bulb converts visible light to ultraviolet radiation

D. coating on the inside surface of the bulb converts ultraviolet radiation to visible light

Use the following information to answer the next question.

The anglerfish is named for the fleshy growth that extends from its head and hangs down to the front of its mouth. The end of this structure glows and acts as a lure for smaller prey. As smaller fish swim up to the lure to investigate, they are snapped up into the waiting jaws of the anglerfish.

7. Light produced by the lure is a result of a process called

A. chemiluminescence

B. bioluminescence

C. incandescence

D. fluorescence

10.5.E3.2 *identify and label the visible and invisible regions of the electromagnetic spectrum*

THE ELECTROMAGNETIC SPECTRUM

Electromagnetic radiation is often described in terms of its wavelength and frequency.
The electromagnetic spectrum uses wavelength, frequency, and photon energy to categorize the types of radiation.

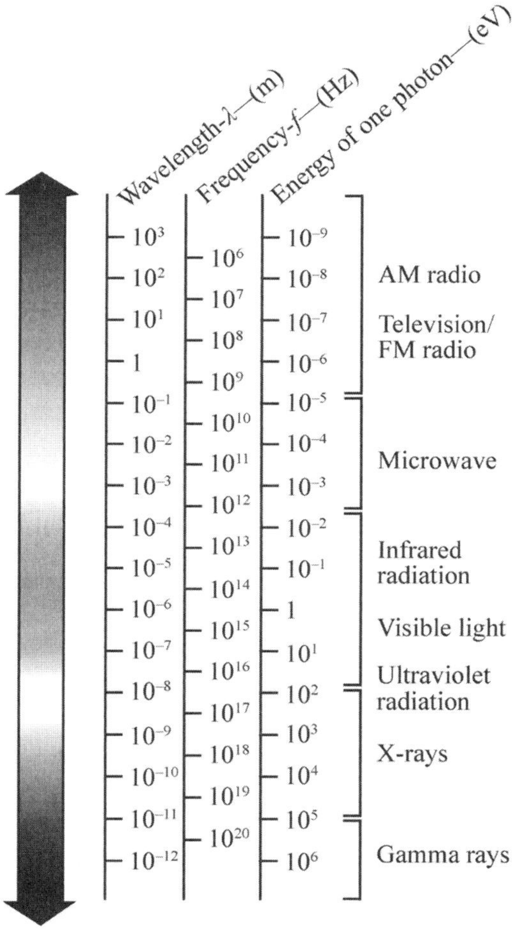

Radio waves have the longest wavelengths, followed by microwaves, infrared radiation, visible light, ultraviolet radiation, X-rays, and gamma rays.

The Visible Spectrum

The visible light spectrum is the region of the electromagnetic spectrum that produces light that is visible to the human eye. The visible part of the EMR spectrum ranges from approximately 380 to 750 nm in wavelength.

The visible spectrum

The visible spectrum is ordered from longest (red) to shortest (violet) wavelength. The order of colors in the visible spectrum is red, orange, yellow, green, blue, indigo, and violet. A useful acronym for remembering the order of the visible spectrum is the name ROY G BIV.

8. From highest to lowest frequency, which of the following lists provides the correct order of electromagnetic radiation?

A. Ultraviolet, microwave, visible light

B. Visible light, microwave, radio

C. Ultraviolet, X-ray, gamma ray

D. X-ray, infrared, visible light

10.5.E3.3 *describe, on the basis of observation, the characteristics and positions of images formed by plane and curved mirrors (e.g., location, orientation, size, type), with the aid of ray diagrams and algebraic equations, where appropriate*

10.5.E2.2 *use an inquiry process to investigate the laws of reflection, using plane and curved mirrors, and draw ray diagrams to summarize their findings*

10.5.E2.3 *predict the qualitative characteristics of images formed by plane and curved mirrors (e.g., location, relative distance, orientation, and size in plane mirrors; location, orientation, size, type in curved mirrors), test their predictions through inquiry, and summarize their findings*

Images Formed by Mirrors

A mirror is an object with a polished, reflective surface. Most mirrors consist of a piece of glass that has one surface coated with a reflective metal like silver or aluminum.

There are three main types of mirrors:

- Plane mirrors
- Converging mirrors
- Diverging mirrors

Characteristics of images formed by all three types of mirrors can be determined using both ray diagrams and algebraic equations.

Images Formed by Plane Mirrors

A plane mirror is a mirror with a flat, reflective surface. A plane mirror reflects images of objects placed in front of it. It does this using light rays coming from the object to create an image of the object that appears to be located behind the mirror. The image formed by a plane mirror is virtual, upright, and of the same shape and size as the object it is reflecting.

Some of the terms used in the discussion of mirrors are illustrated in the given diagram:

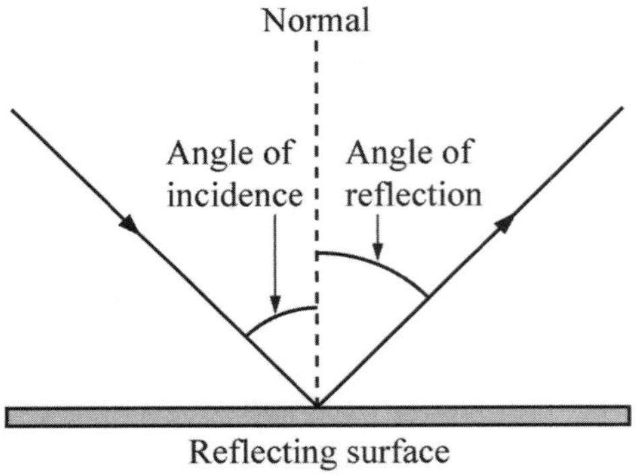

The images formed in all mirrors are governed by two laws of reflection:

- The angle of incidence is equal to the angle of reflection.
- The incident ray, reflected ray, and normal all lie in the same plane.

The given diagram illustrates how an image is formed by a plane mirror.

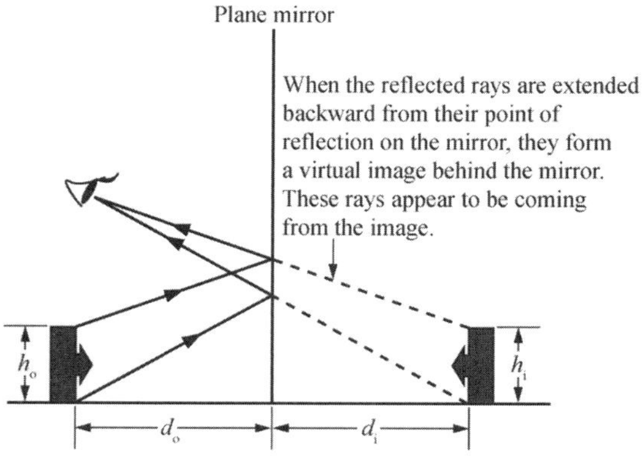

The characteristics of the image formed by a plane mirror are as follows:

- The image distance, d_i, is equal to the object distance, d_o.
- The height of the image, h_i, is equal to the height of the object, h_o.
- The image is laterally inversed (the right side of the object is the left side of the image).
- The image is vertically upright (the top of the object is the top of the image).
- The image is a virtual image. Light rays do not actually pass through a virtual image. When the rays are extended backward from their point of reflection on the mirror, they lead to the apparent position of the image behind the mirror. An observer sees these rays as if they were coming from the image. The brain assumes that the rays come straight from the object that is producing them.

Images Formed by Converging Mirrors

A converging mirror has a concave shape, and the object is placed on the same side as the centre of curvature. The following diagram shows a converging mirror with its centre of curvature, focal point, and principal axis labelled:

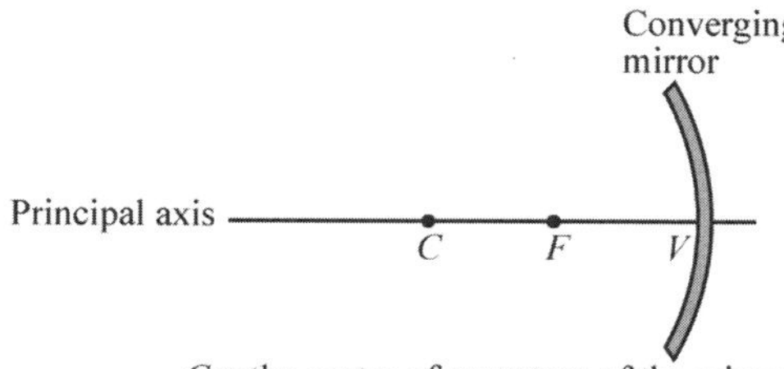

C = the centre of curvature of the mirror
F = the focal point of the mirror
V = the point of intersection of the principal axis with the mirror

There are three rules concerning rays hitting a converging mirror. The application of these rules enables you to determine the position, orientation, size, and type of image formed by a converging mirror. The diagram that follows illustrates each rule.

1. Any ray that is parallel to the principal axis is reflected through the focal point (ray 1 on the following diagram).
2. Any ray that passes through the focal point is reflected parallel to the principal axis (ray 2 on the following diagram).
3. Any ray that passes through the centre of curvature is reflected back along the same path (ray 3 on the following diagram).

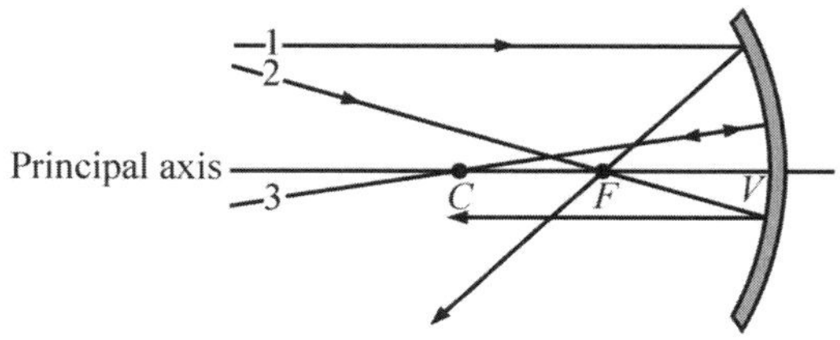

Using any two of the rays in the diagram is enough to locate an image, but the third ray may be used as a check.

This diagram shows the image formed when an object is placed beyond the centre of curvature (C). The object is the thick arrow pointing downward.

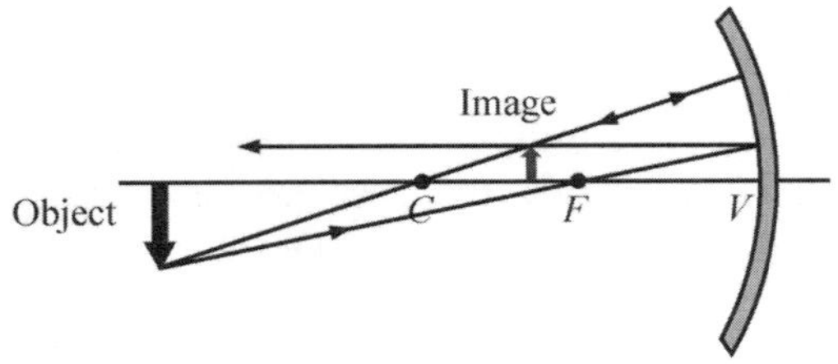

The image formed in this case is real, inverted, and smaller than the object.

This diagram shows the image formed when an object is placed between the radius of curvature and the focal point. The object is the smaller arrow pointing upward.

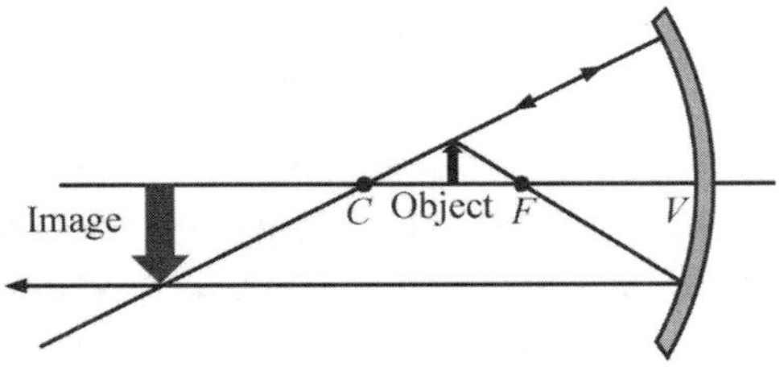

The image formed in this case is real, inverted, and larger than the object.

This diagram shows the image formed when an object is placed between the focal point and the mirror.

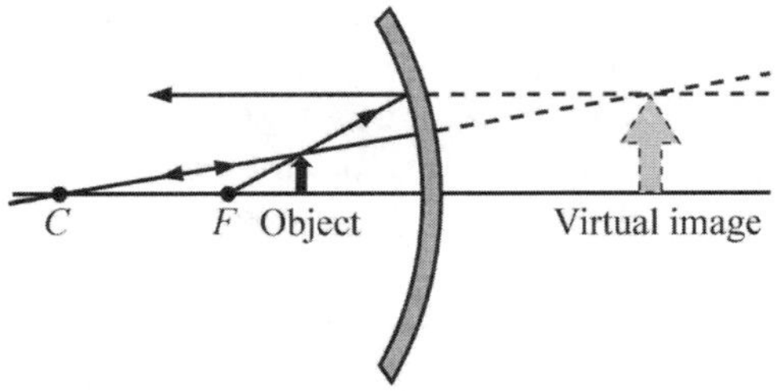

The image formed in this case is on the other side of the mirror, virtual, upright, and larger than the object.

This diagram shows that when the object is placed right at the focal point, the rays do not converge at all; consequently, no image is formed.

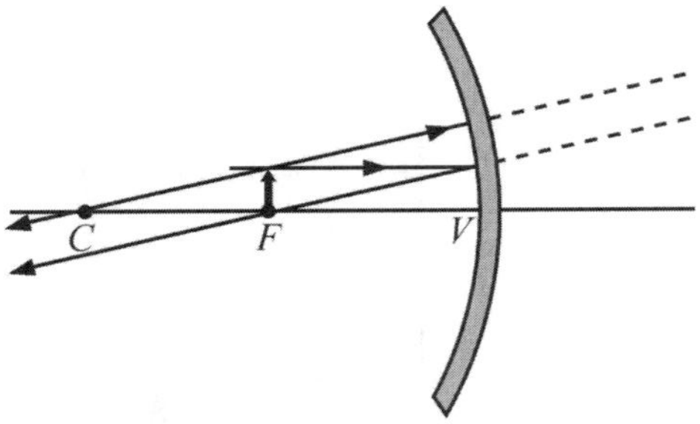

Images Formed by Diverging Mirrors

A diverging mirror is a convex mirror, and the object is placed on the side opposite the centre of curvature. With a diverging mirror, both the focal point and the center of curvature are virtual and located behind the mirror, so rays from the object do not actually pass through them. The apparent position of an image is obtained by extending the rays backward from their points of reflection on the mirror surface. A diverging mirror produces only virtual images.

The given diagram shows an example of an image formed by a diverging mirror:

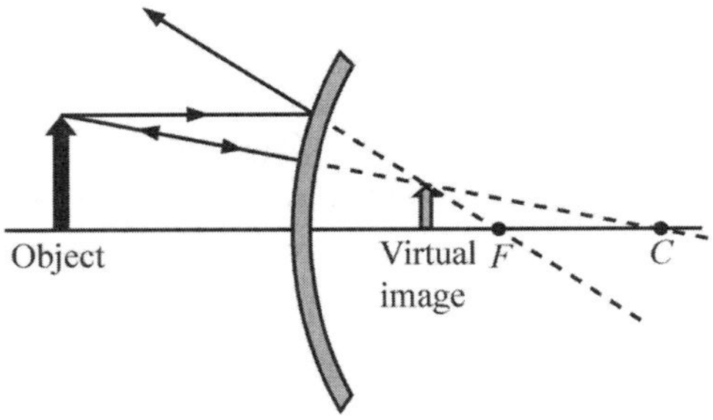

The image is virtual, upright, and smaller than the object. It appears to be behind the mirror.

Diverging mirrors are often used as side-view mirrors in cars and trucks. They have a larger field of view than flat or converging mirrors, and can show objects in an area that is normally a blind spot. Warnings printed on these mirrors state that objects in the mirrors are closer and larger than they appear.

Equations Involving Images in Mirrors

With a plane mirror, the object distance and the image distance are equal: $d_o = d_i$. Also, the height of the object is equal to the height of the image: $h_o = h_i$.

Calculations involving the object and image distances with converging and diverging mirrors are done using the mirror equation, $\frac{1}{f} = \frac{1}{d_o} + \frac{1}{d_i}$, where f = focal length.

Calculations involving the object and image heights with converging and diverging mirrors are done using the magnification equation for mirrors:

$$M = \frac{h_i}{h_o} = -\frac{d_i}{d_o}$$

Whether a value for a particular quantity is positive or negative reveals important information about the type of mirror being used and the type of image obtained. The sign conventions for mirrors are summarized as follows:

- If f is positive, the mirror is a converging (concave) mirror.
- If f is negative, the mirror is a diverging (convex) mirror.
- If d_i is positive, the image is real and is located on the same side of the mirror as the object.
- If d_i is negative, the image is virtual and is located behind the mirror.
- If h_i is positive, the image is upright.
- If h_i is negative, the image is inverted.

Example

An object 5.0 cm in height is placed 11.0 cm from a converging mirror with a focal length of 14.5 cm.
How far is the image from the mirror?

Solution
The object distance, the object height, and the focal length are given.
Use the mirror equation to calculate the image distance:

$$\frac{1}{f} = \frac{1}{d_o} + \frac{1}{d_i}$$

$$\frac{1}{d_i} = \frac{1}{f} - \frac{1}{d_o}$$

$$= \frac{1}{14.5\text{ cm}} - \frac{1}{11.0\text{ cm}}$$

$$= -0.021\ 94\text{ cm}$$

$$d_i = \frac{1}{-0.021\ 94\text{ cm}} = -45.6\text{ cm}$$

The image is 45.6 cm from the mirror.

How tall is the image?

Solution
Calculate the height of the image using the magnification formula:

$$M = \frac{h_i}{h_o} = -\frac{d_i}{d_o}$$

$$h_i = -\frac{d_i}{d_o} \times h_o$$

$$= -\left(\frac{-45.6\text{ cm}}{11.0\text{ cm}}\right) \times 5.0\text{ cm}$$

$$= 20.7\text{ cm}$$

The image is 20.7 cm tall.

Is the image upright or inverted?

Solution
Since h_i has a positive value, the image is upright.

Is the image real or virtual?

Solution
Since d_i has a negative value, the image is virtual.

Is the image on the same side of the mirror as the object, or is it behind the mirror?

Solution
Since d_i has a negative value, the image is behind the mirror.

Use the following information to answer the next question.

The three main types of mirrors are plane mirrors, converging mirrors, and diverging mirrors.

9. Real images can be formed by
   A. plane mirrors only
   B. converging mirrors only
   C. plane and diverging mirrors
   D. converging and diverging mirrors

Use the following information to answer the next question.

An object is located at point C. Point F is the focal point of the mirror.

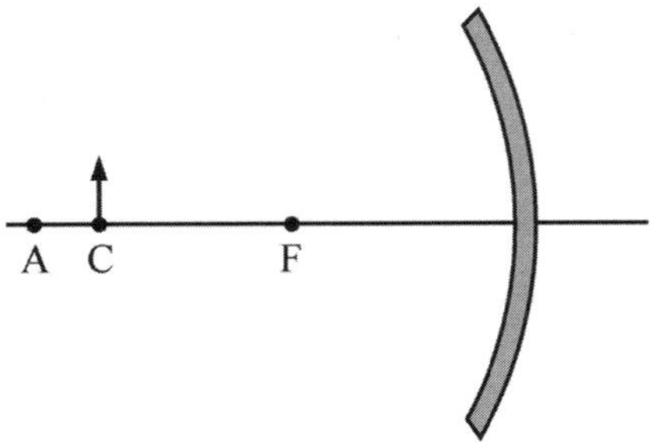

10. The image of the object formed by the mirror will be
   A. located at point A and upright
   B. located at point C and upright
   C. located at point A and inverted
   D. located at point C and inverted

Use the following information to answer the next question.

An image of a cup is formed using a plane mirror.

11. The image formed would show
   A. an upright cup with its handle on the left side
   B. an upright cup with its handle on the right side
   C. a vertically inverted cup with its handle on the left side
   D. a vertically inverted cup with its handle on the right side

Use the following information to answer the next question.

A candle is placed in front of a concave mirror between the centre of curvature (*C*) and the focal point (*F*).

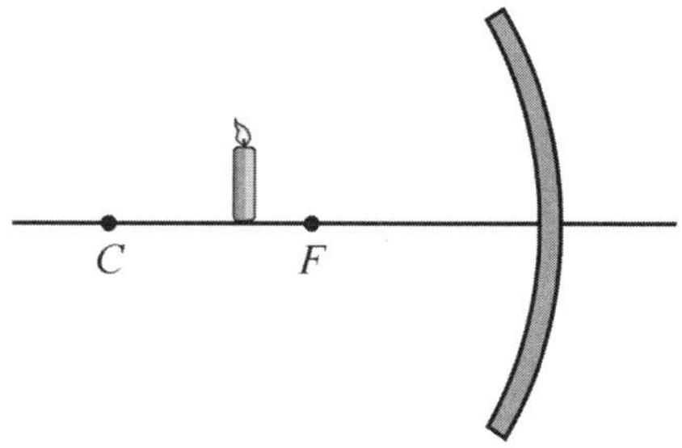

12. The image of the candle formed by this mirror will be

A. upright and larger than the candle

B. inverted and larger than the candle

C. upright and smaller than the candle

D. inverted and smaller than the candle

Numerical Response

13. A convex mirror produced an image 3.0 cm behind the mirror. If the focal length of this mirror is 5.0 cm, at what distance from the mirror is the object placed? __________cm

(Record your answer as a **two-digit** number.)

10.5.E3.4 *explain the conditions required for partial reflection/refraction and for total internal reflection in lenses, and describe the reflection/refraction using labelled ray diagrams*

10.5.E2.4 *use an inquiry process to investigate the refraction of light as it passes through media of different refractive indices, compile data on their findings, and analyse the data to determine if there is a trend (e.g., the amount by which the angle of refraction changes as the angle of incidence increases varies for media of different refractive indices*

10.5.E3.7 *identify the factors, in qualitative and quantitative terms, that affect the refraction of light as it passes from one medium to another*

Behavior of Light at a Boundary Between Two Media

When light travels across a boundary from one medium into another, both refraction and reflection can occur. The relative amount of refraction and reflection depends on the media and the angle at which light strikes the boundary (the angle of incidence).

Refraction of Light

Light rays are bent, or refracted, as they pass from one transparent material into another, depending on the refractive index of each material.

There are several terms that are used when discussing light rays:

- The **normal** is a line that is perpendicular to the boundary between two materials.
- An **incident ray** is a light ray that is travelling through a material toward the boundary.
- A **refracted ray** is a light ray that is travelling from the boundary through a material.
- The **angle of incidence** is the angle between the incident ray and the normal.
- The **angle of refraction** is the angle between the refracted ray and the normal.

These terms can be illustrated using the following diagram:

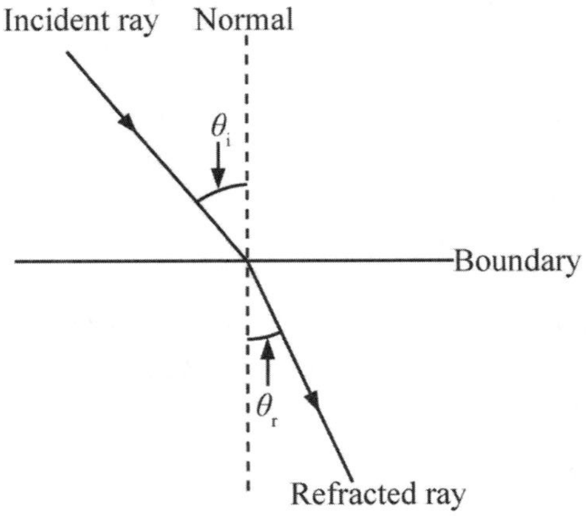

Refraction and Reflection

Ray diagrams are a handy tool for examining the path of light as it passes from one medium to another, such as from water to air or through a lens.

Consider a light ray travelling from water into air. When the angle of incidence is small, a ray diagram can be used to show most of the light is refracted, and very little is reflected.

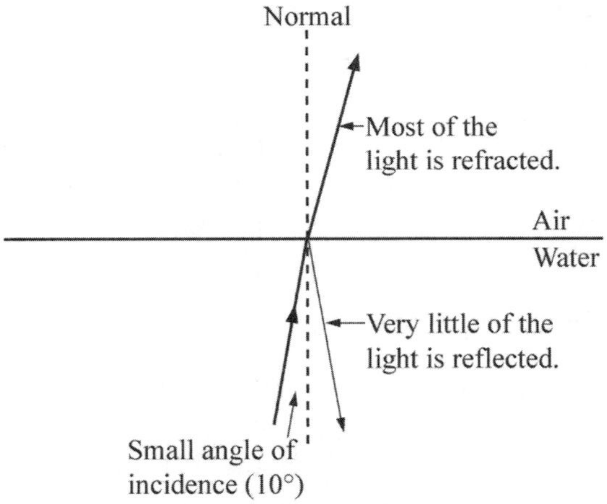

When the angle of incidence is larger, the ray diagram demonstrates that there is less refraction and more reflection.

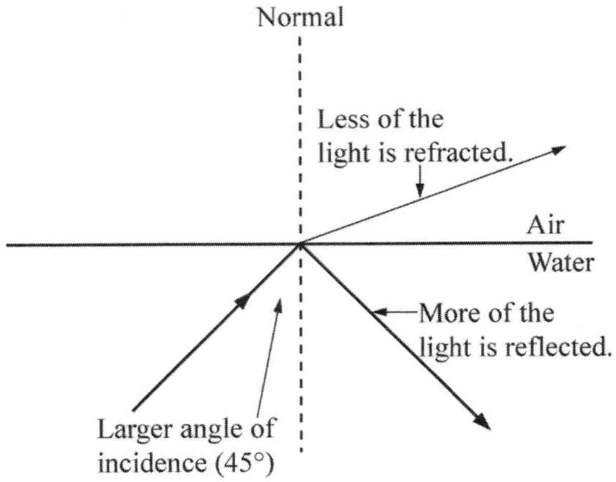

Example

Consider a situation in which you are floating in a boat upon still water. If you look over the edge of the boat into the water, it may be possible to see some weeds or rocks on the lake bottom. In this case the angle of incidence is small, and most of the light coming from the lake bottom is refracted.

If you look into the distance at the surface of the water, you most likely will not be able to see the lake bottom—you are more likely to see reflections of the lake shore or clouds than anything else. This is because the angle of incidence is high. The majority of light reaching your eyes has been reflected off the surface of the water.

Total Internal Reflection

When light travels from a medium with a higher refractive index (more optically dense medium) into a medium with a lower refractive index (less optically dense medium), the angle of refraction will be greater than the angle of incidence.

The critical angle is the angle of incidence that will result in an angle of refraction of 90° to the normal.

When a light ray is shone from water toward air at its critical angle, the refracted ray will travel along the boundary and will not reach the air.

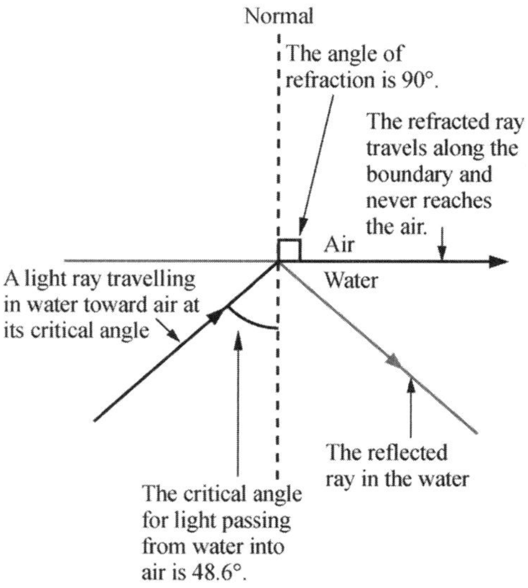

When the angle of incidence is greater than the critical angle, none of the light is refracted (all of it is reflected), and it remains in the more optically dense medium. This phenomenon is referred to as **total internal reflection**.

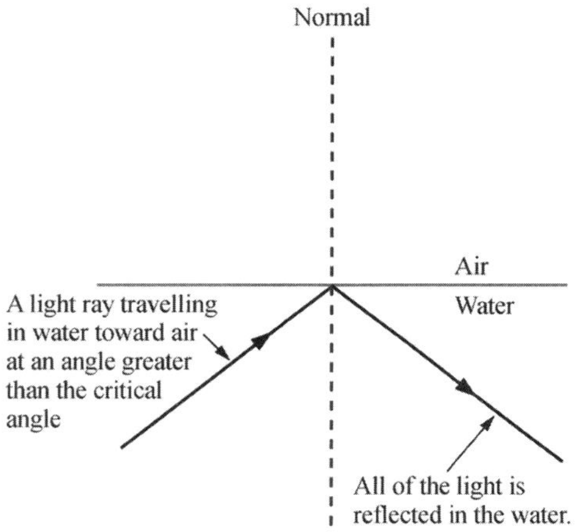

There are two main requirements for total internal reflection:

- The light is inside the more optically dense medium
- The angle of incidence is greater than the critical angle

Total internal reflection cannot occur when light is travelling from a less optically dense medium into one that is more optically dense.

The critical angle for a light ray travelling from one medium to another can be calculated using Snell's law setting the refracted angle at 90°:
$n_1 \sin \theta_1 = n_2 \sin \theta_2$.

Example

The index of refraction of water is 1.333, and the index of refraction of sapphire is 1.760. Calculate the critical angle for a light ray travelling from sapphire into water.

Solution

$n_{\text{sapphire}} \sin \theta_{\text{sapphire}} = n_{\text{water}} \sin \theta_{\text{water}}$

At the critical angle for sapphire (θ_{sapphire}), θ_{water} would be 90.0°.

$$\sin \theta_{\text{sapphire}} = \frac{n_{\text{water}} \sin 90.0°}{n_{\text{sapphire}}} = \frac{1.333 \times 1.00}{1.760} = 0.7574$$

Critical angle = $\theta_{\text{sapphire}} = 49.2°$

The principles of total internal reflection are applied in light pipes and fibre optics.

The core of an optical fibre is made of very pure glass and is about the thickness of a human hair. Surrounding the core is a cladding made of a material with a much lower index of refraction. A plastic coating protects the fibre.

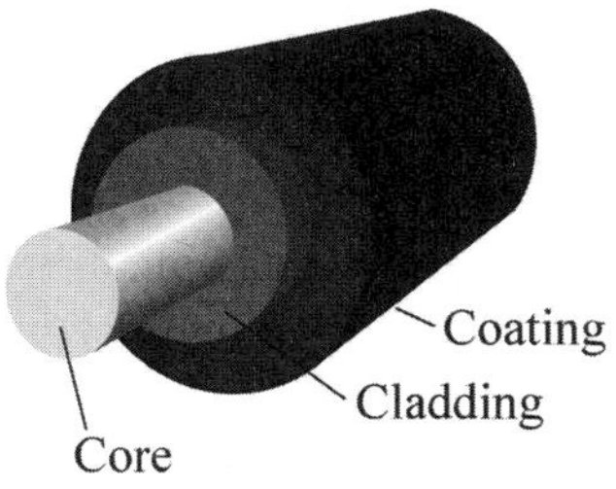

A cross section of an optical fibre

Total internal reflection within the fibres assures that very little light is lost, even over long distances. Huge amounts of data can be transferred using light travelling through fibre optic cables.

Example

The typical value for the cladding of an optical fibre is 1.46. The core value is typically 1.48. What is the critical angle for this optical fibre? What might cause light to be lost from an optical fibre?

Solution

$n_1 \sin \theta_1 = n_2 \sin \theta_2$

$n_{\text{core}} \sin \theta_{\text{core}} = n_{\text{cladding}} \sin \theta_{\text{cladding}}$

$(1.48)(\sin \theta_{\text{critical}}) = (1.46)(\sin 90.0°)$

$\theta_{\text{critical}} = 80.6°$

This is a large critical angle, and consequently light rays must travel fairly parallel to the long axis of the fibre or reflect at angles of incidence greater than the critical angle. A sharp bend in the fibre will cause the angle of incidence to be smaller the the critical angle, and the light ray can leave the fibre.

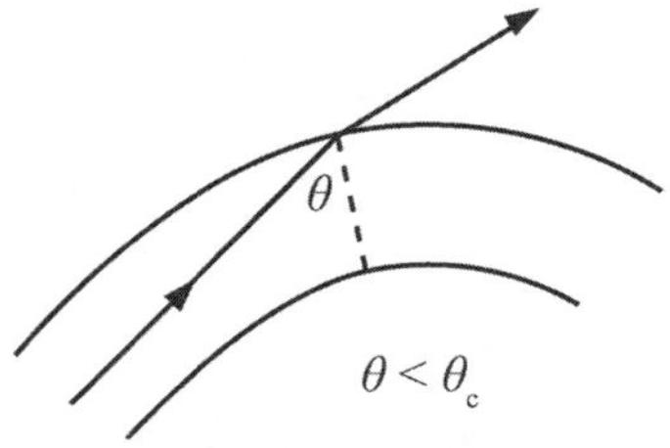

Gemstones have high refractive indexes, and carefully calculating the angle of the facets causes light entering a gemstone from the sides to exit only out of the top facets. This gives a gemstone like a diamond its brilliance and sparkle. The facet angles result in a large critical angle for light rays that are directed toward the sides of the gem.

Use the following information to answer the next question.

The critical angle for a light ray travelling from water to air is 48.6°.

14. When a light ray travels from water toward air at an angle of incidence of 45.0°

A. some of the light is refracted and some is reflected

B. all of the light is refracted and none is reflected

C. all of the light is reflected and none is refracted

D. the light is neither refracted nor reflected

Use the following information to answer the next question.

The index of refraction of water is greater than that of air. A beam of light originates in the water at position II, as shown in the diagram.

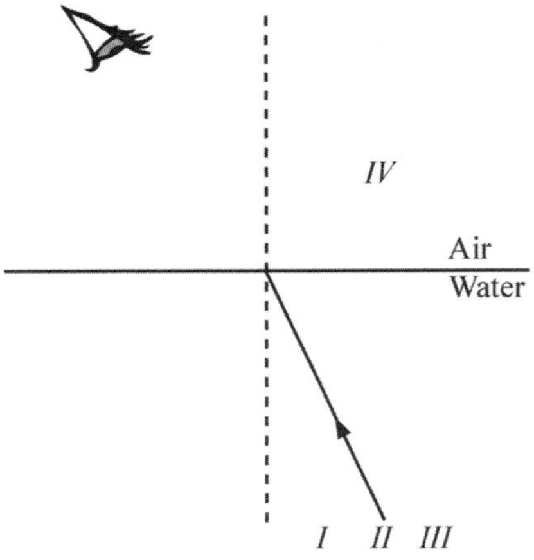

15. An observer above the water would **most likely** see the beam as if it were coming from position

A. I

B. II

C. III

D. IV

Use the following information to answer the next question.

The refractive index of bisphenol A polycarbonate (BPA) is 1.586, and the refractive index of water is 1.333. When a light beam travels from BPA into water, the angle of incidence is 41.5°.

16. What is the angle of refraction for the light beam in water?

A. 33.8°

B. 34.9°

C. 49.4°

D. 52.0°

Use the following information to answer the next question.

When a light ray travels from air into a sample of acrylic glass, the angle of refraction in the glass is 20.0°. The index of refraction of acrylic glass is 1.49.

17. The angle of incidence of the light ray is

A. 13.2°

B. 20.0°

C. 29.8°

D. 30.6°

10.5.E3.5 *describe the characteristics and positions of images formed by converging lenses (e.g., orientation, size, type), with the aid of ray diagrams*

10.5.E2.5 *predict, using ray diagrams and algebraic equations, the position and characteristics of an image produced by a converging lens, and test their predictions through inquiry*

Images and Converging Lenses

The positions and characteristics of images produced by converging lenses can be determined using two main tools: ray diagrams and mathematical equations.

Converging Lenses and Ray Diagrams

A converging lens is a double-convex lens, which is thicker in the center than it is at the edges. Rays passing through a converging lens are deflected toward one another.

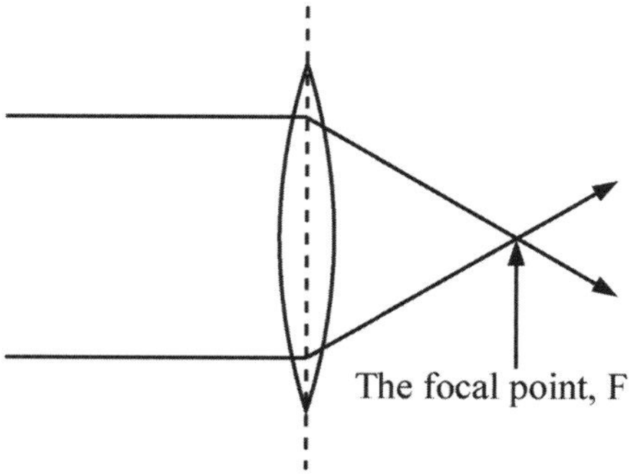

Rays passing through a converging lens will intersect one another at a single point—the focal point. The distance from the center of a lens to the focal point is called the focal length of the lens.

Incident rays move from an object toward a lens. There are three rules concerning incident rays and how a converging lens affects them:

- Any incident ray that is parallel to the principal axis (labelled 1 in the following diagram) will refract through the lens and pass through the focal point on the opposite side.
- Any incident ray that passes through the focal point on the way to the lens (labelled 2 in the following diagram) will refract through the lens and travel parallel to the principal axis on the opposite side.
- Any incident ray that passes through the center of the lens (labelled 3 in the following diagram) will continue in a straight path.

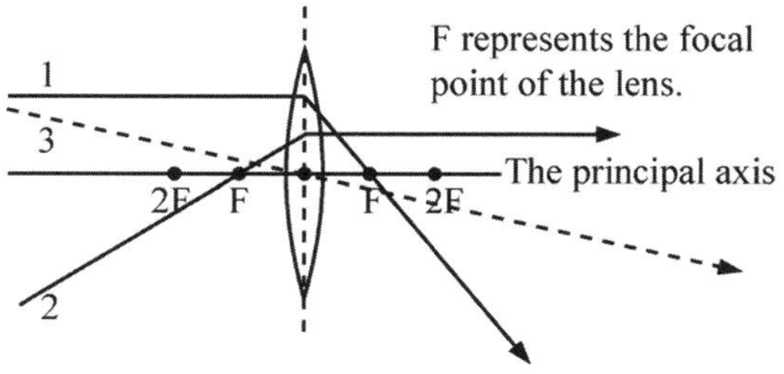

The position and orientation of an image created by a converging lens can be determined using the given three rules to construct a ray diagram.
The following ray diagram shows how the image of an upright arrow outside the 2F point is obtained. Three rays are drawn starting at the point of the arrow at the top of the original object. These rays then converge at the point of the arrow, which is now at the bottom of the image. Light rays from the bottom of the object pass straight though the lens along the principal axis to form the same point on the image.

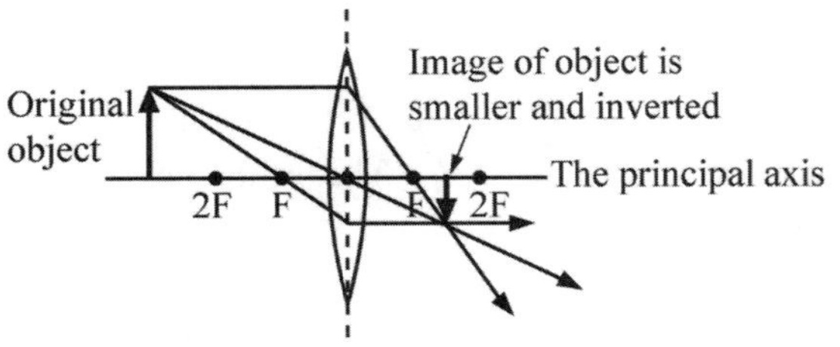

The image formed can be projected onto a piece of white paper held at the position of the image shown on the diagram. This is called a real image.

The following diagram shows the image formed by an object placed between the 2F and F points on the principal axis.

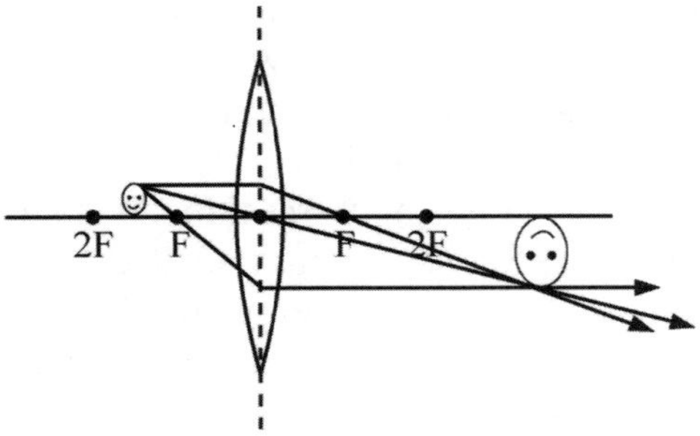

In this case the image is still inverted, but it is larger than the original object. The image here is also a real image.

When an object is placed between the focal point (F) and the lens, no real image results, but a virtual image is formed.

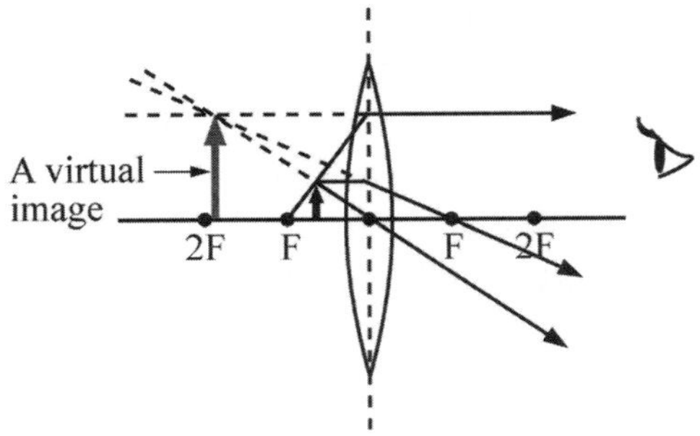

In the given diagram, the rays do not converge after passing through the lens, but if lines are drawn backward from their point of intersection with the center of the lens, they converge at a point on the same side as the object. The rays appear to be originating from this point to the observer.
This forms a virtual image. The virtual image is larger than the object, and would appear to the observer to be on the same side of the lens as the object. A virtual image will not be projected onto a piece of paper.

Because the image is larger than the original object, any object placed inside the focal point will appear to be magnified by the lens. In this way a converging lens can be used as a magnifying glass.

An object placed right at the focal point will not form any image. The rays passing through the lens in this case neither converge nor diverge.

Calculations Involving Converging Lenses

The **thin lens equation** was developed to predict the relative positions of an object and its image, formed by a converging lens. This equation is most accurate when the lens being used is relatively thin.

The thin lens equation is as follows:

$\frac{1}{f} = \frac{1}{d_o} + \frac{1}{d_i}$, in which f is the focal length, d_o is the distance from the centre of the lens to the object, and d_i is the distance from the centre of the lens to the image. For this equation to work properly, all the variables must be in the same unit (for example, all values should be in cm).

Example

An object is 45.5 cm from a lens with a focal length of 16.0 cm. The distance between the image and the lens is __________cm. (Record your three-digit answer.)

Solution

The focal length, f, and the object distance, d_o, are given. Use the thin lens equation to calculate the image distance, d_i.

$$\frac{1}{f} = \frac{1}{d_o} + \frac{1}{d_i}$$

$$\begin{aligned}\frac{1}{d_i} &= \frac{1}{f} - \frac{1}{d_o} \\ &= \frac{1}{16.0} - \frac{1}{45.5} \\ &= 0.0625 - 0.021\ 98 \\ &= 0.040\ 52\end{aligned}$$

$$\frac{1}{d_i} = 0.040\ 52$$

$$d_i = \frac{1}{0.040\ 52} = 24.7 \text{ cm}$$

The **magnification equation** relates the height of the object to the height of its image.

The magnification (M) of a lens is the ratio of the height of the image (h_i) to the height of the object (h_o). The equation also includes the image distance (d_i) and the object distance (d_o).

The magnification equation is as follows:

$$M = \frac{h_i}{h_o} = -\frac{d_i}{d_o}$$

Example

A object that is 8.0 cm tall is placed 30.0 cm from a converging lens. The image is 45.0 cm away from the lens. Calculate the height of the image, and indicate whether the image is inverted or upright. (Record your answer to three-significant digits.)

Solution

You are given the height of the object (h_o), the distance of the object from the lens (d_o), and the distance of the image from the lens (d_i). Use the magnification equation to calculate the height of the image (h_i).

$$\frac{h_i}{h_o} = -\frac{d_i}{d_o}$$

$$\begin{aligned}h_i &= -\frac{d_i}{d_o} \times h_o \\ &= -\frac{45.0}{30.0} \times 8.0 \\ &= -12.0 \text{ cm}\end{aligned}$$

A negative height value means the image is inverted. If the object is above the principal axis, the image will appear below it.

Use the following information to answer the next question.

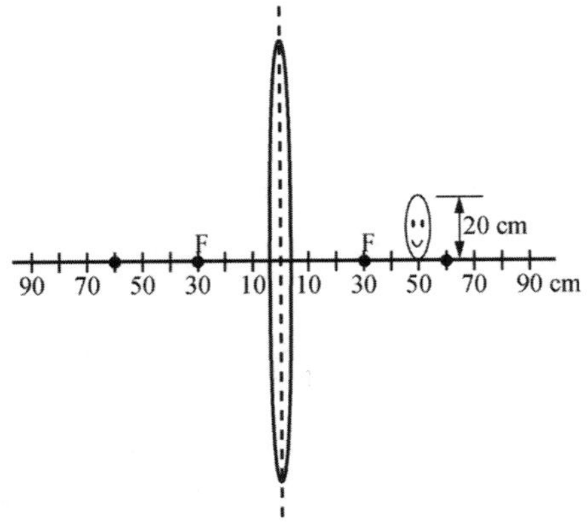

An object is placed on the right side of a converging lens with a focal length of 30 cm.

18. The image of this object formed by the lens will appear

A. upright and about 30 cm to the left of the lens

B. upright and about 73 cm to the left of the lens

C. inverted and about 73 cm to the left of the lens

D. inverted and about 30 cm to the left of the lens

Use the following information to answer the next question.

An image of an object is 82.5 cm from a lens with a focal length of 22.0 cm.

19. The distance from the object to the lens is

A. 3.75 cm   **B.** 17.4 cm

C. 30.0 cm   **D.** 60.5 cm

CHALLENGER QUESTION

Use the following information to answer the next question.

A black arrow is shown on the left side of a converging lens with a focal length of 3.0 cm.

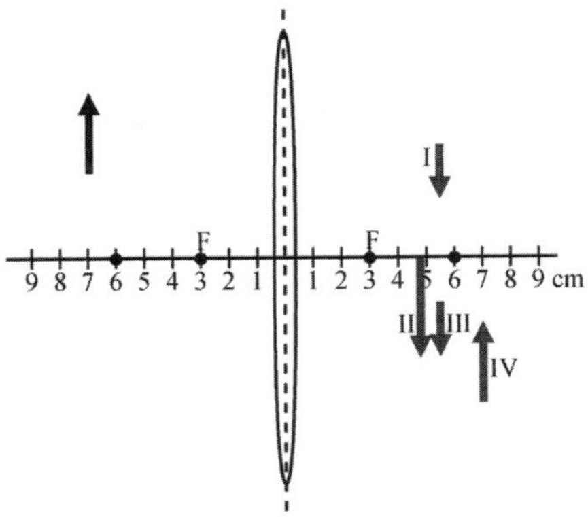

20. Which arrow accurately represents the position, size and, orientation of the image produced by this lens?

A. I   **B.** II

C. III   **D.** IV

Use the following information to answer the next question.

An object is placed 5.0 cm to the left of a converging lens with a focal length of 3.0 cm.

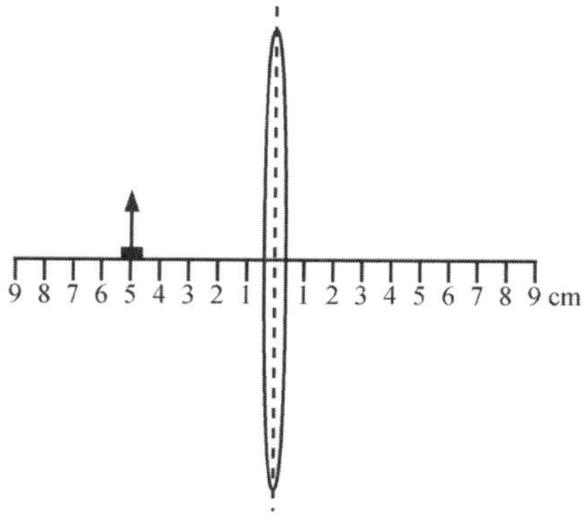

Open Response

21. Using a ray diagram, determine the position and orientation of the image of this object, and include a sketch of the image as it would appear in the diagram.

____
____
____
____
____
____
____

Use the following information to answer the next question.

A real image of a happy face appears on the left side of a converging lens with a focal length of 2.0 cm.

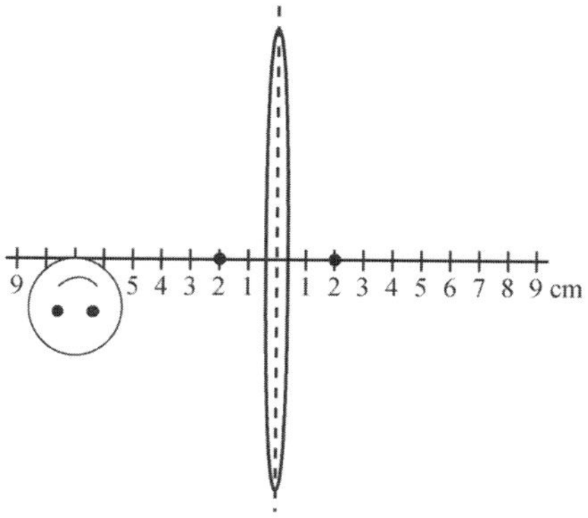

Open Response

22. Using a ray diagram, indicate the position and orientation of the original object, and sketch the object as it would appear.

____
____
____
____
____
____
____

10.5.E3.6 *identify ways in which the properties of mirrors and lenses (both converging and diverging) determine their use in optical instruments (e.g., cameras, telescopes, binoculars, microscopes)*

Some Applications of Lenses and Mirrors

The light-altering abilities of lenses and mirrors can be used to help view and capture images in everyday life. Cameras, binoculars, microscopes, and telescopes all employ the optical properties of either lenses or mirrors.

Cameras and Lenses

A camera records information contained in an image either on film or, in the case of a digital camera, on an electronic sensor. A very simple camera uses a single converging lens to form a real image. The camera is designed so that the image is produced right on the plane of the film or sensor.

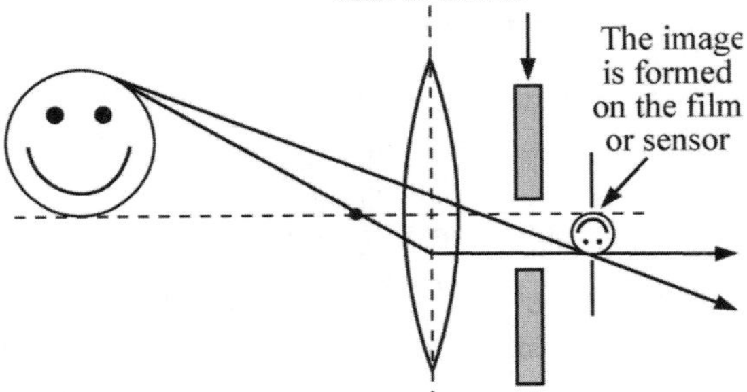

The shutter is opened only when a picture is taken. A typical exposure usually lasts only a fraction of a second. The lens is moved during focusing so that a sharp image is always produced on the plane of the film or sensor.

For a number of reasons, a single converging lens will not produce a high quality image in a camera. What is referred to as the lens of a better camera is actually a combination of several converging and diverging lenses placed in a single tube. These lenses work together to form an image with accurate color and minimal distortion.

A single-lens reflex (SLR) camera uses a plane mirror and prism assembly to send a separate image from the lens to the viewfinder so that the photographer can see the same image as the one that will be recorded on the film or sensor.

Binoculars

Binoculars produce two highly magnified images of a distant object—one for each eye.

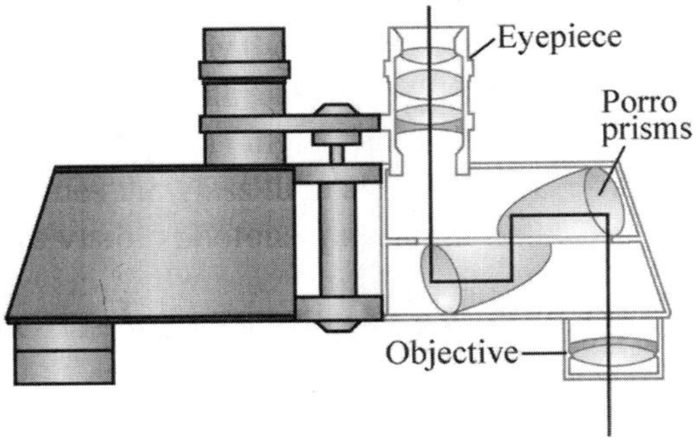

The magnified image formed by each objective lens is redirected to the eyepiece using two prisms. The eyepiece contains lenses that further magnify the image and adjust it so it is upright. Binoculars have a huge range of sophistication, quality, and cost.

Microscopes

Microscopes that are used to view very small objects are called compound microscopes.

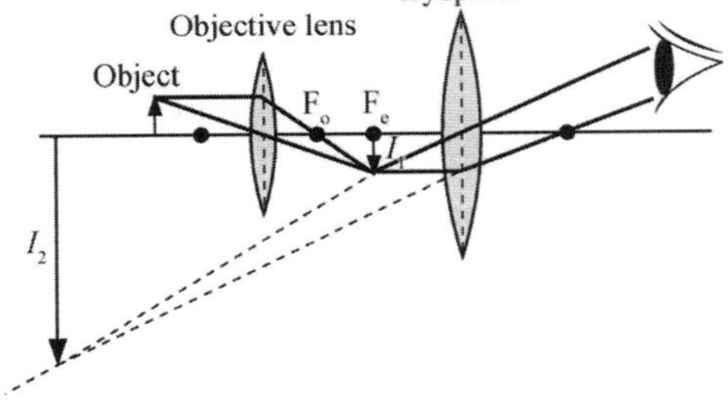

In a compound microscope, an object is first magnified by an objective lens. The image formed by the objective lens (I_1) is situated at the focal point (F_e) of an ocular lens (or eyepiece). The ocular lens uses this image as an object and produces a very large virtual image (I_2).

The total magnification of a compound microscope is calculated by multiplying the magnification of the objective lens by the magnification of the ocular lens. If a 40X objective lens is used with a 10X ocular lens, the total magnification will be $40 \times 10 = 400$X.

TELESCOPES

The two main types of telescopes are refracting telescopes and reflecting telescopes.

Refracting telescopes use a combination of lenses to produce an image of a distant object. There are several different designs for this type of telescope. One type uses two converging lenses: an objective lens and an eyepiece (ocular lens).

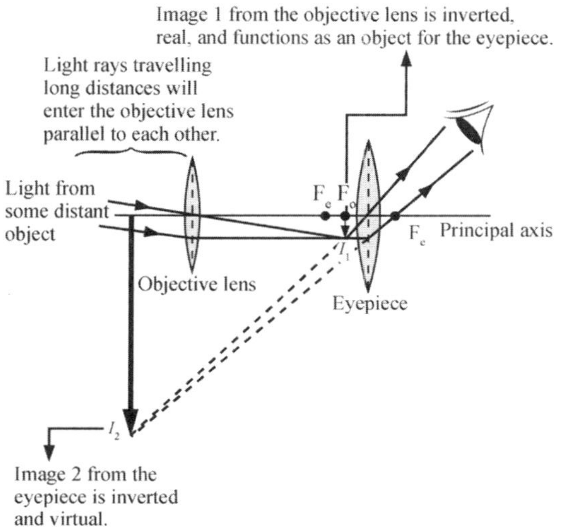

The objective lens produces an image (I_1) of a distant object. A second converging lens acts as the eyepiece. Since the image I_1 is inside the focal point of the eyepiece (F_e), a large virtual image (I_2) is created.

A reflecting telescope uses a combination of mirrors to produce an image. There are several different designs for this type of telescope. A type of design called Cassegrain first uses a primary mirror to initally converge the rays from an object being viewed and then uses a secondary mirror to reflect the rays toward the viewer.

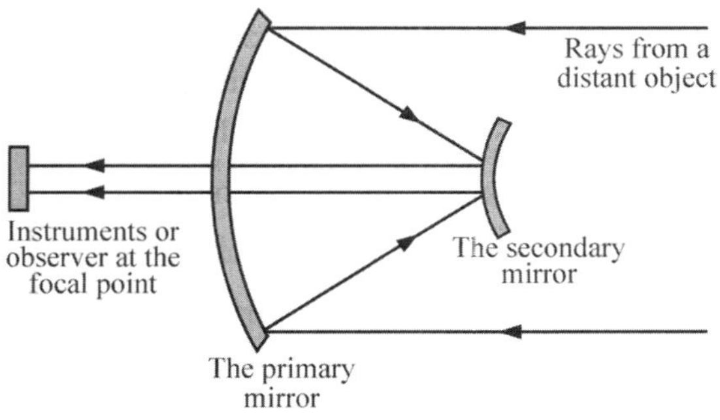

Reflecting telescopes of this design are used in most of the large optical astronomical observatories on Earth and in the Hubble Space Telescope.

Use the following information to answer the next question.

> In a camera with a single convergent lens, the sensor is 6.00 cm behind the lens and the object is 2.50 cm in front of the lens.

23. The effective focal length of the lens is

A. 1.76 mm **B.** 4.29 mm

C. 17.6 mm **D.** 42.9 mm

24. The **primary** role of prisms in binoculars is to

A. increase the effective magnification of the eyepiece lens

B. increase the size of the image formed by the objective lens

C. decrease the size of the image formed by the objective lens

D. change the direction of the rays from the objective lens so that they hit the eyepiece lens correctly

10.5.E2.6 *calculate, using the indices of refraction, the velocity of light as it passes through a variety of media, and explain the angles of refraction with reference to the variations in velocity*

VELOCITY OF LIGHT THROUGH DIFFERENT MEDIA

When a light ray travels from a vacuum into any other medium, its velocity (or speed) decreases. The index of refraction (n) of a given medium is the ratio of the velocity of light in a vacuum to the velocity of light in the medium.

$$n_{\text{medium}} = \frac{v_{\text{air}}}{v_{\text{medium}}} = \frac{v_{\text{vacuum}}}{v_{\text{medium}}}$$

The velocity of light in air is almost the same as it is in a vacuum, so the index of refraction of air (n_{air}) is 1.00.

The velocity of light in air is 3.00×10^8 m/s, while the velocity of light in water is 2.25×10^8 m/s.

The index of refraction of water is as follows:

$$n_{water} = \frac{v_{air}}{v_{water}} = \frac{3.00 \times 10^8 \text{ m/s}}{2.25 \times 10^8 \text{ m/s}} = 1.33$$

The index of refraction does not have a unit because it is simply a ratio.

Example

The velocity of light in air is 3.00×10^8 m/s, and the index of refraction of glycerol is 1.47. Calculate the velocity of light in glycerol.

Solution

$$n_{glycerol} = \frac{v_{air}}{v_{glycerol}}$$

$$v_{glycerol} = \frac{v_{air}}{n_{glycerol}} = \frac{3.00 \times 10^8 \text{ m/s}}{1.47} = 2.04 \times 10^8 \text{ m/s}$$

When light travels from one medium into another, its velocity changes. This causes the ray to bend either toward or away from the normal.

- When a light ray passes from a medium in which it travels fast to one in which it travels more slowly, it will bend toward the normal. In this case the angle of refraction is less than the angle of incidence.
- When a light ray passes from a medium in which it travels slowly to one in which it travels faster, it will bend away from the normal. In this case the angle of refraction is greater than the angle of incidence.

Light travels more slowly in water than it does in air, so when a light ray passes from air into water, it will bend toward the normal.

The relationships between the angle of incidence, angle of refraction, and refractive indexes of media are summarized in Snell's law: $n_i \sin \theta_i = n_r \sin \theta_r$.

Where

n_i = the index of refraction of the incident medium

n_r = the index of refraction of the refractive medium

θ_i = the angle of incidence

θ_r = the angle of refraction

Snell's law can also be expressed in the form $\frac{\sin \theta_i}{\sin \theta_r} = \frac{n_r}{n_i}$.

If a light ray is travelling from air into another medium, air is the incident medium and the index of refraction of air n_{air} or $n_i = 1.00$,

so when air is the incident medium: $\frac{\sin \theta_i}{\sin \theta_r} = n_r$.

The fact that Snell's law applied perfectly to the refraction of light by glass lenses and prisms led many scientists to believe that light was a wave. This belief was held for approximately 300 years when Einstein introduced his explanation of the photoelectric effect in metal by giving light both particle and wave properties, and by predicting the range of allowed energies that light could possess.

Example

A ray of light is travelling from air into liquid benzene. The angle of incidence is 35.0°, and the refractive index of benzene is 1.50.

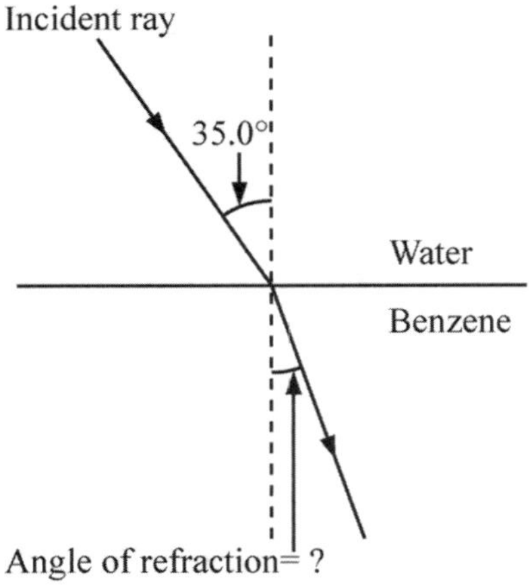

Calculate the angle of refraction of the ray as it travels through the benzene.

Solution

$$\frac{\sin\theta_i}{\sin\theta_r} = n_r$$

$$\sin\theta_r = \frac{\sin\theta_i}{n_r} = \frac{\sin 35.0°}{1.50} = \frac{0.5736}{1.50} = 0.3824$$

$$\therefore \theta_r = 22.5°$$

Another variation of Snell's law can be used to predict the velocity of light as it travels through different media:

$$\frac{\sin\theta_i}{\sin\theta_r} = \frac{n_r}{n_i} = \frac{v_i}{v_r}$$

Example

When a light ray with a 40.0° angle of incidence travels from air into a block of polycarbonate, the angle of refraction is 23.8°.
The velocity of light in air is 3.00×10^8 m/s.
Calculate the velocity of light in polycarbonate.

Solution

$$\frac{\sin\theta_i}{\sin\theta_r} = \frac{v_i}{v_r}$$

$$v_r = v_i\left(\frac{\sin\theta_r}{\sin\theta_i}\right) = \left(3.00 \times 10^8\ \text{m/s}^2\right)\left(\frac{\sin 23.8°}{\sin 40.0°}\right) = 1.88 \times 10^8\ \text{m/s}$$

Use the following information to answer the next question.

The velocity of light in a vacuum is 3.00×10^8 m/s, and the index of refraction of sapphire is 1.77.

25. The velocity of light in sapphire is

A. 1.23×10^8 m/s

B. 1.69×10^8 m/s

C. 3.00×10^8 m/s

D. 5.31×10^8 m/s

Use the following information to answer the next question.

The velocity of light in air is 3.00×10^8 m/s. An emerald has a refractive index of 1.58.

26. The velocity of light in emerald is

A. 1.42×10^8 m/s

B. 1.90×10^8 m/s

C. 4.58×10^8 m/s

D. 4.74×10^8 m/s

Use the following information to answer the next question.

A beam of light travels from air into a flat piece of jade with an angle of incidence of 38.0°. The angle of refraction of the beam in the jade is 21.9°. The index of refraction of air is 1.00.

Numerical Response

27. What is the index of refraction of the jade?__________(Record your answer to **three**-significant digits.)

Use the following information to answer the next question.

Some of the properties of ruby and opal in relation to light are listed as follows:

- The index of refraction of opal is 1.44.
- The index of refraction of ruby is 1.76.
- The velocity of light in opal is 2.08×10^8 m/s.

Open Response

28. Calculate the velocity of light in ruby.

____

____

____

____

____

10.5.E3.8 *describe properties of light, and use them to explain naturally occurring optical phenomena (e.g., apparent depth, shimmering, a mirage, a rainbow)*

Optical Effects of Light Travelling in Different Media

As light passes from one medium to another, or even through areas of different temperature within the same medium, several effects can occur, which can be explained using the properties of light.
These effects include change in apparent position, shimmering, mirages, and rainbows.

Real and Apparent Positions of an Object

When you look at a straight stick that is placed in water, it appears to be bent. This has to do with the refraction of light. When a light ray travels from one medium to another, it changes direction. This is called refraction.

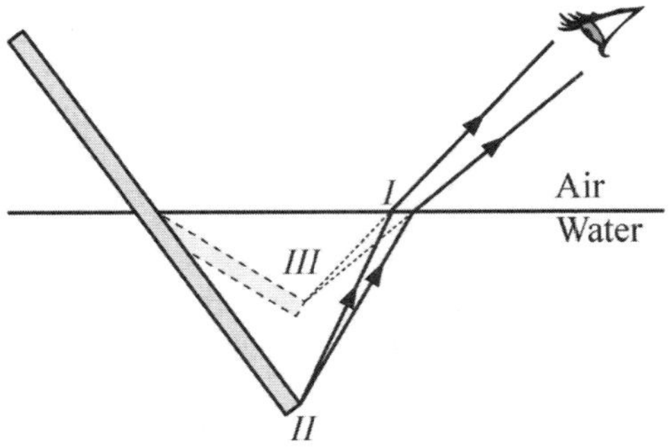

The apparent position of an object in a different medium

In the given diagram, a straight stick is placed in water with its bottom at point *II*. When the light rays from point *II* hit the air at point *I*, they refract and bend away from the normal as they travel toward the observer. The human brain always assumes that rays are straight, when in fact they are sometimes bent. This means you cannot always trust that what you see in regards to the position of an object is actually the object's true position. In this case the observer's brain assumes that the rays coming from point *I* are straight, and therefore originate at point *III*. In this way, the observer sees the stick as bent, with the bottom at point *III* instead of point *II*. Point *III* is called the apparent position of the end of the stick, whereas point *II* is its real position.

Shimmering

You have probably observed what appear to be heat waves being emitted from hot objects and moving upward through the air. These apparent waves are usually caused by the bending of light rays as a result of temperature variations in the atmosphere, which always has local variations in air temperature.
The extent to which air refracts, or bends light, depends on its temperature. Warmer air refracts light a little less than cooler air.

When a ray of light hits the boundary between cool air and hot air (at point *A* on the given diagram), it bends slightly away from the normal. At point *B*, where the ray crosses the boundary back into cooler air, it bends back toward the normal a little bit.
In this way, the movement of a light ray is somewhat distorted as it passes through zones of varying temperatures.

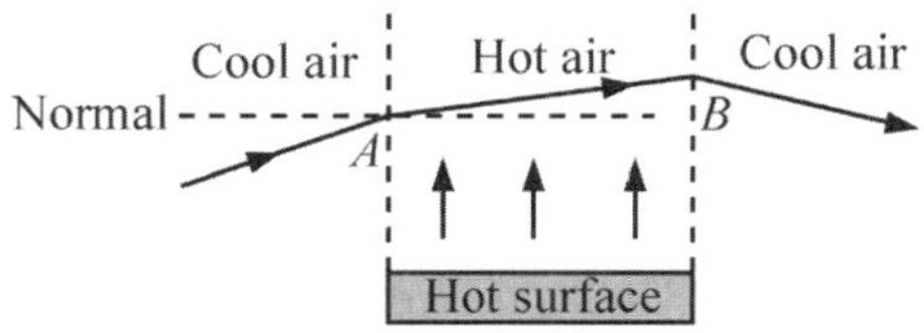

A zone of air passing above the hot surface of an object, like a barbecue, causing a light ray to bend because of differences in temperature

An observer may see these distorted rays as shimmering or heat waves when air passes over a hot surface.

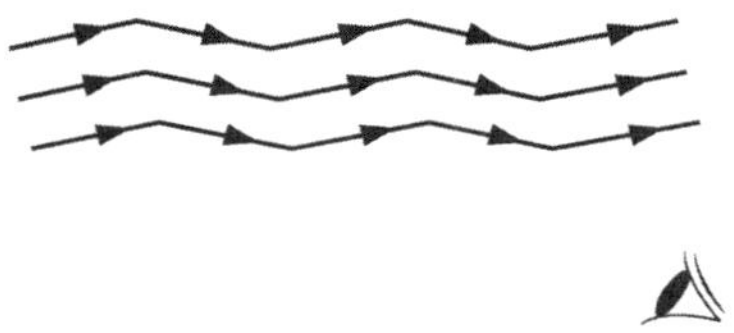

Shimmering caused by distorted light rays as they pass through zones of varying temperature

Mirages

When air sits above a hot surface, it heats up from the bottom. This can cause the air to form layers, with each layer getting slightly cooler from the ground upward. Refraction (or bending) occurs when light travels across a boundary between any two media. The warmer the air is, the less it refracts light toward the normal, or perpendicular to the boundary. Therefore, when a light ray moves across a boundary from cooler air to warmer air, it tends to bend slightly away from the normal.

The given diagram shows consecutive layers of air that get warmer as they get closer to the heated surface of the ground. Light rays travel from the sky toward the observer on the right. As the light rays pass into warmer layers of air, they tend to deflect away from the normal and move in a direction that is closer to being parallel to the ground.
For example, the ray labelled *A* tends to become more horizontal as it moves toward the ground on the left. After moving along the surface of the ground, it bends back upward toward the observer on the right. Your brain will always interpret a ray coming toward you as moving in a straight line directly from its source; therefore, ray *A*, which is carrying light from the sky, appears to the observer to be coming directly from point *B*. The observer then sees an image of the sky that appears to be on, or even below, the surface of the ground. Your brain interprets this image as a body of water. The given diagram is highly exaggerated vertically in order to illustrate the effect, so the image, or mirage, is actually a longer distance from the observer than the diagram indicates.

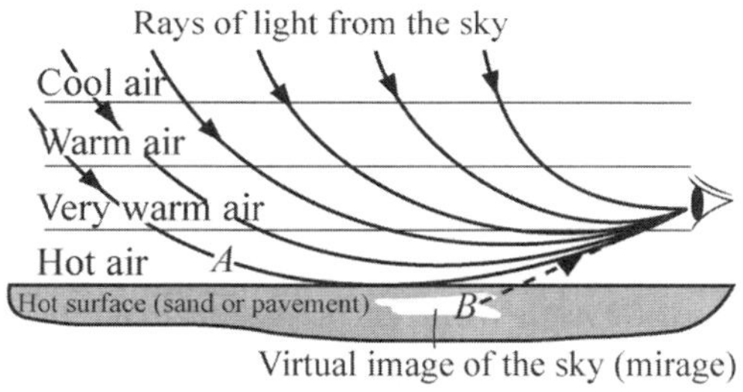

How a mirage is caused

The mirage phenomenon has, throughout history, tricked people into believing that something existed when it really was not there. Indeed, some folk legends and myths are actually based on the appearance of mirages.

RAINBOWS

When a light ray travels across a boundary between one medium and another, it is bent or refracted. White light is actually a mixture of all the various colours of light. When white light is shone into a prism, each colour in the light is refracted at a slightly different angle. In this way, a prism tends to separate white light into its component colours. This phenomenon is known as dispersion of light.

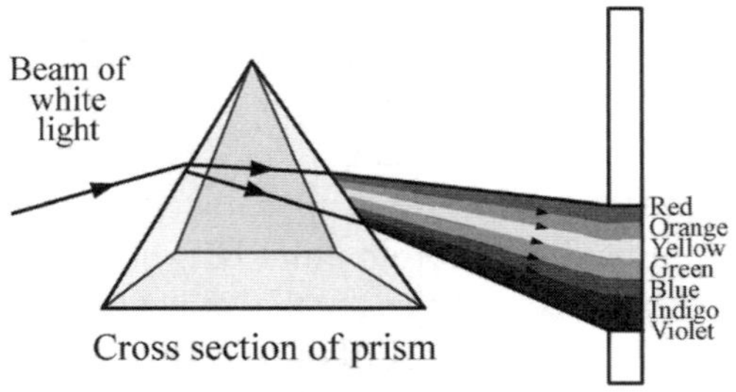

Dispersion of light

The formation of rainbows can be explained using the optical properties of light. Much like a prism, a raindrop refracts each colour of light at a slightly different angle. Some of the refracted light will pass through the raindrop, but some will reflect from the far surface of the raindrop, back toward the observer.

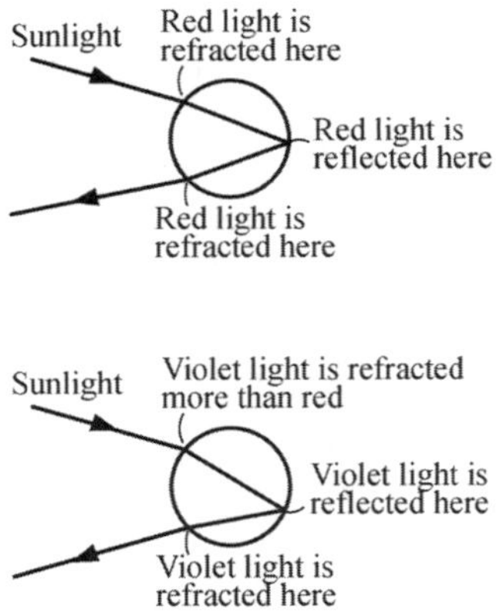

Refraction and reflection of red and violet light in a raindrop

Notice that violet light is refracted more than red light when it enters the raindrop. The reflection of each colour of light takes place at a slightly different location on the far side of the drop. The result is that a ray of each particular colour will reach the observer from a slightly different angle. Any ray of light hitting your eyes is interpreted by your brain as coming in a straight line, directly from its source. The rays of light reflected from the far side of a raindrop appear to be coming from behind the raindrop. Because all raindrops are composed of the same medium (water), the angle of reflection of a particular colour will be the same in every raindrop. In this way, all the red light, for example, seems to come from the same band in the sky in front of you.

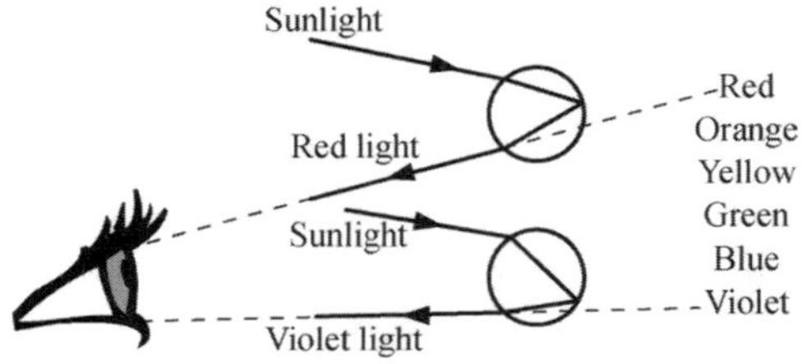

Red and violet light strike an observer from slightly different angles.

The light of each colour between red and violet has its own particular angle through which it reaches the observer. Extending the rays backward leads to a virtual image of where they are coming from—a rainbow.

29. Compared to the optical density of cold air, the optical density of warm air is

A. less than that of cold air, so it refracts light less toward the normal

B. less than that of cold air, so it refracts light more toward the normal

C. more than that of cold air, so it refracts light less toward the normal

D. more than that of cold air, so it refracts light more toward the normal

30. A rainbow is **best** defined as a

A. real image that results primarily from refraction

B. virtual image that results primarily from refraction

C. real image that results from refraction and reflection

D. virtual image that results from refraction and reflection

Answers and Solutions
Physics: Light and Geometric Optics

1. D	7. B	13. 1.9	19. C	25. B
2. OR	8. B	14. A	20. C	26. B
3. D	9. B	15. C	21. OR	27. 1.65
4. OR	10. D	16. D	22. OR	28. OR
5. B	11. A	17. D	23. C	29. A
6. D	12. B	18. C	24. D	30. D

1. D

During laser eye surgery, a small flap on the cornea is cut. A laser is used to reshape the cornea, and the flap is replaced. Reshaping the cornea focuses images on the retina, permanently correcting refractive errors.

2. OR

Infrared sensors detect heat. An animal's body heat is usually significantly greater than the temperature of its surroundings. This is particularly true in mammals and birds, which are warm-blooded. The body temperatures of warm-blooded animals are maintained at constant levels, so it is easy to track these animals using infrared sensors. Reptiles are cold-blooded, and their body temperatures are regulated by the environment. The difference between a reptile's body temperature and its surroundings is not significant enough to be detected by the infrared sensors. Therefore, infrared sensors would be a poor tracking device to use on reptiles.

3. D

A simple microscope uses two convex lenses to form a magnified and erect image of a minute object, as shown in the given ray diagram.

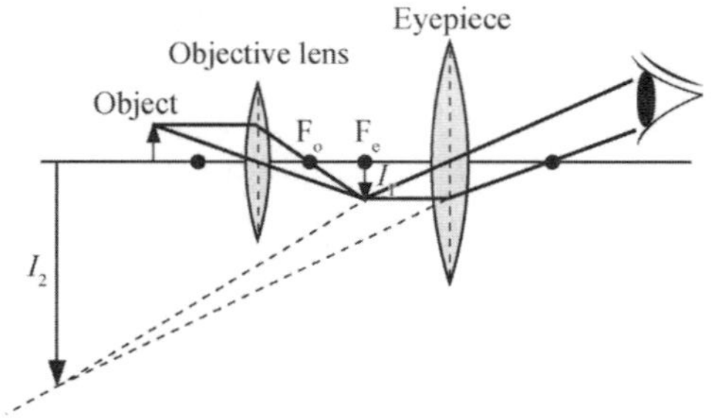

4. OR

There are many possible designs for a solar oven. The outside of the pot used in the oven should be black to absorb the most solar energy. Most solar ovens consist of panels made of a reflective material; this is so the sun's rays not initially absorbed by the pot are reflected and directed back toward the pot. Many designs also use a heat-tolerant, plastic cooking bag around the pot to trap the heated air next to its exterior. In the right climate, a family-sized pot of rice can be cooked in several hours using a solar oven.

The two properties of light that make solar ovens efficient are reflection and absorption.

5. B

A light-emitting diode (LED) consists of an N-type semiconductor connected to a P-type semiconductor. When electrons cross the boundary between the two semiconductors, they enter electron-deficient atoms (holes) found in the P-type semiconductor. Electrons release light as they move into lower energy orbitals in these atoms. Very little heat is produced while an LED is operating, which helps to make these devices very efficient.

6. D

While a fluorescent light bulb is operating, high-energy electrons passing through the bulb cause mercury atoms in the gas to emit energy in the form of ultraviolet radiation. The ultraviolet radiation is absorbed by the coating on the inside surface of the bulb (phosphor), which emits energy in the form of visible light. The process in which a material absorbs one type of electromagnetic radiation and emits a type with a longer wavelength (lower frequency) is called fluorescence.

7. B

Deep-sea anglerfish emit light using the process of bioluminescence, which is the emission of light by a living organism as a result of a chemical reaction.

8. B

In order of decreasing frequency, the electromagnetic spectrum is gamma, X-ray, ultraviolet, visible, infrared, microwave, and radio.

9. B

A converging mirror will form a real image if the object is farther from the mirror than the focal point. It will form a virtual image if the object is between the focal point and the mirror.

Plane mirrors and diverging mirrors can form only virtual images.

10. D

The given ray diagram shows that the image is located at point C and inverted. This situation always occurs for a converging mirror that has an object at the centre of curvature.

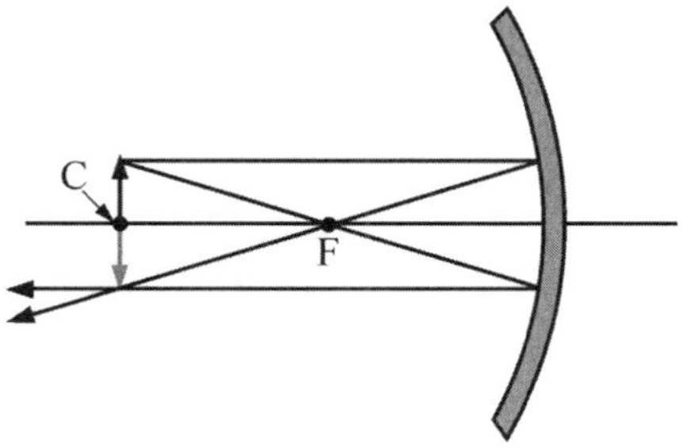

11. A

A plane mirror shows an image that is upright but laterally reversed. This means that the mirror image has the same vertical alignment as the object, but the right side of the object is on the left side of the image.

12. B

A candle positioned between the centre of curvature and the focal point in a concave mirror produces an image that is inverted and larger.

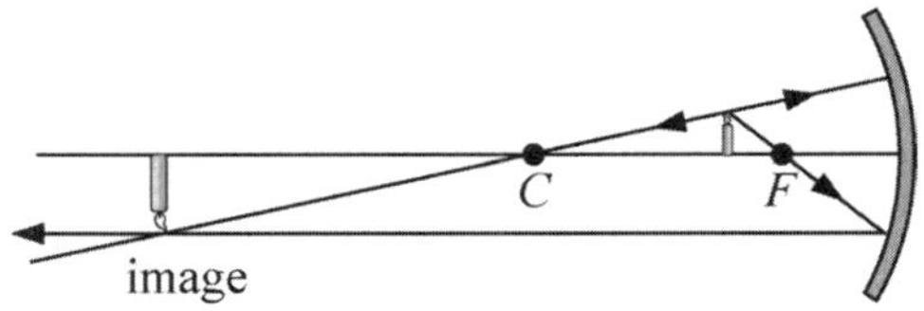

13. 1.9

The distance of the image (d_i) and the focal length (f) are given. Remember that if d_i is behind the mirror, then the value is negative. Also, remember that convex (or diverging) mirrors always produce virtual images (behind the mirror). Use the mirror equation to calculate the distance from the mirror at which the object is placed (d_o).

$$\frac{1}{f} = \frac{1}{d_o} + \frac{1}{d_i}$$

$$\Rightarrow \frac{1}{d_o} = \frac{1}{f} - \frac{1}{d_i}$$

$$\frac{1}{d_o} = \frac{1}{5.0\text{ cm}} - \frac{1}{-3.0\text{ cm}} = 0.533\text{ cm}$$

$$d_o = 1.9\text{ cm}$$

The object is 1.9 cm from the mirror.

14. A

In this case the angle of incidence is less than the critical angle, so refraction and reflection both occur. If the angle of incidence was greater than 48.6° (the critical angle), there would be no refraction and all of the light would be reflected back into the water.

15. C

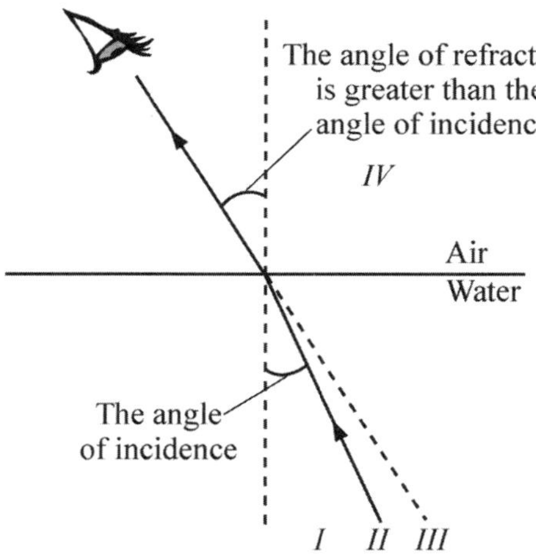

Since the refractive index of air is less than that of water, the angle of refraction in air is greater than the angle of incidence in water.

The brain interprets a beam of light as travelling in a straight line from its source. The beam of light reaching the observer appears to be coming from position III on the diagram.

16. D

According to Snell's law,
$n_w \times \sin\theta_w = n_{BPA} \times \sin\theta_{BPA}$.

$$\sin\theta_w = \frac{n_{BPA} \times \sin\theta_{BPA}}{n_w}$$
$$= \frac{1.586 \times \sin 41.5°}{1.333}$$
$$= 0.7884$$
$$\theta_w = 52.0°$$

17. D

$$\frac{\sin\theta_i}{\sin\theta_r} = \frac{n_r}{n_i}$$

The index of refraction of air $(n_i) = 1.00$.
$\sin\theta_i = n_r \times \sin\theta_r = 1.49 \times \sin 20.0° = 0.5096$
$\theta_i = 30.6°$

18. C

To calculate the distance from the lens at which the image will be formed, draw a ray diagram. First, draw a straight line from the top of the object to the lens. According to the rules of refraction, this light ray will be refracted through the lens and will travel through the focal point. Another line can be drawn from the top of the object directly through the centre of the lens and continuing in the same direction. A third line can be drawn from the top of the object and through the focal point. When this final line enters the lens, it is refracted and will travel parallel to the main horizontal axis. These three lines should all intersect at the same point, which represents the point at which the image will form.

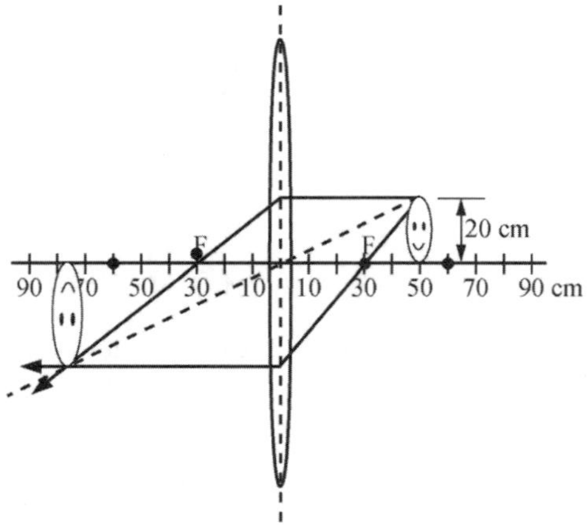

A larger, inverted image appears about 73 cm to the left of the lens.

19. C

The distance from the lens to the object, or object distance d_o, can be calculated using the thin lens equation $\frac{1}{f} = \frac{1}{d_o} + \frac{1}{d_i}$.

$$\frac{1}{d_o} = \frac{1}{f} - \frac{1}{d_i}$$
$$= \frac{1}{22.0} - \frac{1}{82.5}$$
$$= 0.0333$$
$$d_o = \frac{1}{0.0333} = 30.0 \text{ cm}$$

Therefore, the object distance is 30.0 cm.

20. C

Since the object is not on the principal axis, a ray diagram must be drawn to determine the postitions of both the top and the bottom of the object. The diagram also shows why the image is inverted. Arrow III shows the correct image for this object.

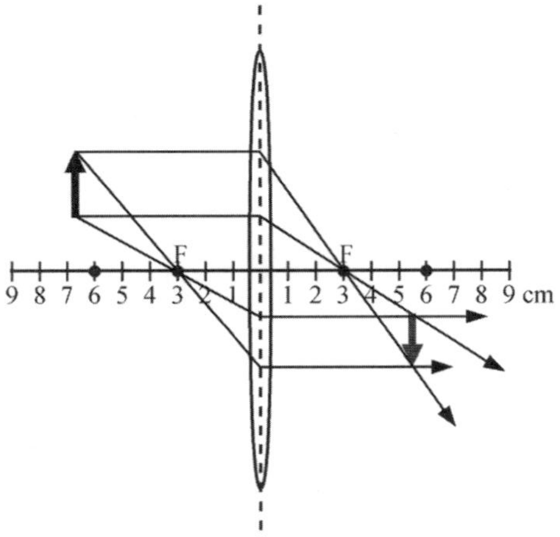

21. OR

Using a ray diagram, a minimum of two lines are required to determine the point of intersection for the image. The first line will travel from the top of the object, parallel to the principal axis and through the lens, at which point it will refract and travel downward through the focal point at 3.0 cm behind the lens. The second line will travel downward from the top of the object through the lens, passing through the focal point 3.0 cm in front of the lens. It will refract as it passes through the lens, and continue parallel to the principal axis as it travels behind the lens. The point at which the two lines intersect indicates the point at which the top of the image will be formed.

Using this technique, a larger, inverted image appears approximately 7.6 cm to the right of the lens.

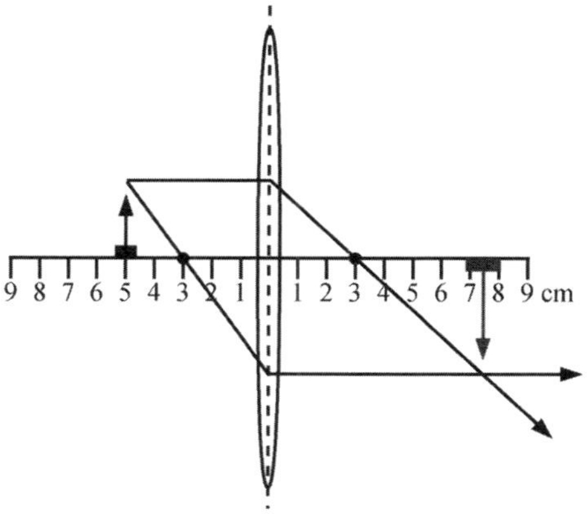

22. OR

The object is upright and smaller than the image. It is located approximately 2.8 cm to the right of the lens.

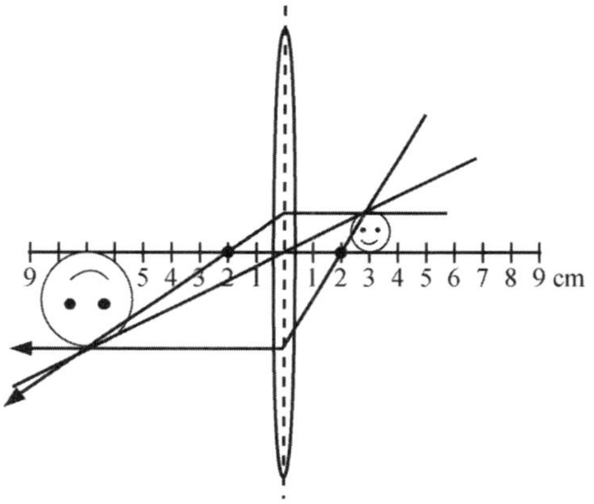

23. C

In a camera, the image is located the same distance from the lens as the sensor, so the image distance is 6.00 cm. The object distance is 2.50 cm. The focal length can be calculated using the thin lens formula $\frac{1}{f} = \frac{1}{d_o} + \frac{1}{d_i}$.

$$\frac{1}{f} = \frac{1}{d_o} + \frac{1}{d_i}$$
$$= \frac{1}{2.50 \text{ cm}} + \frac{1}{6.00 \text{ cm}}$$
$$= 0.5667$$
$$f = \frac{1}{0.5667}$$
$$= 1.76 \text{ cm} \times \frac{10 \text{ mm}}{1 \text{ cm}}$$
$$= 17.6 \text{ mm}$$

24. D

Prisms do not change the size of an image. They are used to guide the rays from the objective lens toward the eyepiece.

25. B

The index of refraction in a medium is given by the following expression: $n_{\text{medium}} = \frac{v_{\text{vacuum}}}{v_{\text{medium}}}$

For sapphire,

$$n_{\text{sapphire}} = \frac{v_{\text{vacuum}}}{v_{\text{sapphire}}} \text{ or } v_{\text{sapphire}} = \frac{v_{\text{vacuum}}}{n_{\text{sapphire}}}$$
$$= \frac{3.0 \times 10^8 \text{ m/s}}{1.77} = 1.69 \times 10^8 \text{ m/s}$$

26. B

The equation that relates velocity of light in a medium to its refractive index is as follows:

$$\frac{n_1}{n_2} = \frac{v_2}{v_1}$$

So, you can say that

$$\frac{v_e}{v_a} = \frac{n_a}{n_e}$$
$$v_e = \frac{n_a}{n_e} \times v_a$$
$$= \frac{1.00}{1.58} \times 3.00 \times 10^8 \text{ m/s}$$
$$= 1.90 \times 10^8 \text{ m/s}$$

27. 1.65

Use Snell's law to calculate the index of refraction of the jade:

$$n_{\text{air}} \times \sin\theta_{\text{air}} = n_{\text{jade}} \times \sin\theta_{\text{jade}}$$
$$n_{\text{jade}} = \frac{n_{\text{air}} \times \sin\theta_{\text{air}}}{\sin\theta_{\text{jade}}}$$
$$= \frac{1.00 \times \sin 38.0°}{\sin 21.9°} = 1.65$$

28. OR

For light travelling in two different media, the equation is $\frac{v_1}{v_2} = \frac{n_2}{n_1}$.

This means that for the velocity of light in ruby, the equation is $\frac{v_{ruby}}{v_{opal}} = \frac{n_{opal}}{n_{ruby}}$.

$$v_{ruby} = \frac{n_{opal} \times v_{opal}}{n_{ruby}}$$
$$= \frac{1.44 \times 2.08 \times 10^8 \text{ m/s}}{1.76}$$
$$= 1.70 \times 10^8 \text{m/s}$$

29. A

When air is warmed up, molecular motion increases and the molecules spread out, leaving more space between themselves. This decreases both the mass density and the optical density of air. Air with less optical density will have a lesser tendency to refract a ray of light toward the normal. The refractive index of warm air is less than that of cold air.

30. D

A rainbow is a virtual image that results from different angles of refraction and reflection of different coloured light in raindrops. It is a virtual image because the observer sees reflected rays that appear to be coming from behind the raindrops. The rays themselves are not travelling through the image; therefore, it is not a real image.

Unit Test

1. Ted has an elongated eyeball, so he wears glasses with corrective lenses in order to see distant objects clearly. The corrective lenses prescribed for Ted's glasses are **most** likely
   A. bifocal **B.** convex
   C. concave **D.** cylindrical

Open Response

2. Thermal imaging detects what kind of radiation emitted by objects and their surroundings?

____
____

3. In order to be functional, optical telescopes use energy from the electromagnetic spectrum in the form of
   A. visible light waves
   B. ultraviolet waves
   C. microwaves
   D. radio waves

Use the following information to answer the next question.

With advances in camera technology, cameras play a significant role in society. Cameras can be found on most cellular phones and computers, at bank ATMs, and on streetlights.

Open Response

4. What are some advantages to the increasing number of cameras present in society, and what is one major concern?

____
____
____
____
____

Use the following information to answer the next question.

The diagram shows an upright letter "A" between the centre of curvature and the focal point of a converging mirror.

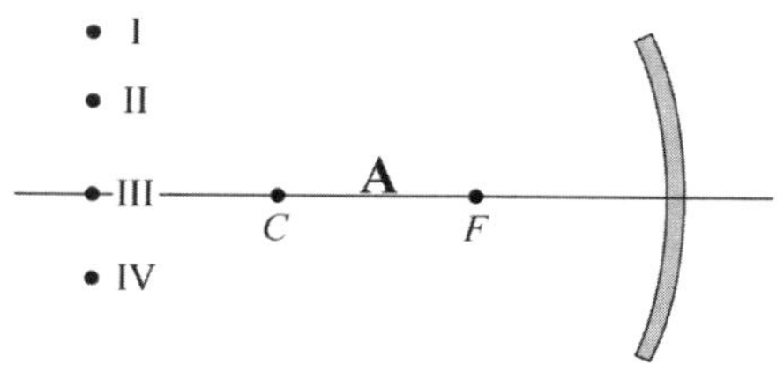

5. The point of the "A" in the image formed by this mirror will be located at
   A. position *I* on the diagram
   B. position *II* on the diagram
   C. position *III* on the diagram
   D. position *IV* on the diagram

Use the following information to answer the next question.

An object is placed 2.0 cm to the left of the centre of a converging lens with a focal length of 3.0 cm.

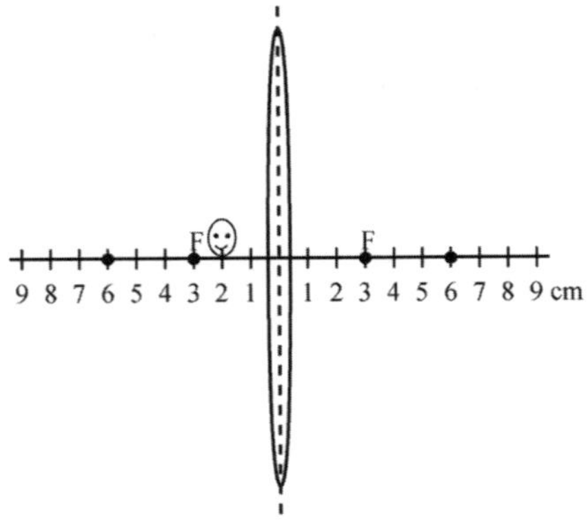

6. The resulting image will be

A. an upright real image to the left of the object

B. an inverted real image to the left of the object

C. an upright virtual image to the left of the object

D. an inverted virtual image to the left of the object

Use the following information to answer the next question.

An object with a height of 20 cm is placed 30 cm to the left of the centre of a converging lens. The image formed is inverted and is 20 cm tall.

7. Based on the given information, the focal length of this lens is

A. 15 cm **B.** 20 cm

C. 30 cm **D.** 60 cm

CHALLENGER QUESTION

Use the following information to answer the next question.

A candle is placed 6.0 cm to the left of a converging lens with a focal length of 2.5 cm. It is located 1.0 cm above the principal axis.

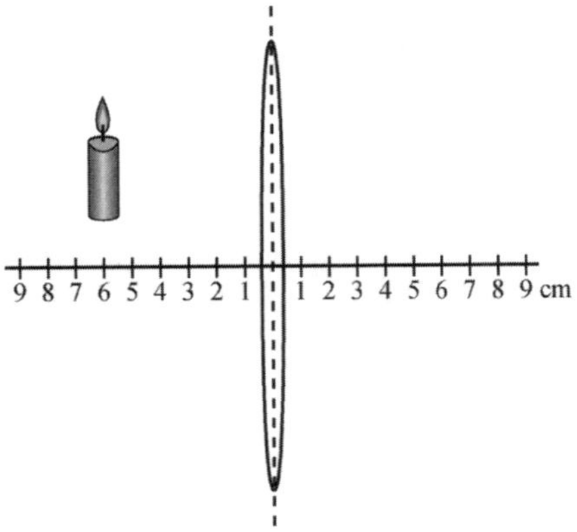

Open Response

8. Use a ray diagram to determine the positions of both the top and bottom of the image, and sketch the image as it would appear.

____

____

____

____

____

____

____

CHALLENGER QUESTION

Use the following information to answer the next question.

The given diagram shows the virtual image formed when a light bulb is placed near a converging lens with a focal length of 3.5 cm.

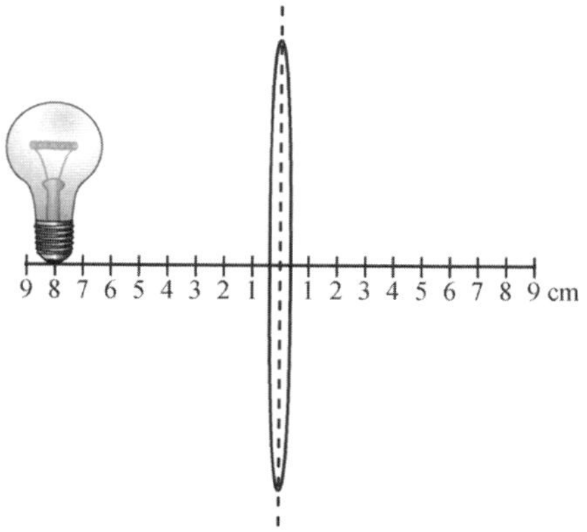

Open Response

9. Use a ray diagram to determine the position, orientation, and size of the original light bulb as compared to the virtual image of the bulb shown in the diagram.

____

____

____

____

____

Use the following information to answer the next question.

A light ray travels from a layer of ethyl alcohol into a layer of benzene with an angle of incidence of 25.0°.

- The velocity of light in ethyl alcohol is 2.21×10^8 m/s.
- The velocity of light in benzene is 2.00×10^8 m/s.

10. The angle of refraction in the benzene is

A. 22.5°

B. 22.6°

C. 25.0°

D. 25.8°

Use the following information to answer the next question.

A beam of light travels from air into a piece of mylar film with an angle of incidence of 26.20°. The angle of refraction is 15.45°.

11. The mylar film has an index of refraction of

A. 1.657 and decreases the velocity of light

B. 0.603 and decreases the velocity of light

C. 1.657 and increases the velocity of light

D. 0.603 and increases the velocity of light

Use the following information to answer the next question.

An underwater flashlight shines a beam of light upward toward the surface of the water at an angle of 24.0° from the vertical.
The index of refraction of water is 1.33, and the index of refraction of air is 1.00.

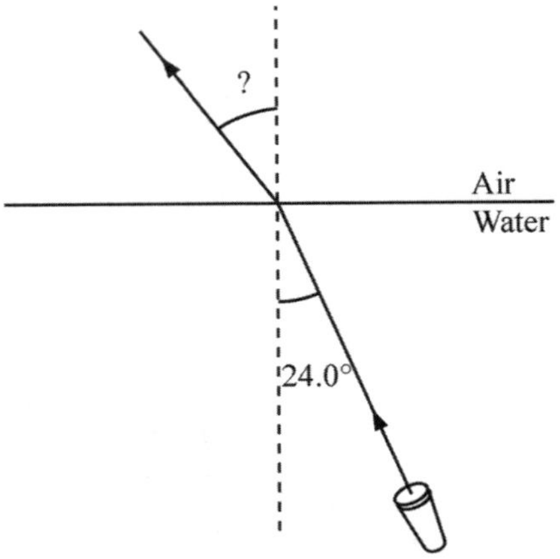

Open Response

12. Calculate the angle the beam forms with the vertical as it travels through the air above the surface of the water.

____

____

____

____

____

CHALLENGER QUESTION

Use the following information to answer the next question.

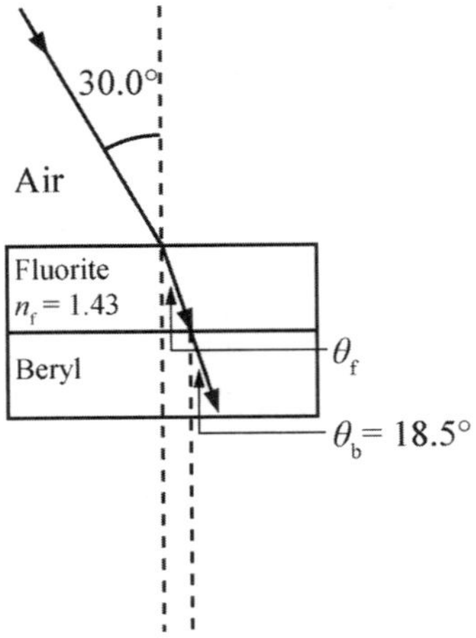

A light ray travels from air into fluorite at an angle of incidence of 30° and then into beryl as shown in the diagram. The angle of refraction in the beryl is 18.5°.
The index of refraction of air is 1.00.
The index of refraction of fluorite is 1.43.
The velocity of light in fluorite is 2.10×10^8 m/s.

Open Response

13. Calculate the velocity of light in beryl.

____

____

____

____

____

____

____

Use the following information to answer the next question.

The given table represents the electromagnetic spectrum in terms of the decreasing frequencies of the waves from left to right. The positions I through to V represent infrared radiation, visible light, ultraviolet light, X-ray radiation, and microwave radiation, but not necessarily in that order.

Gamma rays	I	II	III	IV	V	**Radio waves**

14. In the given table of the electromagnetic spectrum, what is the position of infrared radiation labelled?

A. I
B. II
C. III
D. IV

Open Response

15. A full rainbow shows all the colours of the visible light spectrum. List the colours of the spectrum in order from longest wavelength to shortest wavelength.

____
____
____
____
____

CHALLENGER QUESTION

Use the following information to answer the next question.

A 5.50 cm high object is placed 19.5 cm from a converging mirror with a focal length of 15.0 cm.

16. The image formed by the mirror is

A. 4.50 cm from the mirror and 1.32 cm high

B. 8.38 cm from the mirror and 2.36 cm high

C. 34.5 cm from the mirror and 9.73 cm high

D. 65.0 cm from the mirror and 18.3 cm high

Use the following information to answer the next question.

The indices of refraction (n) for water, vegetable oil, and crown glass are 1.33, 1.47, and 1.52, respectively.

17. Total internal reflection can occur for a ray of light travelling from

A. water into crown glass

B. water into vegetable oil

C. crown glass into vegetable oil

D. vegetable oil into crown glass

Use the following information to answer the next question.

The indexes of refraction (n) of cubic zirconia and acetone are 2.192 and 1.360, respectively.

Open Response

18. Calculate the critical angle of a light ray travelling from cubic zirconia toward acetone.

____

____

____

____

____

Use the following information to answer the next question.

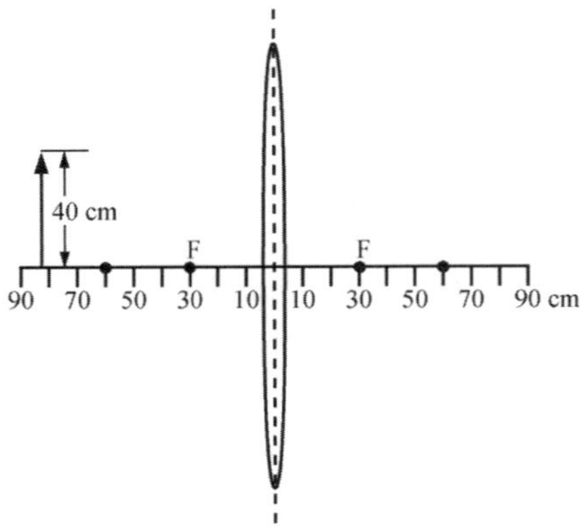

An object that is 40 cm tall is placed 85 cm to the left of a converging lens with a focal length of 30 cm.

19. The image formed by this lens will be

A. 30 cm to the right of the lens and it will be 40 cm in height

B. 47 cm to the right of the lens and it will be 22 cm in height

C. 85 cm to the right of the lens and it will be 78 cm in height

D. 98 cm to the right of the lens and it will be 95 cm in height

CHALLENGER QUESTION

Use the following information to answer the next question.

In a compound microscope, the image formed by the objective lens is 0.32 cm from the centre of the ocular lens.
The image is 13.5 cm from the centre of the ocular lens.

20. The focal length of the ocular lens is

A. 0.31 cm **B.** 0.32 cm

C. 3.05 cm **D.** 3.20 cm

Use the following information to answer the next question.

A compound microscope uses a 40X objective lens and a 15X ocular lens to produce an image of an object. The object is 0.065 cm in diameter.

21. The diameter of the image is

A. 3.58 cm **B.** 39.0 cm

C. 846 cm **D.** 9230 cm

CHALLENGER QUESTION

Use the following information to answer the next question.

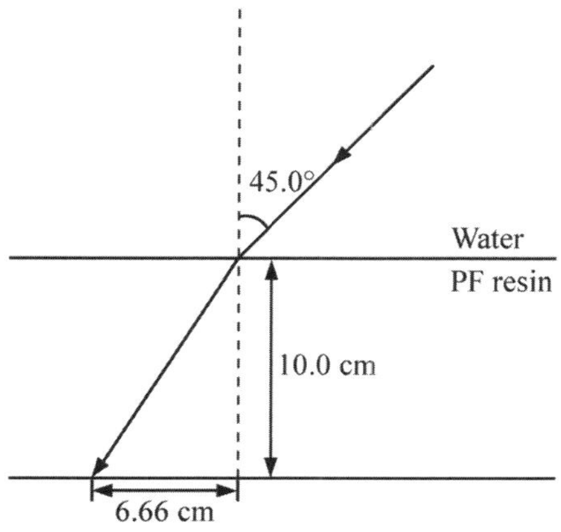

A ray of light passes from water into a 10.0 cm thick sheet of phenol formaldeyde (PF) resin at a 45.0° angle of incidence. The ray exits the PF resin 6.66 cm to the left of the point at which it entered.

22. What is the refractive index of PF resin?

A. 1.42 **B.** 1.50

C. 1.70 **D.** 2.00

Use the following information to answer the next question.

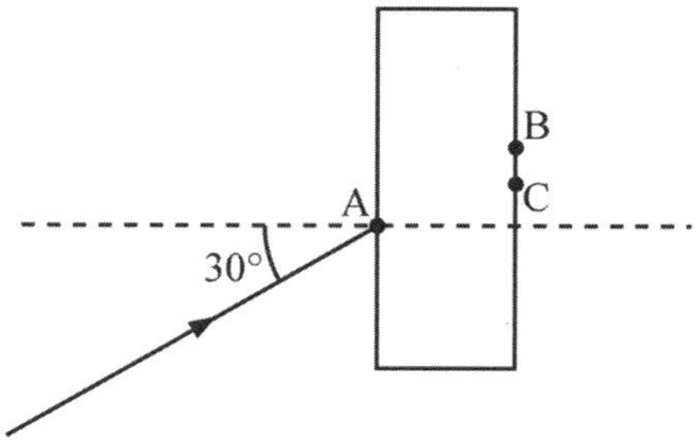

In the given diagram, a ray of light travelling through air strikes a thick piece of glass at point A. The angle of incidence of the ray is 30°.

23. The beam will exit the glass at point

A. B with an angle of less than 30° from the normal

B. C with an angle of less than 30° from the normal

C. B with an angle of 30° from the normal

D. C with an angle of 30° from the normal

24. Which of the following statements **best** defines a mirage?

A. A mirage is a real image caused by differences in the angles of reflection in air of different temperatures.

B. A mirage is a real image caused by differences in the angles of refraction in air of different temperatures.

C. A mirage is a virtual image caused by differences in the angles of reflection in air of different temperatures.

D. A mirage is a virtual image caused by differences in the angles of refraction in air of different temperatures.

Use the following information to answer the next question.

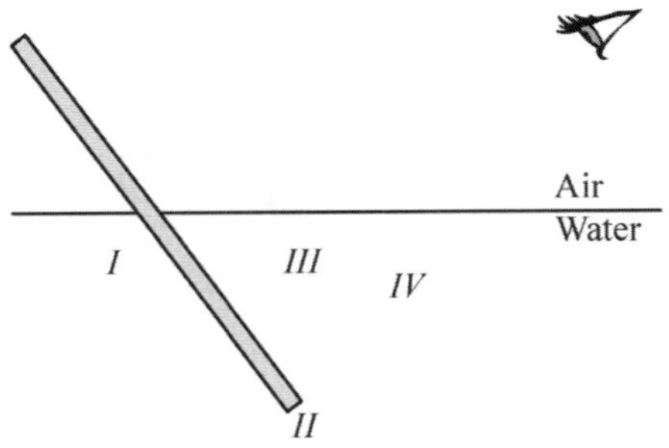

A stick is placed in water as shown in the diagram.

25. An observer on the right will see the bottom of the stick closest to position

A. *I*
B. *II*
C. *III*
D. *IV*

ANSWERS AND SOLUTIONS – UNIT TEST

1. C	6. C	11. A	16. D	21. B
2. OR	7. A	12. OR	17. C	22. C
3. A	8. OR	13. OR	18. OR	23. D
4. OR	9. OR	14. D	19. B	24. D
5. D	10. A	15. OR	20. A	25. C

1. C

Ted suffers from myopia or short-sightedness. Concave lenses are used to correct this disorder. In short-sightedness, rays converge before they reach the retina. Therefore, a concave lens of appropriate focal length is used to make the rays spread out enough to converge at the retina.

2. OR

Infrared radiation is the electromagnetic radiation associated with heat. A thermal imaging device images the infrared radiation that an object emits.

3. A

Optical telescopes refract visible light through a series of lenses or reflect light through several mirrors. All optical telescopes use energy from the visible light portion of the electromagnetic radiation spectrum.

4. OR

There are many advantages to the increasing number of cameras in public. They contribute to security, policing, education, culture, and entertainment.

One of the major concerns with the increasing number of cameras is the loss of privacy. It is very hard to control what people are taking pictures of and where those pictures end up.

5. D

Using a ray diagram, the ray that passes through the tip of the "A" and the centre of curvature, and the ray that starts at the tip of the "A", travels through the focal point, and reflects off the mirror on a path parallel to the principal axis, intercept each other at position IV on the diagram.

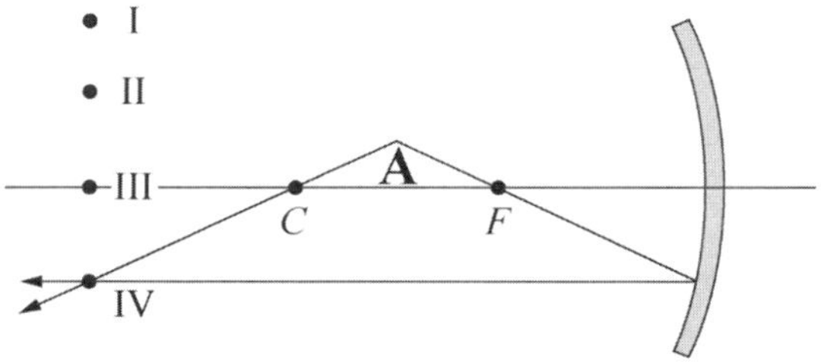

6. C

This situation will create an upright virtual image to the left of the object.

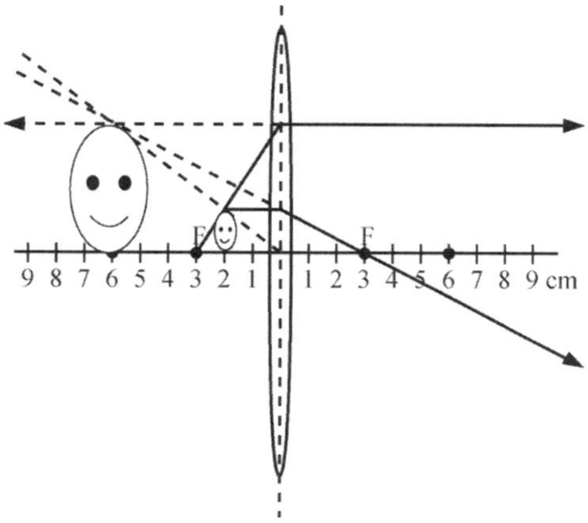

7. A

When light rays strike the surface of a convex lens, they are refracted inward and intersect at a focal point. The rays continue to travel past the focal point to produce an inverted image. If the image produced is the same size as the object, then the image must be the same distance from the lens as the object is from the lens. The focal point must therefore be one-half the total distance, or 30 cm divided by 2.

This situation can be illustrated using a ray diagram.

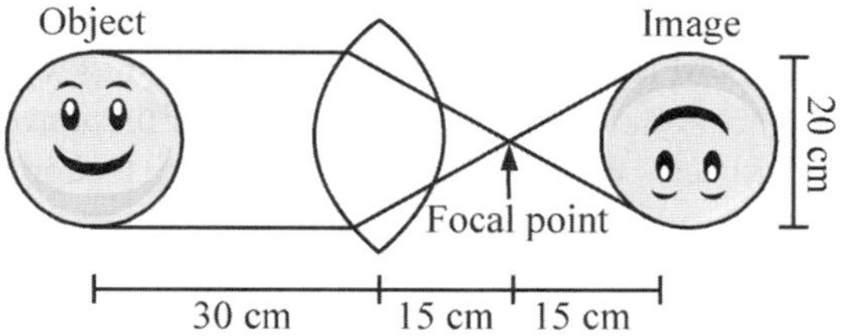

8. OR

The image appears inverted approximately 4.2 cm to the right of the lens.

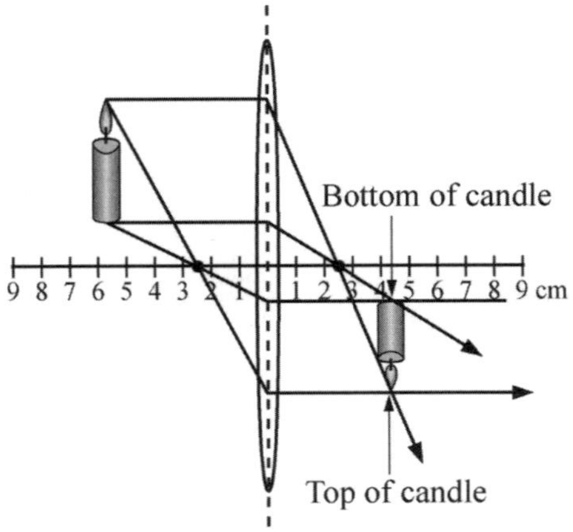

9. OR

The original light bulb is upright, smaller than the virtual image, and located approximately 2.5 cm to the left of the lens.

To an observer on the right side of the lens in the given diagram, the ray represented by the topmost arrow would appear to be coming straight from the top of the bulb, as shown by the topmost, horizontal dotted line. The actual ray is represented by the diagonal solid line angling upward and to the right that passes through the focal point 3.5 cm to the left of the lens. This ray is deflected at its point of intersection with the lens to become the topmost arrow.

Another line is drawn from the other focal point, 3.5 cm to the right of the lens, to the top of the virtual image of the bulb, as represented by the middle dotted line angling downward and to the right. From the point of the intersection of this line with the lens, a short, solid horizontal line representing a second ray is drawn to the left until it intersects the first ray. The point of intersection of these two rays indicates the actual source of the rays: the top of the original bulb. This point is located approximately 2.5 cm to the left of the lens.

The lowermost dotted line, starting at the top of the virtual image and passing through the point of intersection of the principal axis and the lens, also intersects the top of the original light bulb.

The image and the actual bulb are in the same orientation because the bulb is between the focal point and the lens.

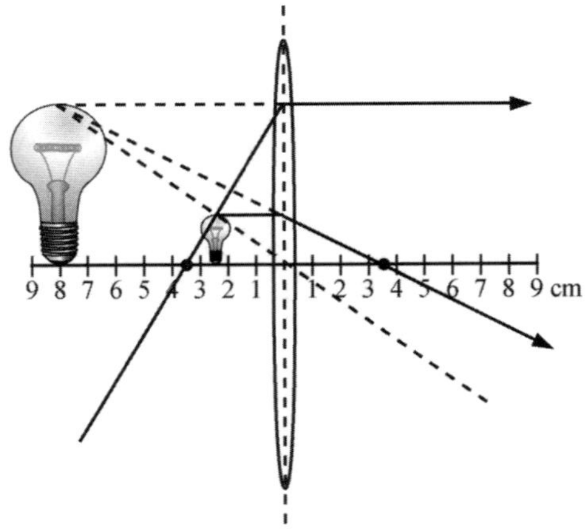

10. A

Using Snell's law and the velocity ratio, the angle of refraction for benzene can be calculated.

$$\frac{\sin \theta_i}{\sin \theta_r} = \frac{v_i}{v_r}$$

$$\sin \theta_r = \sin \theta_i \times \frac{v_r}{v_i}$$

$$\sin \theta_r = \sin 25.0° \times \frac{2.00 \times 10^8 \text{ m/s}}{2.21 \times 10^8 \text{ m/s}}$$

$$\sin \theta_r = 0.3824$$

$$\theta_r = \sin^{-1} 0.3824$$

$$\theta_r = 22.5°$$

11. A

Using Snell's law,
$n_{\text{m}} \times \sin \theta_{\text{m}} = n_{\text{a}} \times \sin \theta_{\text{a}}$.

The index of refraction of air is 1.00.

$$n_{\text{m}}nm = \frac{1.00 \times \sin \theta_{\text{a}}}{\sin \theta_{\text{m}}}$$

$$= \frac{1.00 \times \sin 26.20°}{\sin 15.45°}$$

$$= 1.657$$

Any medium with a refractive index greater than 1.00 will decrease the velocity of light.

12. OR

The indexes of refraction for both water and air are known. The angle of incidence for the flashlight beam is given. Use Snell's law to calculate the angle of refraction as the light passes from the water into the air.

$$n_{water} \times \sin\theta_{water} = n_{air} \times \sin\theta_{air}$$

$$\sin\theta_{air} = \frac{n_{water} \times \sin\theta_{water}}{n_{air}}$$

$$= \frac{1.33 \times \sin 24.0°}{1.00}$$

$$= 0.540\ 96$$

$$\theta_{air} = 32.7°$$

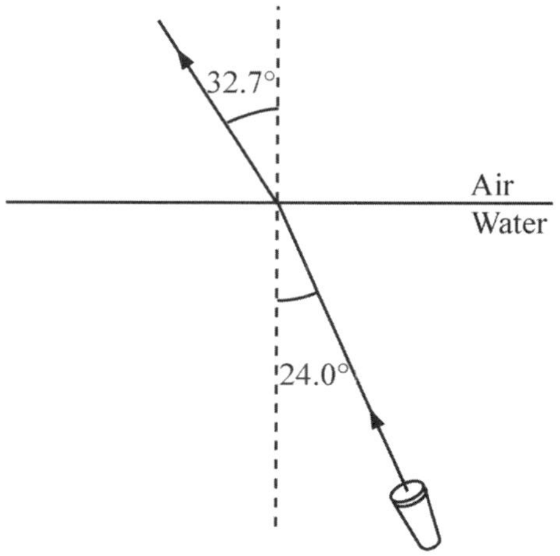

13. OR

Step 1
Calculate the sine of the angle of refraction in the fluorite.

$$n_{air} \times \sin\theta_{air} = n_f \times \sin\theta_f$$

$$\sin\theta_f = \frac{n_{air} \times \sin\theta_{air}}{n_f}$$

$$= \frac{1.00 \times \sin 30.0°}{1.43}$$

$$= 0.349\ 65$$

Step 2
Calculate the velocity of light in beryl v_b using the equation $\frac{v_b}{v_f} = \frac{\sin\theta_b}{\sin\theta_f}$.

$$v_b = \frac{v_f \times \sin\theta_b}{\sin\theta_f}$$

$$= \frac{(2.10 \times 10^8 \text{ m/s}) \times (\sin 18.5°)}{0.349\ 65}$$

$$= 1.91 \times 10^8 \text{ m/s}$$

14. D

In terms of the decreasing frequencies of the waves, the order of the electromagnetic spectrum is shown in the given table.

Gamma Rays	X-Ray Radiation	Ultraviolet Radiation	Visible Light	Infrared Radiation	Microwave Radiation	Radio Waves
	I	II	III	IV	V	

Therefore, the position of infrared radiation is labelled IV.

15. OR

The colours of the visible light spectrum, listed in order from longest wavelength to shortest wavelength, are red, orange, yellow, green, blue, indigo, and violet. An easy way to remember the order of the colours is to remember the name ROY G. BIV, with each letter representing the first letter of each of the colours.

16. D

The object distance is 19.5 cm, the object height is 5.50 cm, and the focal length of the mirror is 15.0 cm.

Step 1

Use the mirror equation $\frac{1}{f} = \frac{1}{d_o} + \frac{1}{d_i}$ to calculate the image distance.

$$\frac{1}{d_i} = \frac{1}{f} - \frac{1}{d_o}$$

$$= \frac{1}{15.0} - \frac{1}{19.5} = 0.015\ 38$$

$$d_i = \frac{1}{0.015\ 38} = 65.0 \text{ cm}$$

Step 2

Use the magnification formula $M = \frac{h_i}{h_o} = -\frac{d_i}{d_o}$ to calculate the object height.

$$h_i = -\frac{d_i}{d_o} \times h_o$$

$$= -\frac{65.0}{19.5} \times 5.50 \text{ cm}$$

$$= -18.3 \text{ cm}$$

The negative value for the image height means that the image is inverted.

17. C

Total internal reflection is possible only when light is travelling from a medium with higher optical density (a higher refractive index) to a medium with lower optical density (a lower refractive index). Crown glass has a higher refractive index than vegetable oil, so this situation can result in total internal reflection.

18. OR

According to Snell's law, $n_z \times \sin\theta_z = n_a \times \sin\theta_a$, where *z* represents cubic zirconia and *a* represents acetone.

At the critical angle for cubic zirconia, θ_z, the angle of refraction of acetone, θ_a, would be 90.0°.

$$\begin{aligned}\sin\theta_z &= \frac{n_a \times \sin 90.0°}{n_z}\\ &= \frac{n_a \times 1.00}{n_z}\\ &= \frac{n_a}{n_z}\\ &= \frac{1.360}{2.192}\\ &= 0.6204\end{aligned}$$

The critical angle of cubic zirconia is $\theta_z = 38.3°$.

19. B

To calculate the distance from the lens at which the image will be formed, draw a ray diagram. First, draw a straight line from the top of the object to the lens. According to the rules of refraction, this light ray will be refracted through the lens and travel through the focal point. Another line can be drawn from the top of the object directly through the centre of the lens and continue in the same direction. A third line can be drawn from the top of the object and through the focal point. When this final line enters the lens, it is refracted and travels parallel to the main horizontal axis. These three lines should all intersect at the same point, which represents the point at which the image will form.

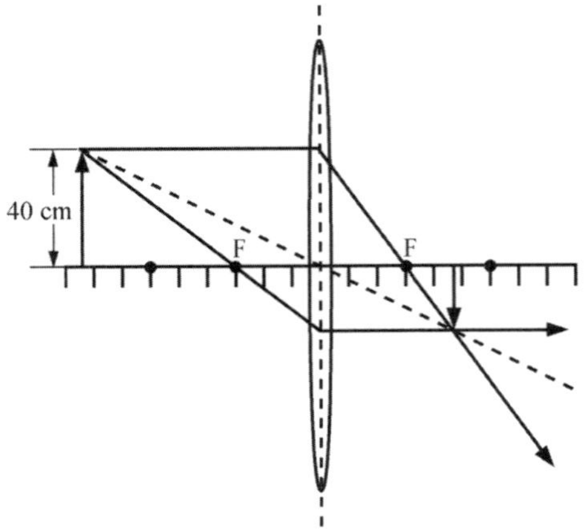

An inverted image that is 22 cm in height appears 47 cm to the right of the lens.

20. A

In a compound microscope, the image from the objective lens acts as the object for the ocular lens, so the object distance of the ocular lens is 0.32 cm.

Calculate the focal length using the thin lens formula $\frac{1}{f} = \frac{1}{d_o} + \frac{1}{d_i}$.

$$\begin{aligned}\frac{1}{f} &= \frac{1}{d_o} + \frac{1}{d_i}\\ &= \frac{1}{0.32 \text{ cm}} + \frac{1}{13.5 \text{ cm}} = 3.199\\ f &= \frac{1}{3.199} = 0.31 \text{ cm}\end{aligned}$$

21. B

The total magnification is $40 \times 15 = 600X$.

Use the given magnification formula.

$$M = \frac{h_i}{h_o}$$

$$h_i = M \times h_o$$
$$= 600 \times 0.065 \text{ cm}$$
$$= 39.0 \text{ cm}$$

22. C

Snell's law is used to calculate the refractive index of PF resin. This law requires that the refracted angle of the medium, in this case PF resin, be known. The refracted angle is between the normal and the ray of light passing through the PF resin, and it can be determined using basic trigonometry and the information given.

$$\tan\theta = \frac{\text{side opposite}}{\text{side adjacent}}$$
$$\tan\theta = \frac{6.66 \text{ cm}}{10.0 \text{ cm}}$$
$$\tan\theta = 0.666$$
$$\theta = \tan^{-1} 0.666$$
$$\theta = 33.66°$$

The refractive index can then be calculated according to Snell's law.

$$n_{PF}\sin\theta_{PF} = n_w \sin\theta_w$$
$$n_{PF} = \frac{n_w \times \sin\theta_w}{\sin\theta_{PF}}$$
$$= \frac{1.333 \times \sin 45.0°}{\sin 33.66°} = 1.70$$

23. D

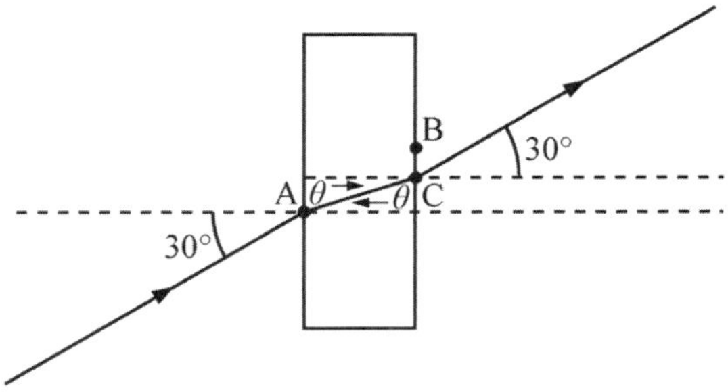

According to Snell's law, the light's velocity will decrease as it passes from air into glass, and the ray will refract toward the normal with an angle of refraction equal to θ_{glass}.

$$\sin\theta_{air} \times n_{air} = \sin\theta_{glass} \times n_{glass}$$

where $\theta_{glass} = 30°$

If the light ray had not refracted, it would have pass straight through the glass to strike point B. Since the ray refracted toward the normal, the light ray will reach the opposite side of the glass at a point lower than point B. Therefore, the light ray would exit the glass at point C.

When the light ray passes from the glass into air at point C, the angle of incidence will be equal to θ_{glass}, so Snell's law states that the angle of refraction into the air must be θ_{air}, or 30°.

24. D

A mirage is a virtual image. Layers of air masses of different temperatures refract light rays at different angles, creating the virtual image in the air.
The diagram illustrates how the differences in the temperatures in the different air layers bend the light rays, causing the formation of a virtual image in the sky.

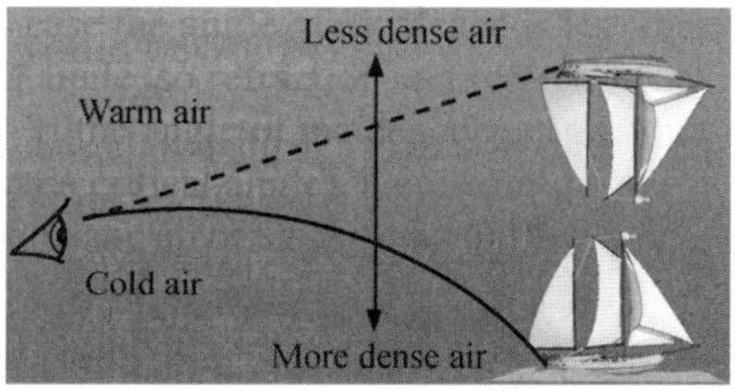

25. C

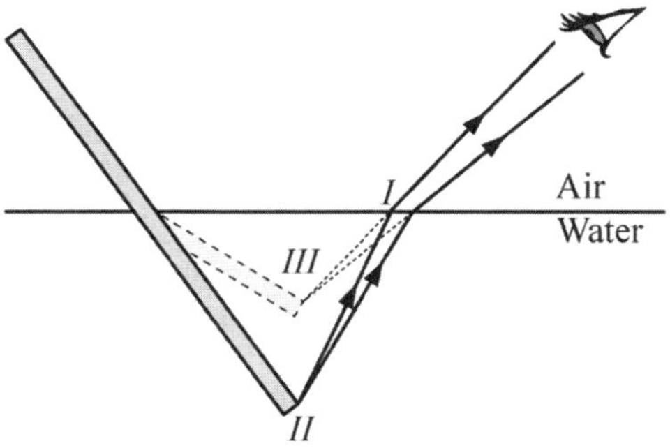

Because light travels more slowly through water than it does through air, the light ray bends away from the normal as it crosses the boundary between the water and the air and travels toward the observer. The human brain assumes that the ray is completely straight. In this case, since the observer's brain assumes that the ray coming from the boundary point (where it is bent away from the normal) is actually straight, the observer sees the light ray originating at point *III*. The diagram shows how refraction would cause the rays coming from the bottom of the stick to appear to originate at position *III*.

NOTES

KEY Strategies for Success on Tests

KEY STRATEGIES FOR SUCCESS ON TESTS

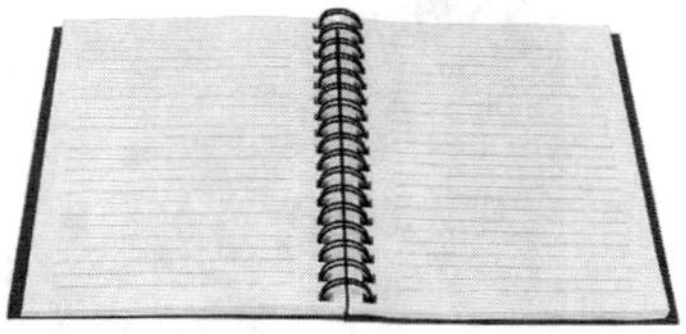

TEST PREPARATION AND TEST-TAKING SKILLS

Things to Consider When Taking a Test

- It is normal to feel anxious before you write a test. You can manage this anxiety by:
  - thinking positive thoughts. Visual imagery is a helpful technique to try.
  - making a conscious effort to relax by taking several slow, controlled, deep breaths. Concentrate on the air going in and out of your body.
- Before you begin the test, ask questions if you are unsure of anything.
- Jot down key words or phrases from any oral directions.
- Look over the entire test to assess the number and kinds of questions on the test.
- Read each question closely and reread if necessary.
- Pay close attention to key vocabulary words. Sometimes these are bolded or italicized, and they are usually important words in the question.
- Mark your answers on your answer sheet carefully. If you wish to change an answer, erase the mark completely and then ensure your final answer is darker than the one you have erased.
- On the test booklet, use highlighting to note directions, key words, and vocabulary that you find confusing or that are important to answering the question.
- Double-check to make sure you have answered everything before handing in your test.

When taking tests, the easy words are often overlooked. Failure to pay close attention to these words can result in an incorrect answer. One way to avoid this is to be aware of these words and to underline, circle, or highlight these words while you are taking the test.

Even though some words are easy to understand, they can change the meaning of the entire question, so it is important that you pay attention to them. Here are some examples.

all	**always**	**most likely**	**probably**	**best**	**not**
difference	**usually**	**except**	**most**	**unlikely**	**likely**

Example

1. Which of the following items is **not** considered abiotic?

A. wind
B. bacteria
C. sunlight
D. precipitation

Helpful Strategies for Answering Multiple-Choice Questions

A multiple-choice question provides some information for you to consider and then asks you to select a response from four choices. Each question has one correct answer. The other answers are distractors, which are incorrect.

Below are some strategies to help you when answering multiple-choice questions.

- Quickly skim through the entire test. Find out how many questions there are and plan your time accordingly.
- Read and reread questions carefully. Underline key words and try to think of an answer before looking at the choices.
- If there is a graphic, look at the graphic, read the question, and go back to the graphic. Then, you may want to underline the important information from the question.
- Carefully read the choices. Read the question first and then each answer that goes with it.
- When choosing an answer, try to eliminate those choices that are clearly wrong or do not make sense.
- Some questions may ask you to select the best answer. These questions will always include words like best, most appropriate, or most likely. All of the answers will be correct to some degree, but one of the choices will be better than the others in some way. Carefully read all four choices before choosing the answer you think is the best.
- If you do not know the answer or if the question does not make sense to you, it is better to guess than to leave it blank.
- Do not spend too much time on any one question. Make a mark (*) beside a difficult question and come back to it. If you are leaving a question to come back to later, make sure you also leave the space on the answer sheet.
- Remember to go back to the difficult questions at the end of the test; sometimes clues are given throughout the test that will provide you with answers.
- Note any negative words like no or not and be sure your choice fits the question.
- Before changing an answer, be sure you have a very good reason to do so.
- Do not look for patterns on your answer sheet.

Helpful Strategies for Answering Open-Response Questions

A written response requires you to respond to a question or directive such as **explain**, **predict**, **list**, **describe**, **show your work**, **solve**, or **calculate.** In preparing for open-response tasks you may wish to:

- Read and reread the question carefully.
- Recognize and pay close attention to directing words such as explain, show your work, and describe.
- Underline key words and phrases that indicate what is required in your answer, such as explain, estimate, answer, calculate, or show your work.
- Write down rough, point-form notes regarding the information you want to include in your answer.
- Think about what you want to say and organize information and ideas in a coherent and concise manner within the time limit you have for the question.
- Be sure to answer every part of the question that is asked.
- Include as much information as you can when you are asked to explain your thinking.
- Include a picture or diagram if it will help to explain your thinking.
- Try to put your final answer to a problem in a complete sentence to be sure it is reasonable.
- Reread your response to ensure you have answered the question.
- Think: does your answer make sense
- Listen: does it sound right?
- Use appropriate subject vocabulary and terms in your response.

About Science Tests

What You Need to Know about Science Tests

To do well on a science test, you need to understand and apply your knowledge of scientific concepts. Reading skills can also make a difference in how well you perform. Reading skills can help you follow instructions and find key words, as well as read graphs, diagrams, and tables. Math skills are also important to success on science exams. Formulas are often used to solve scientific problems. Practicing with formulas is the best way to become good at them. They can also help you solve science problems.

Science tests usually have two types of questions: questions that ask for understanding of scientific concepts and questions that test how well you can solve scientific problems.

How You Can Prepare for the Science Test

Below are some strategies that are particular to preparing for and writing science tests.

- Know how to use your calculator and, if it is allowed, use your own for the test.
- Note-taking is a good way to review and study important information from your class notes and textbook.
- Sketch a picture of the problem, procedure, or term. Drawing is helpful for learning and remembering concepts.
- Check your answer to practice questions that require formulas by working backward to the beginning. You can find the beginning by going step-by-step in reverse order.
- When answering questions with graphics (pictures, diagrams, tables, or graphs), read the test question carefully.
- Read the title of the graphic and any key words.
- Read the test question carefully to figure out what information you need to find in the graphic.
- Go back to the graphic to find the information you need.
- Always pay close attention when pressing the keys on your calculator. Repeat the procedure a second time to be sure you pressed the correct keys.

TEST PREPARATION COUNTDOWN

There is little doubt that if you develop a plan for studying and test preparation, you *will* perform well on tests.

Below is a general plan to follow seven days before you write a test.

Countdown 7 Days before the Test

1. Use "Finding Out About the Test" to help you make your own personal test preparation plan.
2. Review the following information:
   - areas to be included on the test
   - types of test items
   - general and specific test tips
3. Start preparing for the test at least 7 days before the test. Develop your test preparation plan and set time aside to prepare and study.

Countdown: 6, 5, 4, 3, 2 Days before the Test

1. Review old homework assignments, quizzes, and tests.
2. Rework problems on quizzes and tests to make sure you still know how to solve them.
3. Correct any errors made on quizzes and tests.
4. Review key concepts, processes, formulas, and vocabulary.
5. Create practice test questions for yourself and then answer them. Work out many sample problems.

Countdown: The Night before the Test

1. The night before the test is for final preparation, which includes reviewing and gathering material needed for the test before going to bed.
2. Most important is getting a good night's rest and knowing you have done everything possible to do well on the test.

Test Day

1. Eat a healthy and nutritious breakfast.
2. Ensure you have all the necessary materials.
3. Think positive thoughts: "I can do this." "I am ready." "I know I can do well."
4. Arrive at your school early so you are not rushing, which can cause you anxiety and stress.

Summary of How to be Successful During the Test

The following are some strategies you may find useful for writing your test.

- Take two or three deep breaths to help you relax.
- Read the directions carefully and underline, circle, or highlight any important words.
- Survey the entire test to understand what you will need to do.
- Budget your time.
- Begin with an easy question or a question you know you can answer correctly rather than following the numerical question order of the test.
- If you cannot remember how to answer a question, try repeating the deep breathing and physical relaxation activities first. Then, move to visualization and positive self-talk to get you going.
- Write down anything you remember about the subject on the reverse side of your test paper. This activity sometimes helps you to remind yourself that you do know something and you are capable of writing the test.
- Look over your test when you have finished and double-check your answers to be sure you did not forget anything.

NOTES

Practice Tests

PRACTICE TEST 1

1. CAT scans are often more useful than standard X-rays because they
   A. visualize all body tissues and not just bones
   B. provide axial images of the body tissues
   C. are less expensive
   D. are less invasive

2. What disease was virtually eliminated following the development of a vaccine by Jonas Salk in the 1950s?
   A. AIDS
   B. Polio
   C. Measles
   D. Meningitis

Use the following information to answer the next question.

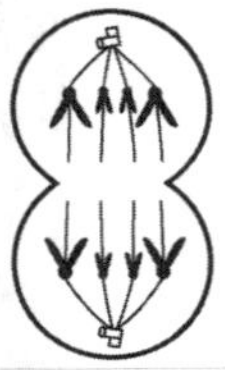

Unknown phase of mitosis

3. Which stage of the mitotic cell cycle is illustrated in the given diagram?
   A. Prophase
   B. Anaphase
   C. Telophase
   D. Metaphase

Open Response

4. Sketch an animal cell, and label the following organelles: nucleus, cytoplasm, vacuole, mitochondria, and cell membrane.

____

____

Use the following information to answer the next question.

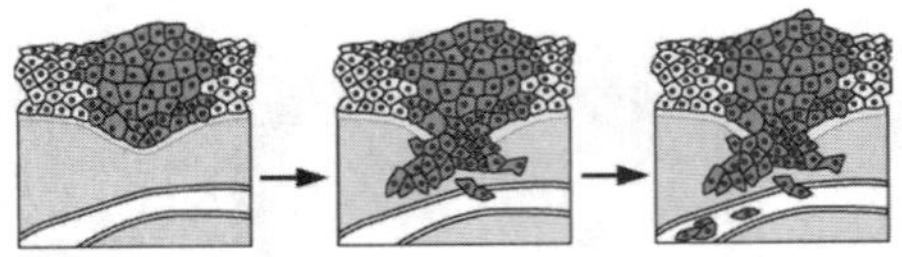

Cross-section of a skin sample

5. What characteristic of cancer cells is illustrated in the given diagram?
   A. Anaplasia
   B. Metastasis
   C. Hyperplasia
   D. Vascularization

Use the following information to answer the next question.

Wheat rust is a disease that affects plants in the wheat and rye family.
Large epidemics of the disease can spread quickly and have a huge economic impact. Field crop plant pathologists in the Ontario Government's Ministry of Agriculture, Food, and Rural Affairs monitor crops closely to detect and treat wheat rust before it can spread.

6. Wheat rust is a plant disease caused by a
   A. virus
   B. protist
   C. fungus
   D. bacteria

State TEST

Use the following information to answer the next question.

The liver has the capability of repairing and regenerating tissue after an injury.

7. The regeneration of new tissue by the liver is made possible by the process of
   A. Mitosis
   B. Meiosis
   C. Dialysis
   D. Homeostasis

8. The scientific term used to describe the process of development from a single unspecialized cell to multiple specialized cells is
   A. differentiation
   B. fractionation
   C. meiosis
   D. growth

Use the following information to answer the next question.

The heart has a natural pacemaker that sends out electrical signals, maintaining the heartbeat. Together, muscle cells and nerve cells form the ___*i*___ that make up the heart, which is ___*ii*___ of the circulatory system.

9. Which of the following charts correctly completes the given statement?

A.

i	*ii*
cells	a tissue

B.

i	*ii*
cells	an organ

C.

i	*ii*
tissues	an organ

D.

i	*ii*
organs	a tissue

10. Which two systems work together to ensure that all the body's cells receive nutrients?
   A. Circulatory system and respiratory system
   B. Respiratory system and excretory system
   C. Circulatory system and digestive system
   D. Digestive system and excretory system

11. Who is responsible for the policies related to the disposal of hazardous substances in Canada?
   A. Government agencies
   B. Small businesses
   C. The police
   D. The public

12. Baking soda is added to vinegar in a glass container. A solid sodium acetate compound settles to the bottom, fizzing carbon dioxide gas appears in the solution, and water is formed. The number of reactants and the number of products in this reaction are
   A. two reactants and three products
   B. three reactants and two products
   C. one reactant and four products
   D. four reactants and one product

Use the following information to answer the next multipart question.

13.

For the following reaction: $2HCl + Sr(OH)_2 \rightarrow ?$

Open Response

a) Predict the products

____

____

b) Complete the balanced equation

____

____

c) Classify the type of reaction

____

____

Use the following information to answer the next question.

A student made the following observations:

- **Observation 1** An egg white changed from clear to white as it was fried.
- **Observation 2** A piece of wet steel wool turned a reddish colour when exposed to air.
- **Observation 3** Some salt dissolved quickly when it was stirred in water.
- **Observation 4** A candle flame gave off heat.

14. All of the above described chemical reactions, **except** for which observation?

A. Observation 1

B. Observation 2

C. Observation 3

D. Observation 4

CHALLENGER QUESTION

Use the following information to answer the next question.

For an assignment, Aden named three molecular compounds from the chemical formulas that were given to her.

Compound	Formula (Given)	Name (Answer)
1	NF_3	nitrogen trifluoride
2	N_2O	dinitrogen dioxide
3	CCl_4	carbon tetra-chloride

15. Which of the compounds did Aden name **correctly**?

A. 1 and 2

B. 1 and 3

C. 2 and 3

D. 1, 2, and 3

Use the following information to answer the next question.

Two important components of insecticides are copper(II) nitrate and copper(II) sulfate. To test for the presence of copper(II) ions in a solution of insecticide, sodium hydroxide is added. When sodium hydroxide$_{(aq)}$ reacts with copper(II) nitrate$_{(aq)}$, the products are sodium nitrate$_{(aq)}$ and copper(II) hydroxide$_{(s)}$.

16. Based on the given information, which of the following indicators is evidence that a chemical reaction has occurred?

A. Appearance of a precipitate

B. Increase in the pH of the solution

C. Decrease in the pH of the solution

D. Ability of the resulting solution to conduct electricity

Use the following information to answer the next question.

The standard form of a balanced equation must contain the smallest whole number of coefficients.

17. The standard balanced equation for the burning of aluminum in the presence of oxygen is represented by

A. $2Al_{(s)} + O_{2(g)} \rightarrow Al_2O_{3(s)}$

B. $4Al_{(s)} + 3O_{2(g)} \rightarrow 2Al_2O_{3(s)}$

C. $2Al_{(s)} + 1.5O_{2(g)} \rightarrow Al_2O_{3(s)}$

D. $4Al_{(s)} + 1.5O_{2(g)} \rightarrow 2Al_2O_{3(s)}$

Use the following information to answer the next question.

__________$NaN_{3(s)} \rightarrow$__________$Na_{(s)}$ +
__________$N_{2(g)}$

The given equation is the unbalanced chemical reaction for sodium azide decomposing into sodium and nitrogen.

Open Response

18. Balance the given chemical equation using the lowest whole number coefficients.

____

____

19. Which of the following reactions is an example of an acid-base neutralization reaction?

A. $NaOH_{(aq)} + HCl_{(aq)}$
$\rightarrow NaCl_{(aq)} + H_2O_{(aq)}$

B. $Zn_{(s)} + 2HCl_{(aq)} \rightarrow ZnCl_{2(aq)} + H_{2(g)}$

C. $NH_4OH_{(aq)} \rightarrow NH_{3(g)} + H_2O_{(l)}$

D. $H_2CO_{3(aq)} \rightarrow CO_2 + H_2O_{(l)}$

Use the following information to answer the next question.

A calcium ion has a charge of 2+. It readily combines with oxygen to form an ionic compound. An oxygen ion has a charge of 2–.
$Ca^{2+}O^{2-}$

20. Which of the following rows gives the formula and IUPAC name for the compound formed by calcium and oxygen?

A.

Chemical formula	IUPAC Name
CaO	calcium oxide

B.

Chemical formula	IUPAC Name
CaO	calcium monoxide

C.

Chemical formula	IUPAC Name
Ca_2O_2	calcium oxide

D.

Chemical formula	IUPAC Name
Ca_2O_2	calcium dioxide

21. The abbreviation IPCC stands for

A. International Panel on Climate Change

B. Intergovernmental Panel on Climate Change

C. International Program for Climate Cooperation

D. Intergovernmental Program for Climate Cooperation

22. Which of the following statements regarding the relationship between global sea rise and anthropogenic climate change is **true**?

A. The global sea level is lower than it ever has been in the past.

B. The rate of global sea rise has doubled in the last decade alone.

C. The global sea level is higher now than it has ever been in the past.

D. The rate of global sea rise has dropped by half over the last decade alone.

Use the following information to answer the next question.

A small container filled with 70°C water is kept inside a larger container filled with water at 20°C.

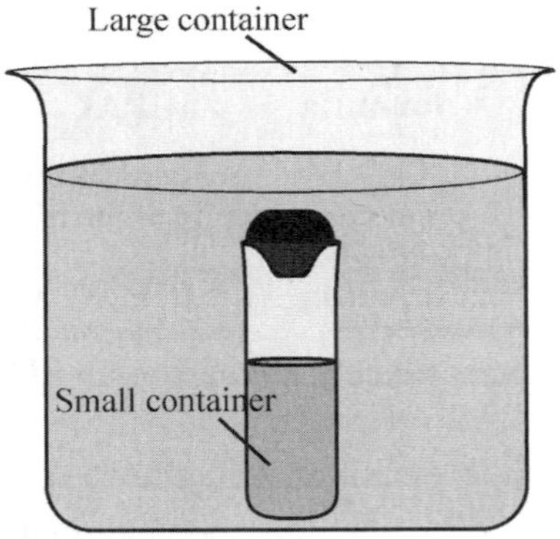

23. After some time, the temperature of the water in the large container has increased to 23°C. The temperature in the large container increased because heat transferred from the water in the small container to the water in the large container by

A. radiation through the glass and convection in the water

B. conduction through the glass and convection in the water

C. convection through the glass and conduction in the water

D. conduction through the glass and radiation in the water

24. If polar ice coverage decreases due to increasing global temperatures associated with climate change, then Earth's albedo will

A. increase

B. decrease

C. be unaffected

D. decrease and then increase

CHALLENGER QUESTION

25. Which of the following statements about the current in the North Atlantic Ocean is **true**?

A. It increases the average annual temperature of the Arctic.

B. It decreases the average annual temperature of the Arctic.

C. It transports cold water from the equator to the North Pole.

D. It transports warm water from the North Pole to the equator.

Use the following information to answer the next question.

A politician gives the following speech: "Climate change is real. Our crops are dying; the rains do not come. The days are hotter, and water is hard to find. Science has provided the evidence. Now it is time for the countries who are creating the problem to do something about it. Our people are powerless and paying for environmental crimes they did not commit."

26. This politician is **most likely** from

A. North America

B. Australia

C. Europe

D. Africa

27. Which of the following sources of energy does not power the thermal energy transfers that shape Earth's climate?

A. Residual thermal energy from Earth's formation

B. Sunlight radiated and absorbed

C. Energy from radioactive decay

D. The burning of fossil fuels

28. Periodically, the coast of British Columbia experiences a year of unusually mild weather. Which of the following natural phenomena is **most likely** responsible for the occurrence of this weather condition?

A. Coriolis Effect

B. Tornado

C. La Niña

D. El Niño

CHALLENGER QUESTION

29. Which of the following statements **best** describes the relative affects of methane and carbon dioxide on climate change?

A. Methane traps more heat per molecule than carbon dioxide, but carbon dioxide is more abundant in the atmosphere.

B. Methane traps less heat per molecule than carbon dioxide, but carbon dioxide is more abundant in the atmosphere.

C. Methane traps more heat per molecule than carbon dioxide, and is more abundant in the atmosphere.

D. Methane traps less heat per molecule than carbon dioxide, and is more abundant in the atmosphere.

30. The weather condition in which cool air is trapped near the ground by warmer air above is called a

A. heat island, which promotes the formation of smog

B. heat island, which promotes the formation of El Niño

C. temperature inversion, which promotes the formation of smog

D. temperature inversion, which promotes the formation of El Niño

31. Contact lenses correct the wearer's vision by focusing the light on the

A. cornea

B. retina

C. pupil

D. lens

32. In extremely hot and dry desert regions, people sometimes see illusions such as water appearing in the middle of the desert. Such illusions are known as

A. garua

B. aurora

C. mirages

D. jet streams

CHALLENGER QUESTION

Use the following information to answer the next question.

A driver notices an image of a stop sign in the convex side mirror of her truck.

33. This image is

A. real, and the sign is actually closer than it appears in the mirror

B. virtual, and the sign is actually closer than it appears in the mirror

C. real, and the sign is actually farther away than it appears in the mirror

D. virtual, and the sign is actually farther away than it appears in the mirror

Use the following information to answer the next question.

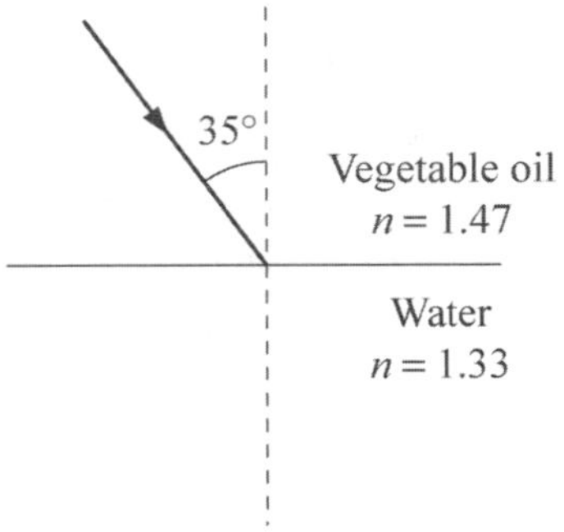

The refractive indexes, n, of vegetable oil and water are 1.47 and 1.33, respectively. A ray of light travels from vegetable oil into water at an angle of incidence of 35.0°.

34. What is the angle of refraction in water?

A. 31.3°

B. 35.0°

C. 38.7°

D. 39.3°

Use the following information to answer the next question.

An object 9.0 cm tall is placed 42.0 cm from a converging lens. An inverted image appears on the other side of the lens. This image is 31.5 cm from the lens.

35. What is the height of the image?

A. 6.8 cm

B. 8.3 cm

C. 9.0 cm

D. 12 cm

Use the following information to answer the next question.

The following information can be used to determine how light and sodium chloride interact.

- The speed of light in a vacuum is 3.00×10^8 m/s.
- The refractive index of sodium chloride is 1.52.

Open Response

36. What is the speed of light in sodium chloride?

____

____

____

____

____

37. Quartz-halogen light bulbs are installed in most automobile headlights and are also used in projectors and outdoor floodlights. Which of the following statements **best** explains why quartz-halogen bulbs, rather than normal incandescent bulbs, are used for these applications?

A. Quartz-halogen bulbs operate at much cooler temperatures than normal incandescent bulbs.

B. Quartz-halogen bulbs consume much less electrical energy than normal incandescent bulbs.

C. Quartz-halogen bulbs are considerably brighter and have longer lifespans than normal incandescent bulbs.

D. Quartz-halogen bulbs are cheaper to produce than normal incandescent bulbs, even though they have shorter lifespans.

State TEST

CHALLENGER QUESTION

Use the following information to answer the next question.

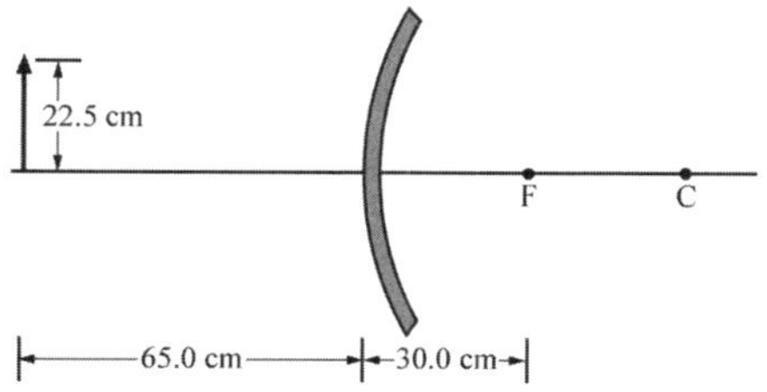

An object 22.5 cm high is placed 65.0 cm to the left of a mirror, as shown in the diagram.

38. The image produced by the mirror is

A. 7.11 cm high and 20.5 cm to the left of the mirror

B. 19.3 cm high and 55.7 cm to the left of the mirror

C. 7.11 cm high and 20.5 cm to the right of the mirror

D. 19.3 cm high and 55.7 cm to the right of the mirror

Use the following information to answer the next question.

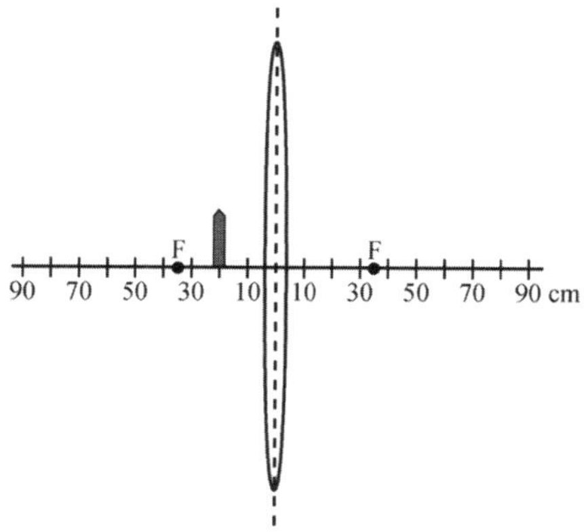

A 15 cm tall pencil is placed 20 cm from a converging lens that has a focal length of 35 cm.

39. The image formed by this lens will be on the

A. opposite side of the lens from the pencil and about 20 cm tall

B. opposite side of the lens from the pencil and about 35 cm tall

C. same side of the lens as the pencil and about 20 cm tall

D. same side of the lens as the pencil and about 35 cm tall

40. When sunlight hits a raindrop, the refraction of violet light is

A. less than red light, and violet appears at the top of a rainbow

B. greater than red light, and violet appears at the top of a rainbow

C. less than red light, and violet appears at the bottom of a rainbow

D. greater than red light, and violet appears at the bottom of a rainbow

State TEST

Practice Test 2

CHALLENGER QUESTION

1. Which of the following statements is **not** an ethical issue related to live organ transplants?
   A. The priority of recipients must be decided for transplant waiting lists.
   B. Someone needs to decide when to take donors off life support.
   C. Animal organs may be used as donor organs in some cases.
   D. The blood type of the organ donor and recipient must match.

Use the following information to answer the next question.

A plant stem was cut and stored in a red-coloured solution for approximately one hour. Afterward, a thin, transverse section was sliced from the plant stem and observed under a microscope.
Some tissues of the sliced section appeared red, while other tissues did not.

2. The tissue that appeared red under the microscope was
   A. cork
   B. xylem
   C. phloem
   D. meristem

Open Response

3. Sketch a cell in telophase as it would appear under a microscope, and describe the major events of the telophase stage of mitosis.

____

____

4. Which of the following cell organelles is present in plant cells but absent in animal cells?
   A. Cell wall
   B. Lysosome
   C. Mitochondrion
   D. Cell membrane

5. Bone marrow continuously produces new red blood cells. Red blood cells differ from bone marrow cells in that bone marrow cells
   A. lack a nucleus
   B. are differentiated
   C. lack mitochondria
   D. are undifferentiated

6. Aaron's Science 10 class is dissecting a worm to view its circulatory and digestive systems. Which system provides the circulatory and digestive systems with protection from the environment?
   A. Integumentary system
   B. Respiratory system
   C. Nervous system
   D. Immune system

CHALLENGER QUESTION

7. Which of the following processes is **not** a role of mitosis?
   A. Formation of sex cells
   B. Asexual reproduction
   C. Repair of tissues
   D. Growth of cells

State TEST

8. Which of the following specialized cell types **cannot** regenerate or be replaced?
   A. Skin cells
   B. Liver cells
   C. Nerve cells
   D. Blood cells

9. In plants, the epidermis provides protection from the outside environment. In vertebrates, this function is performed by the
   A. integumentary system.
   B. reproductive system.
   C. circulatory system.
   D. endocrine system.

10. When a person yawns, which two body systems interact?
   A. Nervous and digestive systems
   B. Nervous and respiratory systems
   C. Digestive and respiratory systems
   D. Circulatory and endocrine systems

CHALLENGER QUESTION

11. How do catalytic converters reduce automobile pollution?
   A. They reduce the amount of fuel required by the vehicle and reduce the amount of carbon dioxide produced.
   B. They convert carbon dioxide to carbon monoxide, reducing the amount of carbon dioxide released.
   C. They convert electrical energy to kinetic energy, reducing the amount of fuel required by a vehicle.
   D. They reduce toxic byproducts in exhaust by providing space for a series of chemical reactions.

Use the following information to answer the next question.

The dissociation of water is shown.
$2H_2O_{(l)} \rightarrow 2H_{2(g)} + O_{2(g)}$

Open Response

12. Sketch the molecular model that represents the given chemical equation.

____
____
____
____
____

Use the following information to answer the next question.

A chemistry teacher weighs and records the mass of several compounds, a container, and the container's lid. She places the chemicals inside the container and seals it. She then shakes the container and the chemicals react vigorously, producing a large volume of brown gas. After a few minutes, she weighs the sealed container.

13. The mass of the container after the reaction will be
   A. equal to the initial mass
   B. equal to the initial mass less the mass of the gas produced
   C. equal to the initial mass plus the mass of the gas produced
   D. equal to the initial mass plus the mass of any remaining gas

14. An aqueous solution with a pH of 0 is
   A. acidic
   B. neutral
   C. alkaline
   D. amphoteric

15. A chemical equation must be balanced in order to obey
   A. Coulomb's law
   B. Mendeleev's periodic law
   C. the law of conservation of mass
   D. the law of conservation of momentum

Use the following information to answer the next question.

Ammonia, NH_3, is dissolved in water and used as a common household cleaner. Ammonia can be produced in a synthesis reaction using hydrogen gas and nitrogen gas.

16. What is the balanced chemical equation for the synthesis of ammonia from hydrogen and nitrogen?
   A. $N_g + 3H_g \rightarrow NH_{3(g)}$
   B. $N_{2(g)} + H_{2(g)} \rightarrow NH_{3(g)}$
   C. $N_{2(g)} + 3H_{2(g)} \rightarrow 2NH_{3(g)}$
   D. $2N_{(g)} + 3H_{2(g)} \rightarrow 2NH_{3(g)}$

Use the following information to answer the next question.

__________ $Sn(NO_2)_4$ + __________
$K_3PO_4 \rightarrow$ __________ KNO_2 +
__________ $Sn_3(PO_4)_4$

Open Response

17. Using lowest whole number coefficients, balance the given equation.

____

____

18. The reaction $CH_3OOH_{(aq)} + KOH_{(aq)} \rightarrow CH_3COOK_{(aq)} + H_2O_{(aq)}$ can be classified as a
   A. synthesis reaction
   B. combustion reaction
   C. neutralization reaction
   D. single replacement reaction

19. Which of the following properties is characteristic of acids?
   A. Bitter taste
   B. Feels slippery
   C. pH greater than 7
   D. Turns blue litmus red

20. The formula for ammonium phosphate is
   A. $NH_4PO_{4(s)}$
   B. $(NH_4)_3PO_{4(s)}$
   C. $(NH_4)_3(PO_4)_{4(s)}$
   D. $NH_4(I)PO_4(III)_{(s)}$

21. Which of the following statements **best** describes the impact of rapid climate change on the polar bear species?
   A. Polar bears would be severely impacted by rapid climate change because they are adapted to a cold-weather habitat.
   B. Polar bears would be minimally impacted by rapid climate change because they are suited to a wide range of habitats.
   C. Polar bears would be severely impacted by rapid climate change because more people would start hunting them for food.
   D. Polar bears would be minimally impacted by rapid climate change because melting sea ice would increase their available habitat.

State TEST

22. Which of the following terms refers to the human influence on a natural process or material?

A. Anthropomorphic

B. Anthropocentric

C. Anthropogenic

D. Anthropologic

Use the following information to answer the next question.

> Climate change scientists do much of their work on computers, creating climate change models.

23. Climate change models are used for all of the following purposes **except**

A. predicting future climate scenarios

B. comparing past and present changes in climate

C. proving that climate change is caused by humans

D. predicting the consequences of increased temperatures

Use the following information to answer the next question.

> Parts of Ontario are located within the Hudson Plains ecozone.

24. Which of the following locations will **most likely** have climatic conditions similar to this ecozone?

A. Africa

B. Siberia

C. Australia

D. Antarctica

25. The seasonal nature of climates are **most affected** by Earth's

A. rotation

B. axial tilt

C. elliptical orbit

D. interior structure

26. The greater the greenhouse effect, the

A. lower the heat produced on Earth

B. greater the heat produced on Earth

C. lower the heat energy leaving Earth

D. greater the heat energy leaving Earth

CHALLENGER QUESTION

Use the following information to answer the next question.

> Over a ___*i*___ period of time, newly uplifted geographic features ___*ii*___ the amount of weathering and the release of atmospheric carbon dioxide, ___*iii*___ the global climate.

27. This statement is completed by the information in which of the following tables?

A.

i	*ii*	*iii*
short	increase	warming

B.

i	*ii*	*iii*
short	decrease	cooling

C.

i	*ii*	*iii*
long	increase	warming

D.

i	*ii*	*iii*
long	decrease	cooling

28. Increasing anthropogenic emissions in the atmosphere have amplified the natural greenhouse effect. Which of the following gases is the **greatest** contributor to the greenhouse effect?

A. Oxygen

B. Ammonia

C. Carbon dioxide

D. Nitrogen dioxide

Use the following information to answer the next question.

Ground level ozone is a major component of smog, which can cause major respiratory problems.

29. Ground level ozone is found in the
- **A.** thermosphere
- **B.** stratosphere
- **C.** mesosphere
- **D.** troposphere

30. Researchers can reasonably predict all of the following effects of climate change **except**
- **A.** a continued rise in average global temperatures
- **B.** a continued decline in polar sea ice levels
- **C.** the end of drought conditions in Australia
- **D.** the increasing intensity of severe storms

31. A film camera and the human eye have comparable structures. What structure of the human eye is comparable to the film in a camera?
- **A.** Cornea
- **B.** Retina
- **C.** Pupil
- **D.** Lens

Use the following information to answer the next question.

The reflection of light (and other forms of electromagnetic radiation) occurs when light waves encounter a surface or other boundary that does not absorb the energy of the radiation and that bounces the waves away from the surface.
The simplest example of visible light reflection is seen in the surface of a smooth pool of water upon which incident light is reflected in an orderly manner to produce a clear image of the scenery surrounding the pool. If a rock is thrown into the pool, the water is perturbed to form waves, which disrupt the reflection by scattering the reflected light rays in all directions.

32. The wave that is bounced back or away from the surface is referred to as the
- **A.** back wave
- **B.** reflected wave
- **C.** refracted wave
- **D.** bouncing wave

CHALLENGER QUESTION

Use the following information to answer the next question.

An object is placed 40.0 cm from a curved mirror. The image appears to be 16.1 cm behind the mirror.

33. The mirror is a
- **A.** diverging mirror with a focal length of 11.5 cm
- **B.** converging mirror with a focal length of 11.5 cm
- **C.** diverging mirror with a focal length of –26.9 cm
- **D.** converging mirror with a focal length of –26.9 cm

State TEST

CHALLENGER QUESTION

Use the following information to answer the next question.

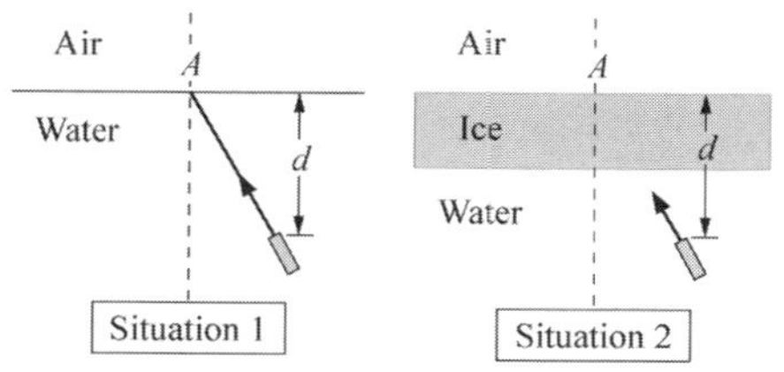

The indices of refraction (n) of water and ice are 1.33 and 1.31, respectively.

In Situation 1, a laser beam travels from water toward air and enters the air at Point A.

In Situation 2, a transparent layer of ice has formed on top of the water, but the position of the laser and its distance from the surface of the air (d), both remain the same

34. In Situation 2, the laser beam

A. enters the air at Point A

B. enters the air to the left of Point A

C. enters the air to the right of Point A

D. enters the ice and is blocked from further movement

Use the following information to answer the next question.

As illustrated in the diagram, a piece of flint glass is placed on top of a piece of borosilicate glass and a ray of light from air strikes the surface of the flint glass at an angle of 45°.

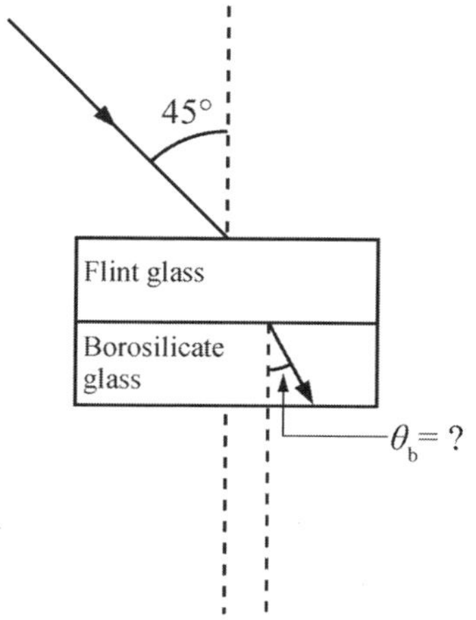

- The index of refraction of air is 1.00.
- The index of refraction of flint glass is 1.61.
- The index of refraction of borosilicate glass is 1.47.

35. The angle of refraction as the ray passes through the borosilicate glass is

A. 23.6°

B. 28.8°

C. 30.6°

D. 50.8°

Open Response

36. Sketch the electromagnetic radiation spectrum in order of increasing frequency, and label the various categories of radiation.

____

____

____

____

____

CHALLENGER QUESTION

Use the following information to answer the next question.

A ray of light from air enters a glass prism as illustrated in the given diagram.

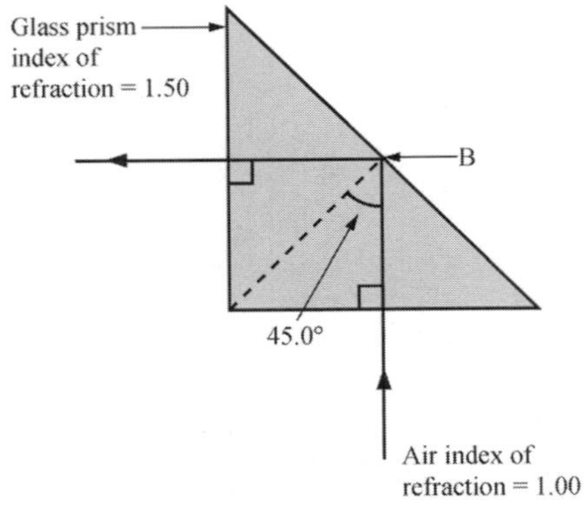

37. Which of the following statements about the refraction of light at point B is **true**?

- **A.** None of the light is refracted into the air because the angle of incidence is less than the critical angle.
- **B.** Some of the light is refracted into the air because the angle of incidence is less than the critical angle.
- **C.** None of the light is refracted into the air because the angle of incidence is greater than the critical angle.
- **D.** Some of the light is refracted into the air because the angle of incidence is greater than the critical angle.

Use the following information to answer the next question.

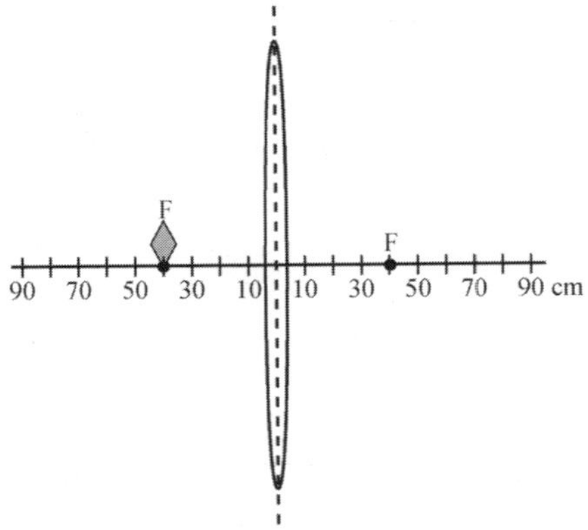

An object is placed 40 cm from a converging lens with a focal length of 40 cm.

38. Which of the following statements accurately describes the result of this placement of the object?

- **A.** A real image will appear 80 cm from the lens on the opposite side.
- **B.** A real image will appear 40 cm from the lens on the opposite side.
- **C.** A virtual image will appear on the same side of the lens as the object.
- **D.** No image will be produced by this object.

39. The eyepiece in a refracting telescope forms a large virtual image of a distant planet. The image formed by the objective lens is located

- **A.** at a distance of twice the focal length from the eyepiece
- **B.** slightly farther from the eyepiece than its focal point
- **C.** slightly closer to the eyepiece than its focal point
- **D.** right at the focal point of the eyepiece

Use the following information to answer the next question.

The index of refraction of water is 1.333 at 0°C and 1.318 at 100°C.

40. Light travelling through water will deflect

A. toward the normal and speed up when water is heated

B. toward the normal and slow down when water is heated

C. away from the normal and speed up when water is heated

D. away from the normal and slow down when water is heated

Answers and Solutions – Practice Test 1

1. B	10. C	17. B	26. D	35. A
2. B	11. A	18. OR	27. D	36. OR
3. B	12. A	19. A	28. D	37. C
4. OR	13. a) OR	20. A	29. A	38. C
5. B	b) OR	21. B	30. C	39. D
6. C	c) OR	22. B	31. B	40. D
7. A	14. C	23. B	32. C	
8. A	15. B	24. B	33. B	
9. C	16. A	25. A	34. D	

1. B

CAT, or CT, is an abbreviation of computerized axial tomography. It is a medical imaging technique that uses a series of X-rays around an axis of rotation to create a series of axial images that can be compiled into a three-dimensional image of the internal body structures.

CAT scans are no more or less invasive than X-rays and are typically more expensive than X-rays, not less. X-rays, like CAT scans, can visualize all types of body tissues, not just bone.

2. B

Poliomyelitis, or polio, is a serious viral disease of the central nervous system that can lead to paralysis and death. Jonas Salk developed a vaccine in the 1950s, and shortly after, Albert Sabin developed an oral vaccine. Since the vaccine was distributed, the number of polio cases has fallen from the hundreds of thousands to just a few each year, virtually eliminating the disease from all except a few developing nations.

3. B

During anaphase, chromosomes are pulled toward the poles. This is being illustrated in the given diagram.

4. OR

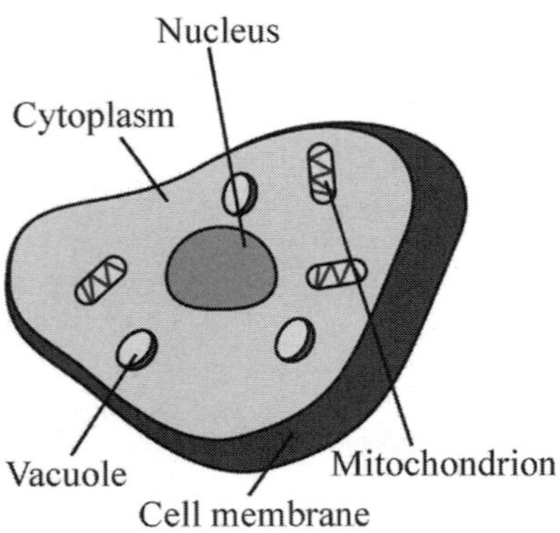

5. B

The migration of cancer cells is called metastasis. A malignant tumour metastasizes by generating small clusters of cancer cells that dislodge from the tumour and are carried by the blood or lymph to other sites in the body. In the given diagram, cancer cells are being dislodged from the tumour and are entering the blood stream to be carried to other sites.

6. C

Wheat rust is caused by the fungus *Puccinia triticina*. Spores of the fungus travel through the air and land on the leaves of the plant. As the fungus develops, it clogs the stomata of the plant, preventing gas exchange and killing the leaves.

7. A

Body tissue is repaired by the division of specialized cells. This division occurs by mitosis.

8. A

In the normal development of an organism, the single cell stage is followed by cell division and cell differentiation. Differentiation produces different cell types that carry out specialized functions. For example, in an adult human, a red blood cell (A) has a different function and structure than a nerve cell (B).

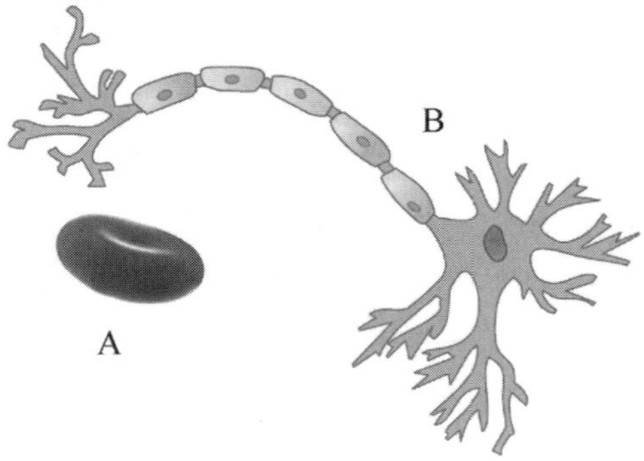

9. C

Groups of similar cells form tissues, and different tissues working together for the same purpose form an organ. Muscle and nerve cells form tissues that make up the heart, an organ of the circulatory system.

10. C

The digestive system breaks down food into nutrients. The circulatory system transports these nutrients in the blood to all the cells in the body.

11. A

All three levels of government—federal, provincial, and municipal—are responsible for setting policies relating to the disposal of hazardous materials. Businesses and the public must follow these policies, and the police may be called in to enforce these policies.

12. A

Baking soda and vinegar are the starting materials or reactants. The products formed during this reaction are sodium acetate, carbon dioxide, and water. There are 2 reactants that take part in this reaction to form 3 products.

13. a) OR

$SrCl_2$ and H_2O

b) OR

$2HCl + Sr(OH)_2 \rightarrow SrCl_2 + 2H_2O$

c) OR

The reaction is a double-replacement reaction.

14. C

In observations 1, 2, and 4, chemical reactions have occurred. The egg changed colour and composition as it cooked. The steel wool changed colour as it rusted. The candle flame gave off heat.
In observation 3, there was no chemical reaction when the salt mixed with the water. The salt dissolved, which is a physical change.

15. B

Aden used the prefixes correctly for NF_3 and CCl_4 but made a mistake in naming N_2O. The correct name for N_2O is dinitrogen oxide, not dinitrogen dioxide.

16. A

The formation of a precipitate, copper(II) hydroxide$_{(s)}$, is an indication that a chemical reaction has occurred.

All ionic solutions conduct electricity, so the reactants and products would both conduct electricity. A change in pH is not an indication of a chemical change.

17. B

A balanced chemical equation must contain an equal number of atoms on the reactant side and the product side. The standard balanced equation must contain the smallest whole number of coefficients. Hence, the balanced equation for the burning of aluminum in the presence of oxygen is

$4Al_{(s)} + 3O_{2(g)} \rightarrow 2Al_2O_{3(s)}$

18. OR

The law of conservation of matter requires that the total number of each type of atom on the reactant side of the equation is the same as the total number of the same type of atom on the product side.

Properly balanced, the equation is
$2NaN_{3(s)} \rightarrow 2Na_{(s)} + 3N_{2(g)}$.

19. A

In an acid-base neutralization reaction, an acid and a base react with each other to form a salt and water. In the given reaction, NaOH is a base, and HCl is an acid. NaOH and HCl react with each other to form sodium chloride (NaCl), or salt and water. Hence, the reaction between NaOH and HCl is an acid-base neutralization reaction. In the reaction with zinc, the given reaction is a single-displacement reaction because zinc replaces hydrogen in hydrochloric acid (HCl) to form $ZnCl_2$. In the reaction with ammonium hydroxide, the decomposition of ammonium hydroxide (NH_4OH) is illustrated. In the reaction with carbonic acid, the decomposition of carbonic acid (H_2CO_3) is illustrated.

20. A

Calcium has a charge of 2+. Oxygen has a charge of 2−. Compounds must be neutrally charged. The simplest ratio of calcium and oxygen that will result in a neutral compound is 1:1, or calcium oxide, CaO.

State TEST

21. B

The abbreviation IPCC stands for the **Intergovernmental Panel on Climate Change**. This organization was established in 1988 through the joint efforts of the World Meteorological Organization (WMO) and the United Nations Environment Programme (UNEP).

22. B

NASA reports that the global sea level has risen 17 cm over the last century. Although sea levels have been higher than they are now, scientists are alarmed that the rate of global sea rise has nearly doubled in the last decade alone. This is a major concern for coastal settlements around the world.

23. B

Recall that heat transfers by three different methods: conduction, convection, and radiation.

Conduction occurs when heat transfers by the contact of two different materials. In this case, heat transfers through the glass by conduction.

Convection occurs when heat transfers within a fluid by the movement of the fluid's particles. Heat transfers throughout the water by convection.

Radiation occurs when heat passes through a material without heating the particles in the material. The transfer of heat by radiation does not directly apply to this example.

24. B

Albedo is the ability of a surface to reflect the sun's rays. Snow and ice reflect more of the sun's rays back toward the atmosphere than soil or bare ground do; they have a higher albedo. If polar ice and snow melt, Earth's albedo will decrease.

25. A

The current in the North Atlantic Ocean is a warm water current. It transports warm water from the equator to the North Pole all year. Thus, this warm water current causes an increase in the annual average temperature of the Arctic.

26. D

The speaker is demanding that the countries responsible for creating the climate change protocol do something about it. This would indicate that the politician is from an area that is not a large contributor to climate change, such as Africa. Many developing nations, including Africa, are not big producers of carbon dioxide or greenhouse gases, but they are suffering the consequences of climate change. They are particularly sensitive to droughts and extreme weather events. Most people in these areas do not have enough money to protect themselves from these effects.

27. D

The thermal processes that shape Earth's climate are driven by three main sources: residual thermal energy from the Earth's formation, sunlight, and energy from radioactive decay of heavy elements in the Earth's core. While the burning of fossil fuels does provide energy, this is a human-made process used to provide for humans' energy needs.

28. D

El Niño is abnormal warming of ocean surface. El Niño is associated with the warming of the tropical Pacific sea surface and is accompanied by changes in winds and air pressure. El Niño is associated with warmer winter temperatures and less precipitation in British Columbia. La Niña is the cooling of the Pacific sea surface. The Coriolis Effect is the deflection of wind and ocean currents in the Northern and Southern Hemispheres. A tornado is a violently circling column of air.

29. A

Methane traps more heat per molecule than carbon dioxide, but carbon dioxide is more abundant in the atmosphere. Although methane is a more powerful greenhouse gas, most efforts are aimed at reducing carbon dioxide levels because it is produced by humans in greater quantities, making it a bigger problem.

30. C

When cold air is trapped below warm air, it is called a temperature inversion because the conditions are the inverse of usual conditions (cold air above warm air). The cold air cannot rise through the layer of warm air above, and therefore traps the smog that may normally rise and be blown away. Temperature inversions are more common in cities found in valleys.

State TEST

31. B

An image is formed when light passes through the eye and is focused on the retina. When the cornea is misshapen or the eye is too long, light is focused in front or behind the retina. Corrective lenses refocus the light on the retina.

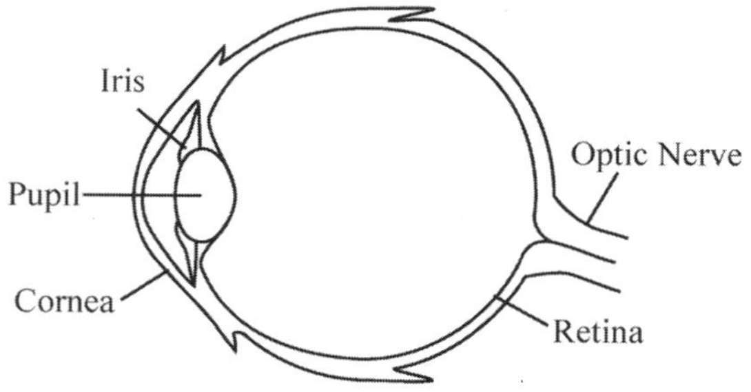

32. C

Mirages generally form over desert regions where conditions are extremely hot and dry.
The atmosphere over such regions refracts light, forming mirages that trick the human eye because the bending of the light creates an image in an unexpected position.

33. B

Convex (diverging) mirrors only form virtual images. The image is significantly smaller than the actual object so it appears as if it is farther away.

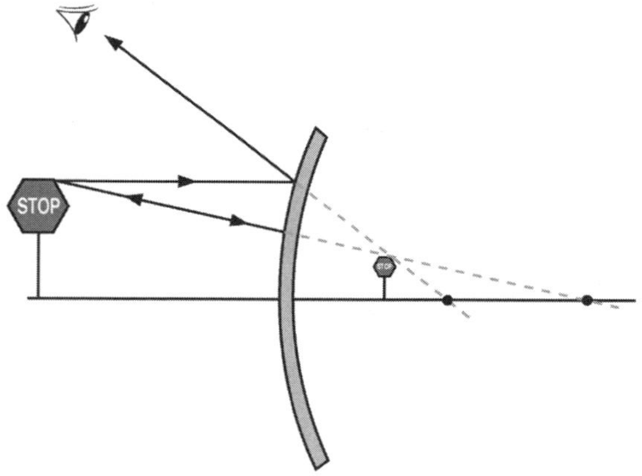

34. D

Calculate the angle of refraction in water, θ_{water}, using Snell's law.

$$n_{water} \times \sin\theta_{water} = n_{oil} \times \sin\theta_{oil}$$

$$\sin\theta_{water} = \frac{n_{oil} \times \sin\theta_{oil}}{n_{water}} = \frac{1.47 \times \sin 35.0°}{1.33} = 0.633\ 95$$

$$\theta_{water} = 39.3°$$

35. A

The object height, h_o, the object distance, d_o, and the image distance, d_i, are substituted into the lens magnification equation. This is then solved to calculate the image height, h_i.

$$M = \frac{h_i}{h_o} = -\frac{d_i}{d_o}$$

$$h_i = -\frac{d_i}{d_o} \times h_o = -\frac{31.5\text{ cm}}{42.0\text{ cm}} \times 9.0\text{ cm} = -6.8\text{ cm}$$

The negative sign on the value simply means that the image is inverted.

36. OR

Light traveling through a medium has a lower speed than light travelling through a vacuum. The greater the index of refraction of a medium (n_{medium}), the more the medium decreases the speed of light.
The ratio of the speed of light through a vacuum to the speed of light traveling through a medium is equal to the refractive index of the medium.
When the medium is sodium chloride, the equation is given as follows:

$$n_{sodium\ chloride} = \frac{v_{vacuum}}{v_{sodium\ chloride}}$$

The equation is rearranged to solve for the speed of light in sodium chloride, the known values are inserted, and its value is calculated.

$$v_{sodium\ chloride} = \frac{v_{vacuum}}{n_{sodium\ chloride}} = \frac{3.00 \times 10^8\text{ m/s}}{1.52} = 1.97 \times 10^8\text{ m/s}$$

Light has a speed of 1.97×10^8 m/s in sodium chloride.

37. C

Most quartz-halogen bulbs have a tungsten filament surrounded by a mixture of an inert gas and a halogen element or compound. Tungsten atoms always evaporate from a hot filament. The presence of the halogen in the gas causes tungsten atoms to deposit back onto the filament. This helps to prolong the lifespan of this type of bulb. Quartz-halogen bulbs are considerably brighter and operate at higher temperatures than normal incandescent bulbs.
The envelope on the outside of the bulb is also quite close to the hot filament. Because ordinary glass would melt at such high temperatures, quartz is often used instead. The transparency and high melting point of quartz make it ideal for these types of applications.

38. C

The diagram shows that the object distance, d_o, is 65.0 cm and the object height, h_o, is 22.5 cm. Since the mirror is a diverging (convex) mirror, the focal length, F, is –30.0 cm.

Step 1
Calculate the image distance, d_i, using the mirror equation $\frac{1}{f} = \frac{1}{d_o} + \frac{1}{d_i}$.

$$\frac{1}{d_i} = \frac{1}{f} - \frac{1}{d_o}$$

$$= \frac{1}{-30.0\text{ cm}} - \frac{1}{65.0\text{ cm}}$$

$$= -0.048\ 72\text{ cm}$$

$$d_i = \frac{1}{-0.048\ 72\text{ cm}}$$

$$= -20.5263\text{ cm}$$

The negative value of the image distance means the image is to the right of the mirror and is virtual. The value can be rounded to –20.5 cm, but the more precise value should be used in the calculation of the image height.

Step 2
Calculate the image height, h_i, using the magnification equation $M = \frac{h_i}{h_o} = -\frac{d_i}{d_o}$.

$$h_i = -\frac{d_i}{d_o} \times h_o$$

$$= -\frac{-20.5263\text{ cm}}{65.0\text{cm}} \times 22.5\text{cm}$$

$$= 7.11\text{ cm}$$

The image produced by the mirror is 7.11 cm high and 20.5 cm to the right of the mirror.

39. D

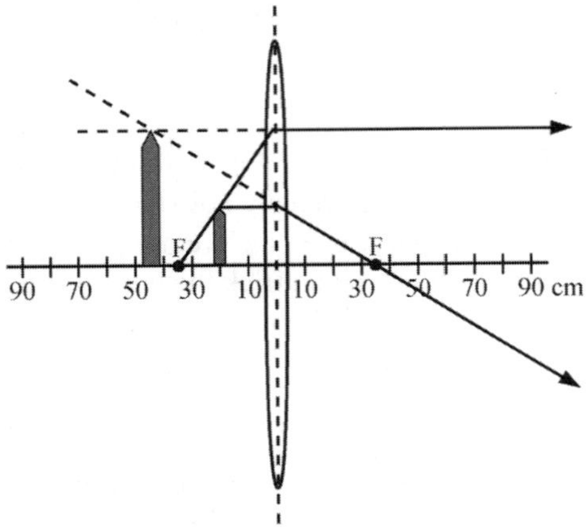

Since the rays travelling to the right side of the lens diverge, there is no real image on the right side of the lens. When these rays are extended backward, they converge at a point about 47 cm to the left of the lens and form an upright virtual image about 35 cm tall. When an object is placed between the focal point and a converging lens, a larger virtual upright image is always formed on the same side of the lens as the object.

State TEST

40. D

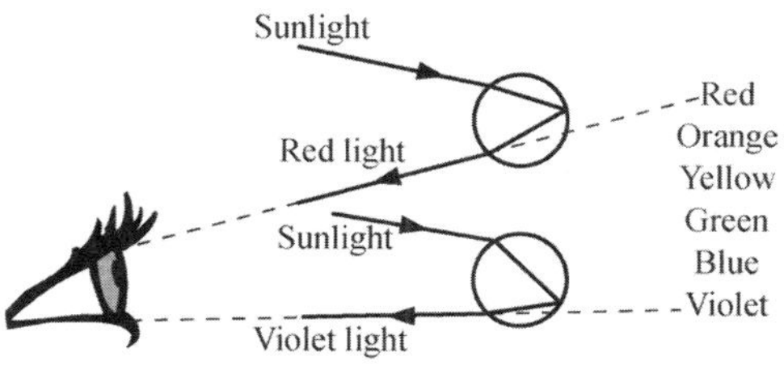

When sunlight hits a raindrop, the raindrop acts like a prism, dispersing the sunlight and separating out its component colours. This is because the reflection of each colour of light takes place at a slightly different location on the far side of the raindrop. The diagram illustrates how violet light has a greater angle of refraction than red light and subsequently reflects from a lower point at the back of the raindrop. (This is illustrated in two separate raindrops for clarity). Because the violet light has a greater angle of refraction than red light and the brain of the observer interprets all light rays to be travelling in a straight line from their point of reflection, the violet light reaching an observer appears lower in the sky than red.

Answers and Solutions – Practice Test 2

1. D	9. A	17. OR	25. B	33. C
2. B	10. B	18. C	26. C	34. B
3. OR	11. D	19. D	27. C	35. B
4. A	12. OR	20. B	28. C	36. OR
5. D	13. A	21. A	29. D	37. C
6. A	14. A	22. C	30. C	38. D
7. A	15. C	23. C	31. B	39. C
8. C	16. C	24. B	32. B	40. C

1. D

The blood type of the organ donor and organ recipient must match in order for the transplant to be successful. This concern is medical, not ethical.

There are often ethical debates surrounding who decides when to take a patient off life support, how to prioritize recipients, and the use of animal organs in transplants.

2. B

In vascular plants, water is transported through the xylem. Since the water provided to the plant was coloured, the xylem tissues appeared red when observed under the microscope.

3. OR

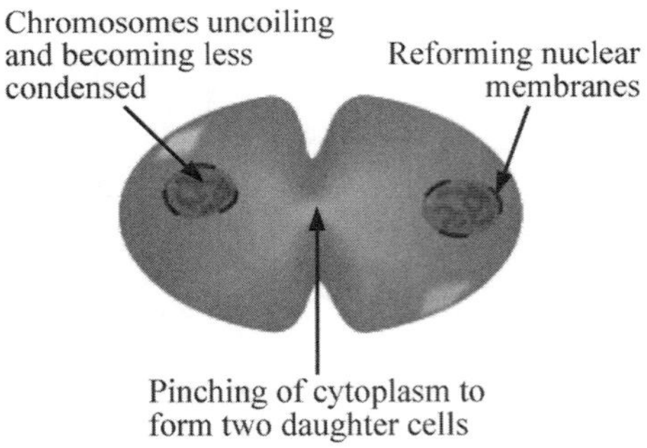

In telophase, nuclear membranes have begun forming around the nuclei of the new daughter cells. The chromosomes uncoil and become less condensed. Cytokinesis occurs, and the cell membrane begins pinching in to separate the two daughter cells.

4. A

Plant cells are characterized by the presence of a cell wall. This wall is very rigid and functions to protect the cell against bursting when the plant cell fills with water. The cell wall is made up of cellulose. Animal cells do not contain a cell wall. Lysosomes, mitochondria, and cell membranes occur in both plant and animal cells.

5. D

Bone marrow cells are undifferentiated cells, also known as stem cells, that possess the power of division. These are unspecialized cells that divide and specialize to form specialized cells. Mammalian red blood cells are specialized, and they lack a nucleus and mitochondria. Bone marrow cells have a nucleus and mitochondria.

6. A

The integumentary system is the worm's skin. It protects the worm from the environment, maintains water balance, and helps the worm to breathe.

7. A

Mitosis is the process by which a cell divides to form two identical daughter cells. Mitosis is responsible for the growth of cells, repair of tissues, and some forms of asexual reproduction. It does not form sex cells. Sex cells have half the number of chromosomes as body cells. They are formed by meiosis.

8. C

Neurons, specialized cells that make up the nervous system, cannot regenerate or be replaced. This is why brain injuries can be so severe, as there is little that can currently be done to help the damaged tissue. Skin and liver cells can both regenerate to heal damaged tissues through mitosis. Blood cells are constantly being renewed by bone marrow.

9. A

In vertebrates, the integumentary system, of which the skin is the major component, performs the same function as the epidermis in plants.

State TEST

10. B

When a person feels tired, the lungs do not take in enough oxygen from the air. This causes a shortage of oxygen in the body. The brain senses this lack of oxygen, and this causes the person to take a long, deep breath called a yawn. The two body systems involved in this process are the nervous and respiratory systems.

11. D

Catalytic converters are attached to exhaust systems, where they provide space for chemical reactions to occur. These reactions change toxic byproducts into less toxic products before they are released by the exhaust system. One of these reactions is the conversion of toxic carbon monoxide to the less toxic carbon dioxide.

12. OR

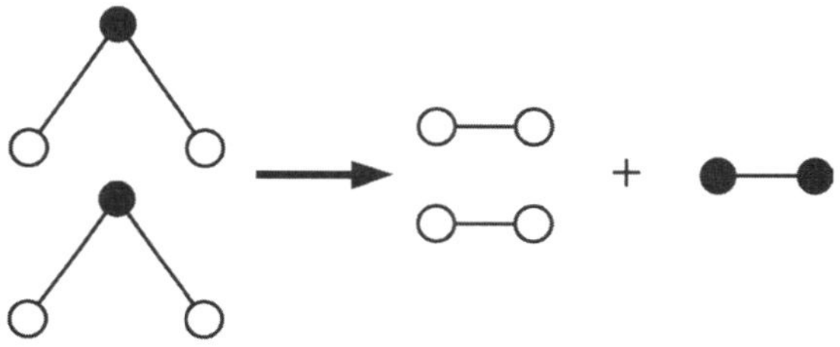

The black circles represent oxygen atoms, and the white circles represent hydrogen atoms.

13. A

The law of the conservation of mass states that the mass of the reactants will equal the mass of the products. Since the container was sealed, none of the gas would have been able to escape, and the mass would remain the same.

14. A

The pH scale ranges from 0 to 14, and it has no units. Solutions with a pH less than 7 are acidic. Hence, a solution with pH of zero is a very strong acid.

15. C

According to the law of conservation of mass, matter can neither be created nor destroyed. Therefore, during a chemical reaction, the total mass of the products remains the same as the total mass of the reactants. In a complete chemical equation, the number of atoms of various elements on both sides must be equal. In other words, the equation has to be balanced or it violates the law of conservation of mass.

16. C

Both hydrogen and nitrogen are diatomic in their elemental form. The balanced equation is $N_{2(g)} + 3H_{2(g)} \rightarrow 2NH_{3(g)}$.

There are two nitrogen atoms and six hydrogen atoms on both sides of the equation.

17. OR

$$3Sn(NO_2)_4 + 4K_3PO_4 \rightarrow 12KNO_2 + 1Sn_3(PO_4)_4$$

18. C

Acetic acid is a weak organic acid. Caustic potash is a strong alkali. A reaction between CH_3COOH and KOH is classified as acid-base neutralization.

19. D

Acids turn blue litmus red. They do not feel slippery, and they may burn your skin on contact. Acids have a pH less than 7 and taste sour. The other alternatives are characteristics of bases.

20. B

Ammonium (NH_4) is a polyatomic ion that has a charge of +1. Phosphate (PO_4) is a polyatomic ion that has a charge of −3. Three ammonium ions (total charge +3) are required to balance one phosphate ion.

To indicate that the 3 refers to both the nitrogen and the hydrogens of the ammonium, the ammonium ion must be in brackets.

The Roman numerals are from Stock's system. They are used in the names of some transition metals, but never in a formula.

21. A

The polar bear is very well adapted to a cold-weather habitat. When the Arctic regions become warmer, it will become harder for the polar bear to hide from prey, and the sea ice that forms an important part of the polar bear's hunting habitat will melt.

22. C

Human-influenced processes or materials are referred to as *anthropogenic*, which means "made by" (*-genic*) "human" (*anthro-*). For example, carbon dioxide emissions released by cars and factories are considered anthropogenic.
Natural emissions from bogs and fens are not anthropogenic.

23. C

Models are computer-generated scenarios that use past and current data to explain the current conditions and predict future scenarios.
Models cannot be used to prove anything; there are too many variables involved in climate change to prove anything. Models can only support the theory that the current climate change is caused by humans by profiling how the climate would have likely changed without anthropogenic greenhouse gas emissions and comparing that scenario to the current one.

24. B

Ecozones are designated based on their shared ecological features, climates, and plant and animal communities. Latitude determines many of these features. Siberia and Ontario have similar latitudes, therefore Siberia would likely have a climatic region similar to the Hudson Plains ecozone.

25. B

The seasons are most affected by the tilt of Earth's axis. During Canada's summer, the North Pole is tilted toward the sun. During Canada's winter, the North Pole is tilted away from the sun.

26. C

The greenhouse effect refers to the atmosphere blocking heat from escaping from Earth. That is somewhat like the glass of a greenhouse blocking the escape of heat. As a result, a greenhouse can become very warm. The most important greenhouse gas is water vapour, however, carbon gases are also important.

The greater the greenhouse effect, the lower the heat energy leaving Earth and the warmer the Earth becomes. A change in the greenhouse effect would not directly impact the amount of heat produced on Earth.

27. C

Over a long period of time, newly uplifted geographic features increase the amount of weathering and the release of atmospheric carbon dioxide, warming the global climate. This process is very slow, occurring over millions of years.

28. C

The most abundant greenhouse gas in the atmosphere is carbon dioxide. Therefore, carbon dioxide is the greatest contributor to the greenhouse effect. It traps the heat that radiates from Earth's surface, leading to rising temperatures.
Although carbon dioxide occurs naturally in the atmosphere, high-level anthropogenic emissions of carbon dioxide have contributed to an amplification of the natural greenhouse effect.

29. D

Ground level ozone is found in the troposphere, the region of the atmosphere closest to Earth's surface.

30. C

Based on current scientific understanding of the greenhouse effect and the impact of greenhouse gas emissions, climate change researchers can reasonably predict that average global temperatures will continue to rise. Given that, they can also reasonably predict that polar sea ice levels will continue to decline and that storm intensity and severity will increase in response to the rising sea's surface temperatures. These predictions are all reasonable because they are broad generalizations based on current, verifiable trends. The prediction about the end of drought conditions in Australia is too specific and relies too heavily on poorly understood interactions of climate dynamics. In fact, scientists are not even certain about what caused Australia's drought in the first place, other than the fact that it is likely related to climate change.

31. B

The light-sensitive film in a camera has the same function as the retina of the human eye. Both the retina and the film are the point at which light must be properly focused in order to form a clear image.

32. B

The incoming light wave is referred to as an incident wave and the light wave that is bounced away from the surface is referred to as the reflected wave. Visible white light that is directed onto the surface of a mirror at an angle (incident) is reflected back into space by the mirror surface at another angle (reflected) that is equal to the incident angle.

33. C

The object distance is $d_o = 40.0$ cm.

Since the image appears to be behind the mirror and the mirror is curved, this must be a diverging mirror. Also, because the image appears to be behind the mirror, the image distance has a negative value, $d_i = -16.1$ cm.

Use the mirror equation to calculate the focal length.

$$\begin{aligned}\frac{1}{f} &= \frac{1}{d_o} + \frac{1}{d_i} \\ &= \frac{1}{40.0} + \frac{1}{-16.1} \\ &= -0.037\,11 \\ f &= \frac{1}{-0.037\,11} \\ &= -26.9 \text{ cm}\end{aligned}$$

A diverging mirror has a negative focal length. This means the focal point is on the opposite side of the mirror to the object.

34. B

Since ice has a slightly lower refractive index than water, the angle of refraction in ice will be slightly greater than the angle of incidence in water. This will cause the ray to enter the air to the left of point *A*.

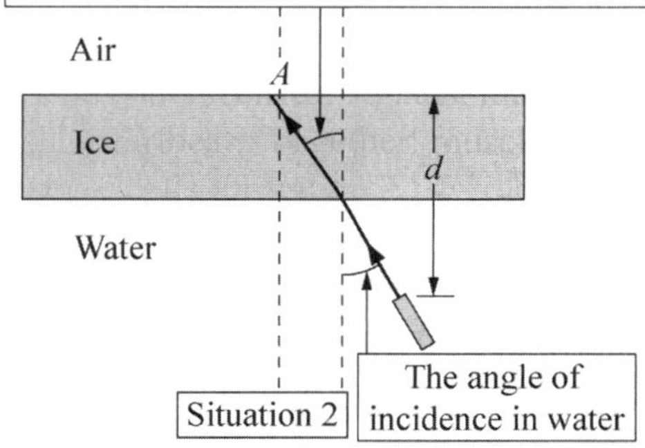

35. B

The general form of Snell's Law is:
$n_1 \sin \theta_1 = n_2 \sin \theta_2$

First, calculate the angle of refraction in the flint glass (θ_f):

$$\begin{aligned}\sin \theta_f &= \frac{n_{air} \times \sin \theta_{air}}{n_f} \\ &= \frac{1.00 \times \sin 45°}{1.61} \\ &= 0.4392 \\ \theta_f &= 26.05°\end{aligned}$$

Next, use θ_f as the angle of incidence and calculate the angle of refraction in the borosilicate glass (θ_b):

$$\begin{aligned}\sin \theta_b &= \frac{n_f \times \sin \theta_f}{n_b} \\ &= \frac{1.61 \times \sin 26.05°}{1.47} \\ &= 0.4810 \\ \sin \theta_b &= 28.8°\end{aligned}$$

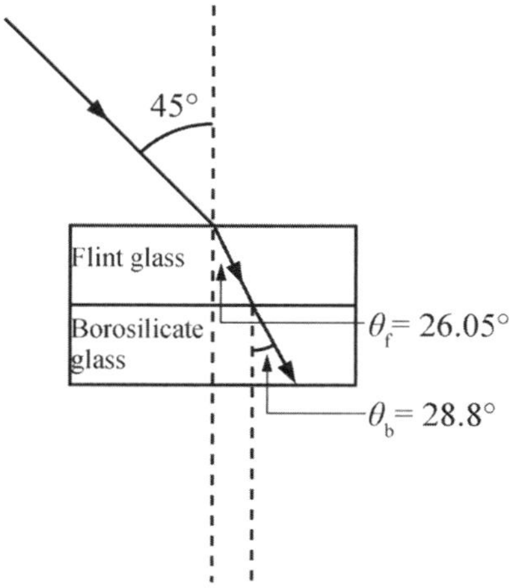

36. OR

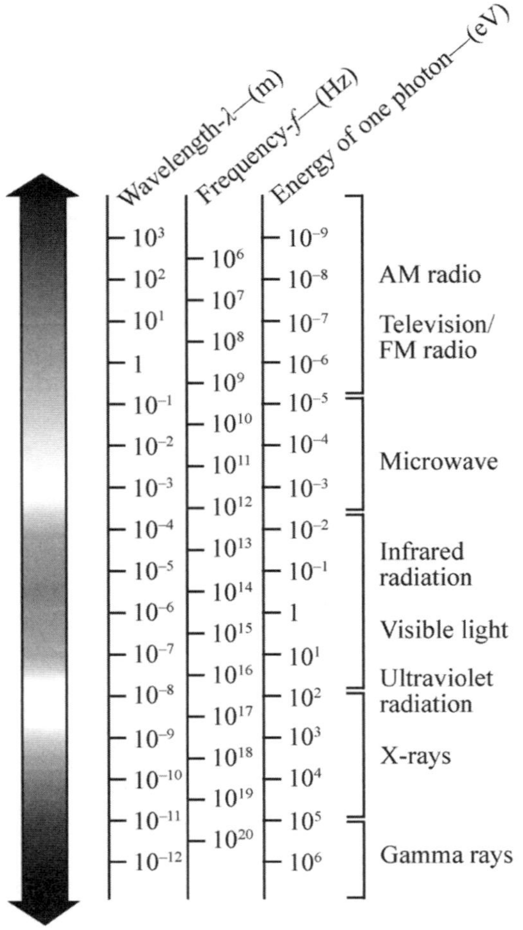

37. C

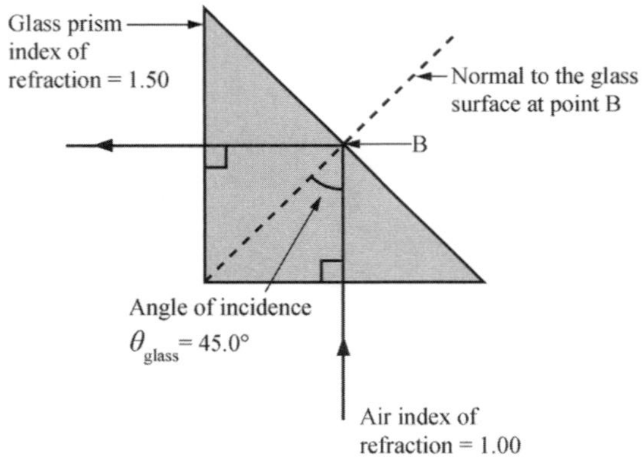

When the light ray hits point B, the relationship between the angle of incidence and the critical angle of light passing from glass into air will determine if there is any refraction. In order to examine this relationship, the critical angle for light travelling from glass into air must be calculated using Snell's law.

Step 1
Determine the critical angle for light travelling from glass into air.
Snell's law describes the relationship between the angles of incidence and refraction and the refractive indices of the two media involved.

$n_{glass} \times \sin\theta_{glass} = n_{air} \times \sin\theta_{air}$

At the critical angle, light will refract along the surface of the glass perpendicular to the normal to the glass surface at point B. This indicates that at the critical angle for glass, the $\theta_{air} = 90.0°$.

Since $n_{air} = 1.00$, $\theta_{air} = 90.0°$, and $n_{glass} = 1.50$, use Snell's law to calculate the critical angle, θ_{glass}.

$$\begin{aligned}\sin\theta_{glass} &= \frac{n_{air} \times \sin\theta_{air}}{n_{glass}}\\ &= \frac{1.00 \times \sin 90.0°}{n_{glass}}\\ &= \frac{1.00 \times 1.00}{n_{glass}}\\ &= \frac{1.00}{1.50}\\ &= 0.6667\end{aligned}$$

$$\begin{aligned}\theta_{glass} &= \sin^{-1}(0.6667)\\ &= 41.8°\end{aligned}$$

The critical angle, θ_{glass}, is 41.8°.

Step 2
Compare the angle of incidence of the ray hitting point B with the critical angle of light travelling from glass to air.
Since the angle of incidence of the ray inside the glass, 45.0°, is greater than the critical angle, 41.8°, the result is total internal reflection. No refraction of light to the air will occur at point B.

State TEST

38. D

When rays are drawn and extended backward, they do not converge at any point. No image is formed in this case.

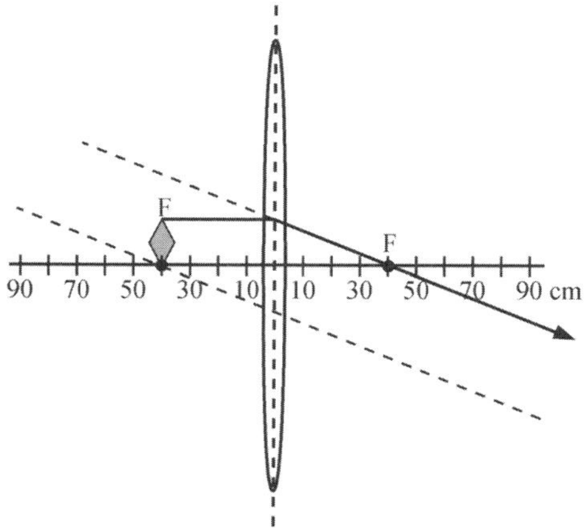

When an object is placed right at the focal point of a converging lens, no images (real or virtual) are formed.

39. C

In order for the eyepiece lens to produce a virtual image, the object must be inside the focal point.

40. C

The higher the refractive index, the lower the velocity of light in the medium. Since the index of refraction of water decreases as it is heated, the velocity of light will increase.

The higher the refractive index, the more a ray will deflect toward the normal. Since the index of refraction of water decreases as it is heated, the ray will deflect away from the normal (the angle of refraction will increase).

CREDITS

NOTES

NOTES

NOTES

NOTES

NOTES

NOTES

RESOURCE INFORMATION *Order online at www.castlerockresearch.com*

SCHOOL ORDERS

Schools are eligible for an education discount. Contact Castle Rock Research Ontario for more information.

THE KEY Study Guides assist in preparing students for course assignments, unit tests, and final or provincial assessments.

***THE KEY* Study Guides** – $29.95 each plus G.S.T.

SECONDARY	ELEMENTARY
Biology 12, University Prep (SBI4U)	Science 8
Canadian and World Politics 12, University Prep (CPW4U)	Math 7
Chemistry 12, University Prep (SCH4U)	Science 7
English 12, University Prep (ENG4U)	Language 6 Reading & Writing
English 12, College Prep (ENG4C)	Math 6
Math 12 Advanced Functions, University Prep (MHF4U)	Science 6
Math 12 Calculus and Vectors, University Prep (MCV4U)	Math 5
Math 12 Data Management, University Prep (MDM4U)	Science 5
Physics 12, University Prep (SPH4U)	Math 4
World History 12, University Prep (CHY4U)	Science 4
Biology 11, University Prep (SBI3U)	Language 3 Reading & Writing
Chemistry 11, University Prep (SCH3U)	Math 3
English 11, University Prep (ENG3U)	Science 3
Math 11, Foundations for College Mathematics (MBF3C)	
Math 11, Functions and Applications, U/C Prep (MCF3M)	
Math 11, Functions, University Prep (MCR3U)	
World History 11, University/College Prep (CHW3M)	
Canadian History 10, Academic (CHC2D)	
Canadian History 10, Applied (CHC2P)	
Civics 10, (CHV2O)	
English 10, Academic (ENG2D)	
Math 10, Academic, Principles of Mathematics (MPM2D)	
Math 10, Applied, Foundations of Mathematics (MFM2P)	
OSSLT, Ontario Secondary School Literacy Test	
Science 10, Academic (SNC2D)	
English 9, Academic (ENG1D)	
Geography of Canada 9, Academic (CGC1D)	
Math 9, Academic, Principles of Mathematics (MPM1D)	
Math 9, Applied, Foundations of Mathematics (MFM1P)	
Science 9, Academic (SNC1D)	

The **Student Notes and Problems (SNAP)** workbooks provide complete lessons for course expectations, detailed explanations of concepts, and exercises with complete solutions.

SNAP Workbooks – $29.95 each plus G.S.T.

SECONDARY
Physics 12, University Preparation (SPH4U)
Physics 11, University Preparation (SPH3U)
Math 10, Academic, Principles of Mathematics (MPM2D)
Math 9, Academic, Principles of Mathematics (MPM1D)
Math 9, Applied, Foundations of Mathematics (MFM1P)

Visit our website for a tour of resource content and features or order online at www.castlerockresearch.com

5250 Satellite Drive, Unit 11
Mississauga, ON L4W 5G5
E-mail: Ontario@castlerockresearch.com

Phone: 905.625.3332
Fax: 905.625.3390

CASTLE ROCK
RESEARCH CORP